Metapattern

Metapattern

Context and Time
in Information Models

Pieter Wisse

ADDISON–WESLEY

Boston • San Francisco • New York • Toronto • Montreal
London • Munich • Paris • Madrid • Capetown
Sydney • Tokyo • Singapore • Mexico City

Many of the designations used by manufacturers and sellers to distinguish their products are claimed as trademarks. Where those designations appear in this book, and Addison-Wesley was aware of a trademark claim, the designations have been printed with initial capital letters or in all capitals.

The author and publisher have taken care in the preparation of this book, but make no expressed or implied warranty of any kind and assume no responsibility for errors or omissions. No liability is assumed for incidental or consequential damages in connection with or arising out of the use of the information or programs contained herein.

The publisher offers discounts on this book when ordered in quantity for special sales. For more information, please contact:

Pearson Education Corporate Sales Division
One Lake Street
Upper Saddle River, NJ 07458
(800) 382-3419
corpsales@pearsontechgroup.com

Visit AW on the Web: www.awl.com/cseng/

Library of Congress Cataloging-in-Publication Data

Wisse, Pieter.
    Metapattern : context and time in information models / Pieter Wisse.
        p.   cm.
    Includes bibliographical references and index.
    ISBN 0-201-70457-9 (alk. paper)
    1. System design   2. Metapattern (Information modeling)   3. Object-oriented
    methods (Computer science)   4. Computer software—Reusability   I.   Title.
    QA76.9.S88 W58 2000
    005.1'2—dc21

                                                        00–056928

ISBN 0-201-70457-9
Text printed on recycled paper
1 2 3 4 5 6 7 8 9 10—CRS—04 03 02 01 00
First printing, November 2000

Contents

Preface

Focused Analysis Tool

Metapattern is an exciting new approach to conceptual information modeling. It is a technique for meta-information analysis and modeling that emphasizes reusability. With the metapattern, analysis is recognized as a critical activity in its own right during information system development. The metapattern is not a method for technical design or software engineering; it is a highly focused analysis tool. But precisely because it provides powerful support for analysis, the metapattern helps focus all other development and management activities during the complete life cycle of systems. Overall success results from the great precision now available in modeling, particularly through the combination of a finely grained concept of time stamping and a recursive, simple but formal concept of context.

The metapattern views conceptual information models as analysis patterns. It is particularly valuable for aligning complex and variable requirements, even across a multitude of organizations with different processes. The concepts of *context* and *time* are critically important in these models, allowing for their adjustment (or readjustment) to time-induced and/or situational changes that the model must account for in order to maintain its integrity. Models scale to meet all such variety.

A professional analyst using the metapattern leads the way in the development of the much-needed flexible, adaptable systems that reflect the nature of the next information age. An entirely new breed of design patterns and software components may be derived from the metapattern and the concrete analysis patterns it helps specify. Any information system implementing analysis patterns that have been developed with the metapattern can enjoy a greatly extended life cycle. A special contribution to longevity is that, with the right definition of meta-information, different information systems, including legacy systems, may be provided with unambiguous interfaces over time. They may thus act, and continue to do so, in concord.

Practical Orientation

This book, written by its original designer, explains the metapattern. Included are many practical examples—that is, a large number of specific analysis patterns—covering a wide range of applications. More than 170 figures capture the main ideas, with the accompanying text sketching background, considerations, and details.

Although the metapattern is basically simple, particularly once the variety offered by contexts is fully understood, its current novelty may present you with some quite natural problems. How do you become familiar with the metapattern and its use without unnecessary effort? The distribution of any innovation is characterized by such communication dilemmas. In this case, some understanding of the metapattern's general theory is a precondition to fully understanding its practical applications. On the other hand, through the exposition of specific practical applications, the understanding of the theory is greatly enhanced.

The *Introduction* following this *Preface* is designed to help you get underway. By the time you arrive at Part I, you will be equipped with a preliminary interpretation scheme that you can develop gradually as you progress.

In textbook fashion, the book begins with a theoretical explanation of the metapattern's most fundamental characteristics. This theoretical part has been kept to the absolute minimum. Practical applications are discussed as soon as possible. Where relevant, such applications provide recognizable opportunities from your daily practice, thereby extending treatment of the theory of the metapattern.

As another service to the reader, the metapattern is applied to practical problems and/or to existing patterns as their proposed solutions. Few books have been written on conceptual information modeling. Nonetheless, important problems and patterns have already been documented elsewhere. Their authors have used familiar approaches; that is, entity-attribute-relationship (EAR) modeling and modeling with object orientation (OO). Comparisons of results should assist you in understanding what is fundamentally different about the metapattern.

And where the metapattern covers new ground, at least the points of departure are known (and, as existing literature is explicitly referred to, verifiable).

The Book and Its Parts

The metapattern is described herein in five parts, each focused on explaining a specific hypothesis.

In Part I, *Design of the Metapattern*, the main concepts and structure are explained in five chapters. We explain the primary concepts of context (Chapter 1) and intext (Chapter 2) first. Together, they form the building blocks of all specific analysis models and, when reusable, analysis patterns. Next, we apply these two fundamental concepts to type (Chapter 3), time (Chapter 4), and compositions (Chapter 5). These additional three concepts are also fundamental, but to a lesser extent than context and intext. The hypothesis underlying Part I is that the recognition of multiple contexts results in a powerful approach to conceptual information modeling. By paying consistent attention to the aspect of time, we augment the approach even further.

Part II, *Conceptual Solutions*, compares the metapattern with traditional object orientation. An excellent source of challenging problems for discussion is *Advanced Object-Oriented Analysis & Design Using UML*. In that collection, J. J. Odell has published a series of his columns containing clear presentations of OO's most pressing conceptual problems. The four chapters of Part II restate Odell's important problem definitions and provide short descriptions of his solutions, followed by one or more alternatives according to the metapattern. It leads to the conclusion that the metapattern is richer than purely object-oriented approaches to information modeling. Part II argues for this hypothesis by consistently providing elegant context-oriented solutions for various outstanding problems in OO conceptual modeling.

Part III, *Pattern Analysis and Design*, has reuse as its main theme. Awareness is growing that conceptual information models can also be reusable. Opportunities can be turned into real profit when the modeler has reuse in mind during the first stages of modeling. A reusable information model is synonymous with a pattern. Literature is now becoming available about such concrete patterns (*Data Model Patterns* by D. C. Hay, *Analysis Patterns* by M. Fowler, and *Business Process Engineering* by A.-W. Scheer). Part III takes a representative selection of patterns as described and prescribed by these authors. Where applicable, we add suggestions for accommodations, and given a reasonable opportunity, we often present completely different patterns to indicate new directions for information systems. Each of these books is reviewed in two chapters; thus, Part III consists of six chapters. The guiding hypothesis of Part III is that the metapattern offers a frame of reference for understanding and analyzing a variety of specific patterns.

In Part IV, *A Case of Financial Accounting*, the author presents in two chapters his original work on analysis patterns for financial accounting systems. Chapter 16 is a summary and Chapter 17 an extension of the generic information models from his earlier book *Aspecten en Fasen*, published in Dutch. The hypothesis of Part IV is that the metapattern is eminently suitable for designing innovative patterns for financial accounting systems.

Part V, *Metapattern and Pluriformity*, provides powerful modeling heuristics. The contents of the previous parts are drawn together in a single, last chapter. What often seems a contradiction should be taken by the professional modeler as an opportunity. Of course, information systems must fit their environment and help it develop. For the exposition in this book, the relevant information environment is a complex organization, meaning that information systems must agree with the pluriformity, plurality, and variety of organizations. But doesn't this raise a contradiction with application of patterns; that is, with reuse of information models? The hypothesis for Part V, in fact, for the whole book, strongly suggests that the metapattern helps increase uniformity in the structure for information systems, while simultaneously enabling the systems' pluriform behavior. The key to those advantages lies with using parameters for contexts. As this book makes abundantly clear, it is made possible through the definition of context as a formal variable *within* information sets, instead of seeing context, often implicitly and therefore unrecognized, as an informal presupposition that is kept outside.

Audiences

The book is mainly targeted at professionals involved with conceptual information modeling. It also aims at those aspiring to enter the modeling profession and to their teachers.

The subdivision into parts makes it possible for each audience to organize the reading experience differently; it attempts to collect, in one book, information for both practical and theoretical (academic) purposes. The practically oriented reader may later want to turn his or her attention to the more theoretical parts to enhance understanding of the metapattern. Academically inclined readers are invited to study the more practical parts, since that is where proof of the metapattern really lies.

Scientists can make a fundamental study of the metapattern on the basis of Parts I and II. The explanation is not exhaustive, but has enough of a formal character to support research into the claims about the metapattern. Part V offers a wider meaning of the concept of infrastructure for information (and information systems). Paradoxically, this increased uniformity in infrastructural terms has positive effects for pluriformity of organizational processes.

Parts III and IV are intended for *conceptual modelers* of information systems who seek specific conceptual (information) patterns. The examples do not pretend to absolute validity. The entire book puts emphasis on the *meta*pattern; that is, on the modeling approach and not so much on the results; specific patterns must often be tailor-made. Part I, and to a lesser extent Part II, provide professionals with a succinct reference to aspects of the metapattern approach to information modeling.

Part V offers important guidelines for *policy makers*. The metapattern allows for increased integration of different aspects of information processing. This coordination mechanism acts in parallel with the opportunity for distributing other aspects, thereby favoring autonomy. Based on increases in both standardization and flexibility, a more powerful balance and management mix for information systems in particular and organizational processes in general result.

The entire book serves users of KnitbITs® as an introduction. This tool construction technology from Information Dynamics, an independent company based in the Netherlands that is involved in the research and development of complex information systems, incorporates the metapattern philosophy. It enables flexible development of specific tools; that is, applications. KnitbITs users, therefore, are mainly *developers* of information systems. From this book they can gain a general understanding of the conceptual origin of the standardized features regarding context, time, and validity.

As the final audience, I want to mention *anyone* who understands that the last word about conceptual information modeling has not been said, written, or modeled. The metapattern attempts to proceed by a vital step, thereby expressing both a small and large ambition.

Acknowledgments

IBM Netherlands and the Dutch Ministry of Foreign Affairs each contracted Information Dynamics to design and develop prototypes based on early precursors of the metapattern and KnitbITs. Pieter Dekker, Jan Koster (both from IBM), Wim van de Lubbe and Hans Möller (both of the Ministry of Foreign Affairs) represented these organizations. In my capacity as president of Information Dynamics, I am grateful to them for the business opportunities they offered. Personally, I want to thank them for the space they allowed for intellectual development.

My thanks also go to Jan van Heijst, at the time consulting with the Task Force Foreign Residents of the Police Organization in the Netherlands, for his spirited encouragement. I have made a special friend whose life courage and sense of humor (are they essentially the same quality?) I greatly admire. He inspired the informal case study presented in the *Introduction*.

To Martin Dooms I do not have to explain the reasons for my gratitude.

The important, innovative work on KnitbITs has so far been done by Information Dynamics' employees Ivar de Jong (earlier) and Martijn Houtman (now). Their suggestions for improved software constructions have also fundamentally contributed to the approach to conceptual information modeling called the metapattern. I value their excellent work, for which I gladly express my gratitude.

A remark made by Henk Gazendam, professor of information systems at the University of Twente, Netherlands, about one of my other texts led me to the idea to frame my approach to conceptual information modeling in the patterns movement. He also mentioned A.-W. Scheer to me, thereby pointing to his work, and through a specific book's title led me to consider D. C. Hay's work. The work of both of these authors is discussed in Part III.

The authors of the books reviewed here deserve special mention. Odell, Scheer, Hay, and Fowler have made important ideas publicly accessible so that others may build on them. I recommend that every serious modeler study their work. They have provided me with the needed background to expound the metapattern in ways that make it easier to understand for many readers. Through them I also gained inspiration to develop alternative models and patterns. Whatever criticism I direct at their work is meant respectfully. I express the hope that they, and others, will feel encouraged to continue constructive discussion to advance conceptual information modeling.

Jim Odell kindly referred me to Addison-Wesley for publication. He also read an earlier version of Parts I and II of my manuscript. Contrary to his (too) modest suggestion, I maintained Chapters 7 through 9, since I have received favorable reactions to sketching the metapattern against the background of his work. I decided not to forgo the highly valued pedagogical opportunity of an extensive discussion of Odell's book.

Through Odell's introduction, I also corresponded by e-mail with Haim Kilov. Kilov kindly drew my attention to the Reference Model for Open Distributed Processing (RM-ODP). I am glad for the opportunity to compare the metapattern with RM-ODP (see Appendix B).

Paul Becker, my acquisitions editor at Addison-Wesley, and Ross Venables, assistant editor, have guided me pleasantly and professionally through the process of preparing the manuscript for publication. Ross let me feel that, however long a publishing decision might take, it would be positive. I have greatly benefited from the reviews Paul solicited. I respect the reviewers' anonymity. It makes me all the more grateful for their insightful, consistently constructive comments, by which they have certainly helped me write a better book. I would also like to thank several other people who were essential in the completion of this book: Jacqui Doucette, who managed the project; copyeditors Suzie Rodriguez and Pat Menard, who dealt with the idiosyncrasies of English being my second language; Kim Arney, who coordinated the book's production in the most helpful manner to me; and Carol Noble, whose professional proofreading added the finishing touch.

For my family I reserve the deepest feelings, but can find the least appropriate words to express them. There are indeed limits to conceptual information modeling and this happy realization, I believe, makes life really and fully human.

Valid criticism the reader must direct only to me, for I am solely responsible for this book's contents. Still, I hope that, if nothing more, at least my effort meets with some praise. The difficulty in opening a new approach has been succinctly formulated by A. H. Maslow in his wonderful book, *The Psychology of Science*: "Knowledge has an embryology, too." Naturally, at its birth, the metapattern cannot yet be fully grown, but its promise should be clearly visible. I hope this book helps bring it to maturity.

Introduction

Advancing in an Important Profession

Conceptual information modeling, or analysis, is now an important profession in its own right, one much in need of responsible, dedicated practitioners. As you read this book, which explains the unique modeling approach of the meta-pattern, you will benefit by attaining a higher level of professionalism.

You are presented here with a simple, yet powerful method of visualization. It will assist you when forming and, equally important, communicating essential concepts. The metapattern is your conceptual tool when participating as a change agent in the increasingly complex development processes of today and the future.

If you take conceptual information modeling seriously, this book is for you. You can begin with the many patterns provided in this book, extending or modifying them. Or you can start from scratch and apply the metapattern to develop your own models/patterns.

Imaginative Realism

To benefit from this book, you need common sense and imagination, characteristics that are far more important than any academic degree you may have acquired. What higher education might have done is better prepare you for practicing abstraction, but if you aren't skilled in abstraction to begin with, conceptual modeling is not the right profession for you.

As for common sense, conceptual modeling is always about your world, including your own place in it. You must be realistic to maintain a proper perspective, as models, too, are means to live in our world, not ends.

Models are also necessary for changing, and best of all, improving your part of the world. That is why a professional modeler must be creative. Modeling is all about finding a realistic expression for imagination.

Conceptual Priority

As a corollary, a predominantly technological orientation will only frustrate the achievement of conceptual information models that really work. So far, implicitly or explicitly, conceptual modeling has mostly been positioned as an extension of software engineering.

Here, the emphasis is firmly reversed, with the author gladly admitting that he has not written a serious computer program since attending college. This is like an architect who continues a career in design rather than construction. Though a room needs walls, it will never attain a living quality when its design is taken as merely the sum of its constructive parts.

Of course, a conceptual information modeler cannot help being strongly influenced by technological constraints and opportunities. Otherwise, her or his work would even not be realistic. But the modeler should always stress the conceptual nature of information. Who needs information? Why? When? What does it *mean*? Conceptual modeling should finally gain priority and determine the concerns of construction and implementation, not the other way around.

Required Background

So you needn't be a skilled computer programmer to qualify as a professional, responsible modeler. Instead, the way people learn is fundamental to successful conceptual information modeling. That is why you should be particularly interested in social complexity, and in the way people deal with it while leading integrated lives. Your models eventually lead to tools those people will use to live their particular realities.

You will be able to design better models when you consistently respect real complexity. When you possess an orderly mind, your models will be neither too complex nor too simple to cover relevant information requirements. You needn't be a qualified psychologist, sociologist, or mathematician for that. Most importantly, you must be curious about the world.

Still, to appreciate the benefits of the metapattern, it does help to have an idea of the conceptual side of object orientation (OO). At the same time, however, you should be ready to leave several of OO's main tenets behind. The same flexibility is helpful with respect to entity-attribute-relationship (EAR) modeling. For with its radical emphasis on context orientation, the metapattern definitely goes beyond both relational modeling and traditional object orientation.

Essential Characteristics

Drawing attention to problems with EAR and OO is far from new. But the metapattern solves them elegantly at a conceptual level.

You may gain some idea of how you can apply the metapattern from a summary statement of its three essential characteristics:

context is a structural concept

Through its partial identities, an overall object may be contained by a variety of contexts. Different contexts facilitate a corresponding, unambiguous variety of information object behavior. Multiple contexts within the information model most elegantly fulfill the increasingly relevant requirement of multiple classification.

time is factored at every meaningful node

As a matter of routine, the period(s) of existence of information objects (meaningful nodes) at each level of granularity versus aggregation is kept track of. Because meta-information is modeled just like any information, the increasingly relevant requirement of dynamic classification is fulfilled by default.

validity is factored at every meaningful node

Errors, intentional or not, are a fact of life. Mistaken information is not removed but maintained with a nonvalid status. The new information entered as a correction takes on the status of valid. Combined with time-factoring, a comprehensive audit trail results by default.

Power

These characteristics, taken together, make the metapattern a powerful approach to conceptual information modeling. The metapattern supports multiple and dynamic classification, as well as a high level of accountability. Because this is achieved through fully operational concepts *within* a single modeling approach, a modeler applying the metapattern can keep conceptual information models robust, compact, and yet flexible, even when dealing with increasingly complex information requirements. Again, this book will show you how.

An Informal Case Study

A simplified—and, at this stage, necessarily informal and playfully reduced—case study is described next, extending through the sections whose titles start with "case study." It is included at the beginning of the book to offer you a first glance at how results might be obtained with the metapattern. The single emphasis is on the use of multiple contexts. Contexts, in the metapattern way, are fundamental to consistent information management of time and validity. Details follow in the main text.

Case Study: Resident Foreigners

For as long as human communities have existed, they have exchanged members. A person can elect, or be forced, to stay in a community different from his original one, or might seek refuge elsewhere.

With the introduction of nation states, persons were attributed with a formal nationality. A person who resides in the area corresponding to a national state is, based on her or his own nationality, officially classified as either a national or a non-national. A non-national resident is a foreigner.

This case study concerns one of many democratic nation states that registers information about foreigners. A foreigner whose residence is officially authorized is allocated a title of residence, allowing her or him particular rights and duties under the control of the nation state in which she or he resides. An example of a right could be eligibility for Social Security payments or guaranteed access to health care. A duty might be the payment of taxes due. These rights and duties may vary with the title of residence. Usually, rights and duties are mostly identical for nationals and foreigners, although some are different.

Several government organizations are involved with resident foreigners. The police, in the nation state under consideration, is a decentralized organization in its own right with 25 regional police forces. Every police force maintains its own information about foreigners residing in that region. A wide range of information may be registered about any foreigner to properly support the allocated tasks of the police.

As different organizations keep their own information systems—some dedicated to foreigners, others established for all eligible residents—duplication of information and related efforts is enormous. The fact that each organization strives to be self-contained is the source of much inefficiency. Most important, though, the service to foreigners becomes less than optimal. A foreigner must often supply identical information to each organization. This compromises the information's quality, which has to be guarded by additional efforts. The author had the privilege to raise this complex issue while working as an external consultant to a police staff unit.

Case Study: All Persons

From the perspective of universal human rights, the most important step in streamlining government information systems is to recognize that a foreigner is *not* fundamentally different from a national. A nation state must treat them all equally as simply, by definition, *persons*. But a difference should remain as the basis for some other, often important, differential treatment. After a foreigner's work permit expires, for example, he or she must leave the country. Or, after a war, the refugee should repatriate. Whether they do so is, of course, another matter—which is why the police must be involved with foreigners.

With *person* as the basic object type, differences can easily be established through subtypes. In this case, relevant subtypes of person are *national* and *foreigner*, as shown in Figure I-1.

Case Study: All Contexts, No Subtypes

The metapattern can be understood informally as a stubborn refusal to admit such subtypes into a conceptual information model. As happens with any outright refusal, however, the required differences do not go away. What, then, takes the functional place of subtypes? The answer is contexts.

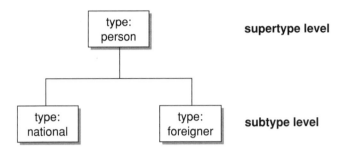

Figure I-1 *Traditional object orientation: differences appear through subtypes*

A context exists as the result of a need to make behavior specific. By the way, *behavior* here is meant in both a static and a dynamic sense. The metapattern does not fundamentally distinguish between state itself and state change. Why? Because the instructions for change are always stated statically. That is, as prescriptions they should also be considered as a state.

From the perspective of the nation state, a national may have to be treated differently from a foreigner. This leads to the contexts of nationalship and foreignership, within which a particular person becomes an object (see Figure I-2). A person existing inside nationalship must behave as a national; inside foreignership, as a foreigner.

Such a model may be represented more simply. The contextual differentiation of behavior is not infinite, and is constrained by what may be loosely called a coordination domain. A context is unique within such a domain, which may be viewed for practical reasons as an information system (note that a configuration of information systems again yields an information system). What counts is the extent of coordination. With this informal notion, a context such as foreigner-

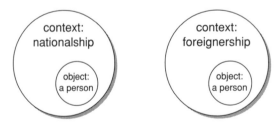

Figure I-2 *Metapattern: differences appear through contexts*

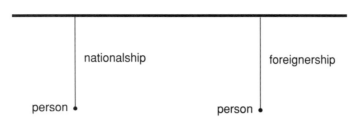

Figure I-3 *Coordination domain as ground for contexts*

ship is grounded; the same ground then applies in this modeling case for nationalship. As shown in Figure I-3, these different contexts are considered to originate in a downward progression from their common ground; nonetheless, within different contexts nodes all representing persons may appear.

What is lacking here, as compared to the subtyping approach, is person as a separate type. This can be dealt with by assuming a corresponding context, personship, as shown in Figure I-4.

The behavior of this last, most general context should be limited to what is universal among persons. The context of foreignership would then be used, as indicated, for behavior specific to being a foreigner. And, obviously, the context of nationalship would restrict behavior of its objects to what concerns nationals.

The general context of personship in particular highlights the possibility that one and the same object occurs in several contexts. Someone is a person first and a foreigner second. This may be shown by a derivative relationship. In Figure I-5 the contexts are also renamed. As a result, the nodes no longer require names. Each node's cardinality—the number of possible object instances within a particular context—is indicated.

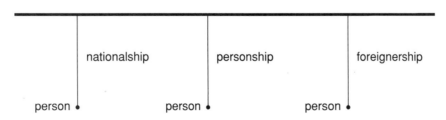

Figure I-4 *Adding a general context*

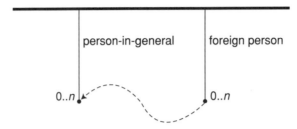

Figure I-5 *Derivation between contexts; specifying instance cardinalities*

Case Study: The Primacy of Title of Residence

The conceptual model, however, has still not captured the coexistence of similarities and differences between nationals and foreigners. It turns out that residence rather than nationality is the prime operating variable for government action. It thus seems wise to try modeling with residence as a context. Corresponding nodes, derived from persons-in-general, represent persons-as-residents. An important property of residents would then be their title of residence (see Figure I-6).

But what if the title of residence is a composition? Its components could be nation state of residence, nationality of resident, reason for residence, and duration of residence. With such contents every resident could be attributed one or more titles of residence, not just so-called foreigners.

From the perspective of a specific title of residence, a person would be called a national when the first two components converged. If nation state of resi-

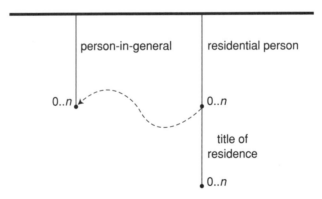

Figure I-6 *What is the critical context?*

dence and nationality of resident diverged, the person would be considered a foreigner. Government actions would thus be directed by the particular title of residence. Irrespective of applying the metapattern, it should be noted that flexibility is greatly increased by eliminating any explicit occurrence of something like nationalship or foreignership from the model's structure. Instead, the more flexible structure permits the required information to be supplied by content.

The next step in modeling is to promote title of residence to the conceptual center stage of government relationships with persons. For example, the fiscal treatment of a person is based on residence and perhaps possessions. In another example, the right to vote is similarly grounded.

It makes sense to use names different from title of residence in those other contexts. Through a direct derivation, their origin is obvious, anyway. Such an overview is shown in Figure I-7.

An abstraction, now within reach, leads away from nation state as the only type of government. By changing nation state of residence to governmental area, the model also applies to municipalities, federal governments, and so on.

Case Study: Continued Integration

Yet another level of conceptual integration may be reached by including, for example, bodies corporate. A body corporate also shows diverse behaviors, many of which share previously stated contexts with persons-in-general.

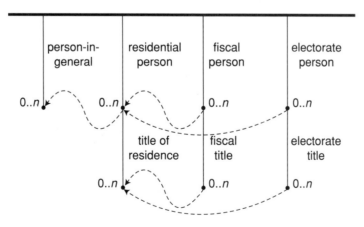

Figure I-7 *Chains of derivational relationships*

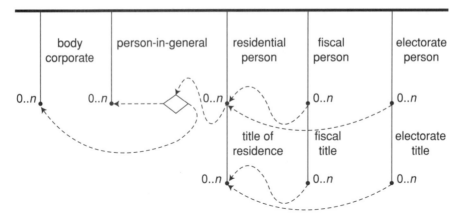

Figure I-8 *Extra-contextual differences, intracontextual similarities*

Figure I-8 shows that the conceptual model extension is extremely simple. When a node for a fiscal person is established, a choice regarding the derivative relationship must be made. A particular fiscal person, electorate person, and so on, is derived from either a person-in-general or a body corporate. The contexts for personship-in-general and (in)corporateship have been kept separate on the assumption that characteristic behaviors are different.

Figure I-8 shows another major advantage of the metapattern. As different contexts are juxtaposed, *all* previously defined contexts are available for derivative relationships. In traditional modeling, additional subtypes would have to be introduced—even when fiscal behavior of a body corporate is identical to a person-in-general's fiscal behavior. Juxtaposition of contexts makes it possible to arrive at consistently singular behavioral descriptions.

Robust Conceptual Models

The models shown in our informal case study were originally suggested by experiences of a small police staff unit. The objective was not to reorganize all information systems of all government organizations. However, the playful exploration of many related information systems ensured that the police information system is optimally scoped. When the range of action might be extended, the original conceptual information models are already up to the task of increased coordination while maintaining relevant differences. Context as constituted by the metapattern is a very natural concept for this purpose.

Paradigm Shift

To learn how to apply the metapattern well, you must understand why you might need it. Throughout this book you'll find examples of the modern problems that traditional modeling approaches cannot adequately solve. Such cases provide clear evidence for a different kind of solution.

The metapattern *is* different. It not only solves many tough modeling problems elegantly, it also creates additional opportunities for information systems. This paradigm shift is further explained in the following sections, whose titles start with the word "shift." Once you accept the necessity of a fundamental difference, you will appreciate the paradigm shift underlying the metapattern.

Shift: A Small Taste of Philosophy

As an experienced or aspiring conceptual modeler you undoubtedly show a philosophical inclination. How else could you be creative about concepts? As such, you probably feel comfortable about returning to basics or seeking a new and improved conceptual foundation. But does the metapattern really reflect such a paradigm shift? Readers in search of an extended inquiry into the metapattern's philosophical roots should read the essay in Appendix A.

Shift: Explaining the World

How you believe the world exists on a fundamental level is known as your ontology. The word *ontology*, which is derived from ancient Greek, means "knowledge of being."

With an ontology, or an ontological paradigm, you inquire into what you consider essential. Other knowledge may then be grounded on such essentials. Another way of putting it is that an ontology covers axioms—or, as some prefer to call them, first principles. An ontological paradigm is, at heart, always a matter of belief. And what people believe to be the essentials of their world may vary.

Many people believe that absolute objects, or entities, make up the world. This works well in daily life. But conceptual information modeling is already different from what normal people normally do.

Shift: Behavioral Diversity

The metapattern way of explaining the world denies the absolute existence of objects. Please note that objects are still believed to exist—very much so, in fact.

It is their *absolute* existence that is removed as the one and only starting point for explaining the world. This is done for a practical purpose, for behavior is often, and increasingly, diverse.

How can different behaviors be attributed to a single object? The metapattern assumes that specific behavior is always determined by an object *being in a situation*. The same object in different situations will show different behaviors. Take yourself as an example. Overall, you surely feel you are one and the same person regardless of the situation you find yourself in. Yet, your behavior at home might be different from how you behave at work, in your car, and so on. Variety is a characteristic of behavior. The metapattern is all about balancing variety of behaviors while maintaining an object's basic unity.

Shift: Situation Is Context

In order to keep an object's perspective, the term *context* is preferred to *situation*. As explained earlier, though the metapattern leaves absolute existence of objects behind, the existence of contexts is assumed to be even more essential. It means that any object may exist in several contexts. By definition, the object's behavior in one context is different from its behavior in all other contexts.

So, by placing the concept of context before that of object, the difference of the metapattern is of an ontological nature. It's reassuring to know that your previous ontological concepts remain completely valid *after* you have introduced contexts, so you lose nothing. In fact, you gain: Your world view as a modeler becomes enriched by a greater degree of freedom. This happens when you accept the paradigm shift of the metapattern toward multiple contexts. The single perspective is replaced by a dual perspective, with objects no longer believed to exist absolutely and contexts given priority.

Shift: Is It Really New?

Indeed, there is nothing new about taking context into account for modeling. The term *context* is encountered frequently enough in serious modeling approaches. The metapattern's innovation is the *radical* importance attributed to the concept of context. Also essential is this concept's implementation—context as an open-ended recursion of object-relationship pairs. How this is achieved is explained fully later. With multiple contexts for any object, differentiating behavior is a straightforward matter.

Even this detailed approach, using recursive pairs of object and relationship instances for context description, might not be absolutely new. As far as the author knows, however, the metapattern's squarely ontological meaning of context, and its consistently recursive implementation by means of object and relationship instances, have never before been applied to conceptual information modeling. The concept of context as explained in this book is offered here as new—in the context of concept, at least.

For its ingredients the metapattern is heavily indebted to many disciplines, all contributing important ideas. These include traditional modeling approaches such as hierarchical and network database management, entity-attribute-relationship modeling, and object-oriented modeling. A more remote example is Gestalt psychology. The parallel is striking, as a particular Gestalt, or appearance, shows up as foreground (behavior) against an equally particular background (context). Still, underlying several appearances may well be a single, overall object. Gestalt psychology really is the arch-example of a dual perspective.

Shift: On Communicating New Ideas

The metapattern is successful in meeting new, often much more complex information requirements. But the inevitable departure from earlier approaches to modeling raises a problem in communication. What is new about the metapattern is described as often as possible in terms already known by the reader. The paradox is that understanding any innovation's value requires going beyond what was known before. It is for this reason that the reader is especially urged to reconsider the basic concepts brought to modeling.

Conceptual Modeling

We stated earlier that ideas about software engineering have largely controlled the perception of conceptual information modeling. This view of conceptual modeling has limitations. Therefore, before details of the metapattern can be fully appreciated, conceptual modeling should be repositioned. What, then, *is* conceptual modeling? The remainder of this *Introduction* attempts to provide an answer. However, before we tackle the question we need to add new terminology, providing an opportunity to rehearse the essentially multicontextual nature of the metapattern.

Information Models and Patterns

Information and communication technology are increasingly applied in various tools for various activities. Those tools are artifacts; that is, they are first and foremost human constructs. This means that people are deeply involved in, and responsible for, decisions about information systems.

The intention(s) with a particular information system must be reflected in the choice of relevant structure and information. It takes professionals, acting on behalf of and together with all stakeholders, to assemble conceptual models. In this book, such conceptual models of information sets are called conceptual information models. When a particular model is suitable as a representative example for various situations, or when it is even widely applicable without modification, it can justifiably be called a pattern.

Ontological Principles

Every information model rests on an ontology, a certain idea about reality. This idea remains mostly hidden, if only because the modeler is often unaware of the workings of his or her knowledge principles. The mark of a professional modeler is that she or he tries to be aware of how her or his knowledge functions. It is precisely this interest in epistemology (another word with a classical origin) that hints that every modeler has at least a small taste for philosophy. Do strange words deter you—words like *ontology* and *epistemology*? It only takes a little extra effort to fully grasp them. But then, grasping meanings is what conceptual modeling is really all about.

The ontological principle behind modern information models, almost without exception, is that objects (or even object types) have a privileged status. A certain object is supposed to exist completely independently, and this principle holds for all objects. Because a world view of all independent objects is untenable, however, objects are then fitted with relationships among them. This, as it were, compensates for the knowledge procedure of postulating separate objects. A more balanced (less unbalanced?) conceptual information model results.

An alternative ontological proposal for conceptual modeling is to consider *context*—not object—as the first principle. This is the very paradigm shift of the metapattern. As a consequence, an object can only exist *within* one or more contexts. Objects keep their relationships. Based on the new principle, however, a relationship between context and object is added. This knowledge procedure also has a compensating quality, since it defines even context as object. Advantages for compact information modeling follow.

An Idea Whose Time Has Come

Actually, given the current state of the world, it is logical to declare *context* a fundamental concept for information modeling. And *time*, too. Most people will increasingly experience the world as multifaceted and highly pluriform. And accelerating changes make the world ever more dynamic. In fact, modern information and communication technology itself is now a prime driver of this post-modern human condition.

With growing diversity, uniform concepts no longer hold sufficient variety for private and organizational affairs. By superimposing the concept of context, and especially by doing so combined with the concept of time, we give earlier uniform concepts enough room to shift their meanings to pluriform usage. What this book hopes to explain is that a contextualized object is different from an absolute object as assumed by traditional object orientation.

It may sound odd to label as traditional a movement that only recently gained momentum. But already a paradigm shift—from object orientation to, say, object-in-context orientation—is needed to keep conceptual information modeling in step with the times.

Outline of the Metapattern

To make the reader comfortable with the experience of encountering familiar-but-also-unfamiliar concepts, we present an additional outline of the conceptual modeling approach, called the metapattern.

The metapattern is about the formalization of context and time in information models. This book concentrates completely on *conceptual* information modeling.

Social psychologists have known for a long time that the overall behavior of a person is never completely consistent. Rather, consistency is limited to what is called—in metapattern terms—a context. But this does not mean that modelers should apply the opposite idea and postulate as many different persons as there are relevant contexts. Overall, it is also still one indivisible person.

Putting contexts first elegantly solves the problem (whereas subtypes solve it crudely). The type that determines behavior is no longer for an object-as-such but for an object-in-context. Actually, context *is* type. This shift in the meaning of type has advantageous consequences; first, for all conceptual modeling; second, and practically, for operational information systems.

Additionally, according to the metapattern, provisions for change are present at the smallest relevant scale of information. This means that, for any point in time, any aggregation of information can be unambiguously reported. When the time of relevance changes, the dynamics of information become visible.

The Approach

As a result of the changed ontological principle, contexts explicitly appear *in* the information model, allowing for increased variety in the approach to information modeling. By emphasizing *approach*, something called a metamodel comes into view. In step with the need for growing reuse, it is called the *metapattern*. It is purposely not written as Metapattern, with a capital M, for there is no single approach to modeling. It is instead *the* metapattern, which is practical in the context of this book. The definite article expresses the firm conviction that the modeling approach presented here as the metapattern is, in many ways and for many information requirements, more powerful than what existed before.

Tools for Life, or Living for Tools

We have so far written about conceptual information modeling without defining it. In attempting to do so, it's helpful to suggest an opposition, as shown in Figure I-9.

A person positioned on one side (left, in Figure I-9) would be focused on her or his life in general. Tools only appear in such a life to support it. Tools are only

Figure I-9 *Opposition between life and tool orientations*

the means to an end. Life contains many uncertainties; its overall quality is imprecise. You will appreciate this complex quality when you accept that each person, yourself included, essentially leads a *social* life. Many aspects escape control, illustrating life's uncertainty.

On the opposite side (right, in Figure I-9) stands a person completely focused on tool making. Her or his life is lived in the service of those activities—inside the box, so to say. Here, tools are the end, and the tool maker's living is the means. A consistent quality of tools requires the elimination of uncertainty; precision is not only valued, but necessary.

In Praise of Imprecision

An information system is also a tool. Highly skilled professionals, specialized in applying technology, develop construction modules and secure their configuration. Increasingly, they use (and, when necessary, modify) research from software libraries. Because these specialists focus on technological issues, they require unambiguous specifications to develop a perfectly matched implementation (that may later be varied through technology).

When actual construction work is highly specialized, as with complex information systems, drawing up specifications can be difficult. With tool specifications, technological experts are involved to ascertain the required precision. But somewhere the focus changes in a fundamental way. When a tool specialist is asked to make specifications from a life perspective, the result is life specified with all the precision of a tool. But real life, being imprecise at heart, is not a tool. Instead, imprecision of life must be respected. It needs a different mindset from that of a tool maker.

Another kind of precision is required for what the metapattern allows to be documented. The enormous variety of real life can be adequately described with multiple contexts, and with any context consisting of an ordered collection of object and relationship instance pairs.

From Two Oppositions to One Continuum

A conceptual modeler must first understand life and its foremost requirements. Basically, this understanding is a quality of the modeler's mind—that is, a true conceptual model is purely subjective. But this does not really work when development tasks are so complex that several people, each contributing particular skills, are needed for successful completion. This introduces communication: What the modeler puts down in a communicable form is also known as a conceptual model.

In a way, capturing the conceptual models in a modeler's mind onto an external medium is already ruled by a dual perspective. On the one hand, the focus should be firmly on life, rather than tool, leading the modeler to neglect the precision required by tool technology. Yet, the purpose of the modeling effort is to make a tool available.

The traditional way out of this dilemma has been to force the issue in favor of tool-focused precision. This has led to conceptual schemas that hardly deserve the name. From a life point of view, concepts have been technologically over- and underspecified, with the result of often missing the original point altogether.

In developing the metapattern we do not want to make this mistake. First of all, the whole process of tool development should be viewed as a continuum, rather than constituted by two separate, and opposite points. Second, the fundamental orientation should remain at the end of the life problem. That is why the metapattern is firmly positioned at that end of the development continuum. As a language to express life's information requirements conceptually, the metapattern supports necessary and sufficient precision. But with complex information systems we have a precision different from that corresponding to the tool focus. The metapattern offers to bring a basically life-oriented model to a point along the continuum where the focus may switch. Metapattern-based models, with their characteristic precision, should then be translated into implementation models with equally characteristic, but necessarily different, precision. These dynamics are summarized in Figure I-10.

Looking at the continuum between life and tool, we can clearly see that the metapattern supports many implementation issues. This is to be expected when, eventually, a tool must result. However, any implementation issue treated may not be (too) dependent on specific technology. In general, though, it's only right that generalized principles of technology appear as conceptual constraints. Which constraints warrant such generalization depends partly on technological development. When they cannot be avoided, they might as well be dealt with conceptually—at the earliest possible stage along the continuum of tool making for life.

An influence in the opposite direction also exists, as Figure I-10 indicates. At first, issues may only be dealt with conceptually. The metapattern concept of context is a prime example. In general, it can then be translated onto construc-

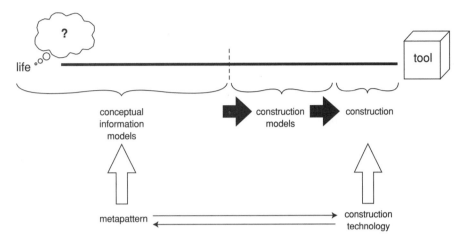

Figure I-10 *Orientation dynamics*

tion technology. When this succeeds, tool features are yet again standardized from the application of technology. Without provisions at the level of general tool technology, such features would have to be developed specifically for each tool. Technology for implementing metapattern-based conceptual information models needs to exhibit *pervasive* support of contextuality, and of temporal and validity issues. This book will prepare your understanding of such characteristics of tool construction technology. Knowing the technology is available will make you more confident in conceptual information modeling.

Development Toward Objectivity

In successful development, models change character from being completely subjective as concepts in a single mind, through being increasingly inter-subjective as concepts shared by stakeholders, to being completely objective as embodied in a tool. All too often, the intrinsically subjective origin is denied. When the tool focus is enforced throughout development, rather than recognizing a continuum with a life focus at the opposite end, all models at all stages are supposed to be objective. This really does not help. It is even a fundamental obstruction to successful communication.

At the early stages of developing a complex information system, stakeholders as a rule entertain divergent concepts. They must become sufficiently converged or shared. In a conceptual sense, stakeholders are better described as shareholders. A conscious, constructive agreement about their disagreement is often the decisive step toward more shared concepts. This is the critical contribution to success that conceptual information modeling must make. The conceptual modeler is a vital change agent. The other important contribution of conceptual information models is to facilitate translation onto technologically precise construction/implementation models that are as objective as possible.

Conceptual precision needs for its expression as few constraints as possible. The precision measures belonging to the tool focus often stifle imagination. A conceptual modeler needs ample room for creativity, as a new idea or concept can only originate in an individual mind. Only after it has been conceived can the modeler proceed to share it. The informal case study, presented earlier in this *Introduction*, serves as an excellent example of using a real problem to invent new concepts. Who had ever heard of residential persons? And of applying titles of residence universally, thereby making residential person and title of residence pivotal concepts? Indeed, they are inventions, or, according to German philosopher H. Vaihinger (1852–1933), fictions. They can bring an elegant solution—a tool—closer to the original problem. An intermediary problem is finding stakeholders to agree on concepts. When stakeholders sufficiently accept new concepts *as if* they were objective—that is, when they all assume that corresponding objects really exist—it is possible to draw up precise tool specifications, a requirement dictated from the tool focus. Most important, the precondition is met that the tool will be used successfully, for any tool must always be placed (back) in the context of life.

What the Metapattern Is, and What It Is Not

The metapattern provides relevant precision to express information requirements directly related to a (social) life focus. It is definitely not an all-encompassing modeling approach. Its power is in its focused ambition—that is, in its conceptual information modeling.

However, the metapattern does support implementation, albeit indirectly. Some generic implementation issues, known for current implementation technologies, have been abstracted into conceptual constructs.

Specific implementation issues are always dealt with separately when translating a conceptual information model to an implementation/construction model. This translation can only be negated at the cost of extending the life focus to tools, or the tool focus onto life. It leads to messy tools, or to a disappointing life, and probably both. Those problems are avoided by understanding what conceptual information modeling is, as opposed to tool specification. Again, the metapattern supports conceptual modeling.

An Independent Profession

Whenever development processes mature beyond a certain complexity, sooner or later the proposed duality of focus appears. It does not seem humanly possible for an individual to be successful at all stages of the continuum. For this reason, the built environment is served by architects and contractors.

This book is written from the conviction that a high-quality information environment urgently needs recognition and deployment of conceptual information modelers as independent professionals. The author unequivocally states that he is not a software engineer, although he respects them highly. Once conceptual modelers and software engineers respect their fundamentally different focuses, they will see the need to cooperate, not compete, for success.

Part I

Design of the Metapattern

Chapter 1

Contexts

The design of the metapattern identifies several concepts in a characteristic semantic structure. This chapter develops a basic concept—that of context— and elaborates upon the connections among context, object, and relationship, which result in an even wider definition of object as seen from the dual meta-pattern perspective.

1.1 Contexts with Object

An object behaves according to a particular situation; that is, its behavior can change from one situation to another. For instance, if you only know Bill as your next-door neighbor, you might be surprised to see him in action at work or visiting his mother. It is this behavioral variety, and the need to model it conceptually, that has resulted in the assignment of primacy to the situation rather than to the object. Another word for situation is *context*.[1] Thus, primary attention shifts to what is *around* an object.

We use the term *context* because most people seem familiar with it in the sense of appreciating why something is not always completely the same thing. Meta-pattern is a technique for information modeling that emphasizes flexibility and reusability. It helps the modeler strike a deliberate balance between general

---

1. Actually, the equivalence of situation and context reflects a limited orientation. Though limited, it is optimally suited when the ontological status of an objective reality does not pose problems. In fact, human behaviors in daily life, including most conceptual information modeling in practice, can easily rest on the assumption of *the* objective reality. But a more general, philosophical orientation should recognize the difference between situation and context. In a new book, tentatively entitled *Semiosis & Sign Exchange, Conceptual Grounds of Business Information Modeling*, I have developed such themes in depth.

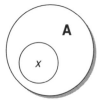
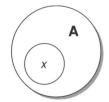
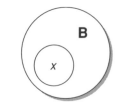
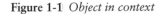

Figure 1-1 *Object in context*   **Figure 1-2** *Object in multiple contexts*

structure (abstraction) and instances (concreteness) of information. The resulting conceptual models will always optimally accommodate requirements. The metapattern presumes that an object's behaviors are completely different from one context to another. Odd as it may look, the absence of *any* shared properties by an object among its contexts exemplifies the metapattern. The minimal mechanism that holds the object's contextual identities together is explained at the end of this chapter.

Suppose a particular context **A** exists. And suppose that the equally specific object *x* is contained by **A**. An example would be Bill (*x*) at work (**A**). This relationship is shown in Figure 1-1.

Another context, say **B,** could also contain the object *x*. This is shown in Figure 1-2. Bill (*x*) is either at work (**A**) or at home (**B**).

Contexts **A** and **B** may overlap, as in Figure 1-3. This happens when Bill works at home.

However, any overlap can be reduced; in this case, to three disjunct contexts. One context applies strictly to work behavior, the second to home behavior, and the third to behavior in which work and home are mixed. These derived contexts are defined using the accepted notation of set theory. In general, the set containing all elements outside any set **A** is denoted by $\bar{\text{A}}$ (see Figure 1-4).

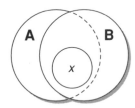

Figure 1-3 *Object in overlapping contexts*

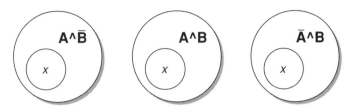

Figure 1-4 *Conversion to disjunct contexts*

Because reductive conversion is always possible, contexts are always assumed to be disjunct for simplicity's sake.

1.2 Instances and Types

It is important to distinguish between instances and types when necessary. To call an object a person, for example, usually means that a particular *object instance* is referred to, which obeys the *object type* of person. For example, Bill is a particular person. John is another, and equally particular, person. As unique individuals they are both regarded as instances. When object instances are required to share properties—but not necessarily actual property values—they belong to the same object type.

Listing relevant instances or elements defines a set by extension. Following the extensional approach, set members may, or may not, share their properties. In contrast, a type intentionally specifies a set—that is, through conditions that must hold valid for elements to qualify as set members. The assumption that Bill is of the person type, unambiguously specifies his properties. With the person type assigned to John, he too will exhibit exactly the same properties.

The context in which the term *object* appears often makes it immediately clear whether that object's instance or type is meant. To avoid clutter, we use this implicit procedure throughout this book.

1.3 Object with Contexts

Figure 1-1 suggests that object *x* exists in context **A**. Simultaneously, however, the idea of context leads to an independent consideration of the object. This suggests an explicit relationship; that is, between a context and an object. Let's

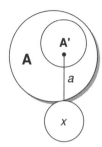

Figure 1-5 *An explicit relationship between object and context*

call the relationship between context **A** and object *x*, *a*. Thus, Bill (*x*) is an employee (*a*) at Case Study Corp. (**A**). For an easier overview, put *x* below **A**, formally retaining *a* within the context (see Figure 1-5). As part of **A**, something of a subcontext **A'** originates, where

A = {*a*, **A'**}

Because relationship *a* remains part of context **A**, every context of *x* is unique. A relationship *b* that could connect *x* to **A'** would lead to a different context. Bill (*x*) could also be retired (*b*) from Case Study Corp. (**A**). This also holds for relationship *a* between object *x* and another context **B**. Indeed, this reflects that Bill (*x*) is also an employee (*a*) of Trial & Error Inc. (**B**).

The formal distinction between context **A** and subcontext **A'** only continues to be specified in the text if the argument may be confusing. If an explicit relationship appears, it is simpler to use only a single capital letter to indicate a subcontext.

In another schematic convention, the line representing the relationship runs into the same set the object seems to have left *because of* that relationship.

For context **B**, everything said about **A** holds true. Therefore, object *x* can be involved in relationships with various contexts. Figure 1-6 shows the abstraction with two contexts.

Figures 1-1 and 1-5 are equivalent, as are Figures 1-3 and 1-6. In both Figures 1-5 and 1-6, the context has been objectified: context and object are placed apart. An explicit relationship between them is required to maintain a view on their original synthesis.

With the relationship subsequently defined as part of its context, an object is best positioned to show its unique behaviors. Note that *behaviors* is plural. An object's behavior may be specified on the basis of several relevant contexts.

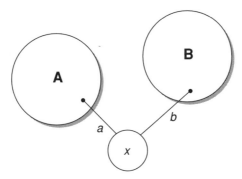

Figure 1-6 *An object's relationships with multiple contexts*

1.4 Reality and Information Objects

The question as to the degree to which reality and information concur defies a comprehensive theoretical answer. For most practical purposes, it is highly "realistic" to interpret information *as if* it represents reality. The information objects should then be considered representatives of real-world objects. But what about contexts and relationships?

According to the metapattern, it's also *as if* they exist. Are they actually objects? With the metapattern, contexts and relationships also have information objects as their "representatives." This is what we meant earlier when we stated that contexts are objectified for the purpose of information modeling. And relationships are, too. However, the formalization of relationship is kept straightforward throughout this metapattern exposition. It is established from the perspective of objects (including, at this stage, whole contexts). Thus, a particular relationship marks a difference between objects while it maintains them in an overall structure. For this purpose, the information object acting as a relationship is everywhere represented by a named link. Together with objects, relationships help form contexts. At the same time, a particular relationship also *appears* in a certain context. The meaning of a named relationship is therefore always clear.

1.5 Recursiveness in Context

The explicit relationship between context and object raises the question of how the connection inside the context is established. For that purpose, as a matter of design, another object is assumed. In other words, not only is a context generally objectified but its structure also consists of objects and relationships.

The metapattern's flexibility is shown by the overall application of object and relationship as building blocks in information modeling, including modeling of contexts.

Let x be the original object and let y be the object added inside the context to serve as a hook for the relationship established between object x and context $\mathbf{A}$ (Figure 1-7). Bill (x) is an employee (a) in the Purchasing Department (y) inside Case Study Corp. $(\mathbf{A})$.

The assumption of object y is a powerful procedure. As a principle, recall that context is given primacy (existence before object). In information models, however, a context is treated *as if* it consists of objects (and their relationships). This results in objects also being elements of contexts—in objects recursively forming a particular context.

Previously, through relationship a, object x was placed below "its" context $\mathbf{A}'$. To keep things simple, context is almost everywhere called $\mathbf{A}$ again. (Using the same name in no way changes the principle.) The same procedure can be applied to object y. Drawing on the original context $\mathbf{A}$, the overall metamodel is as presented in Figure 1-8.

Parsing the context of x in the manner described can be propagated in $\mathbf{A}''$ by assuming an object z. Bill (x) is an employee (a') in Purchasing (y), which is a department (a'') of Facilities (z), which is a division (a''') of . . . Case Study Corp. $(\mathbf{A})$. Thus, the original $\mathbf{A}$ is gradually broken down or decomposed, resulting first in $\mathbf{A}'$, then in $\mathbf{A}''$, and so on.

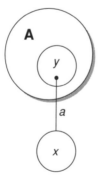

Figure 1-7 *An object's partner in a contextual relationship is another object*

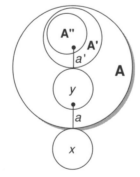

Figure 1-8 *Every object is taken outside its context through a relationship*

The structure of the context—an ordered collection of relationships and objects—is equivalent to a hierarchical classification schema. As such, a context *classifies* the objects it contains. The context as a so-called whole, and the object as a so-called part, together represent just one classification type.

It should now be clear that a positive (as in positivist science) definition of context is impossible. There does not exist something-out-there-in-the-world which only needs to be labeled properly. The metapattern view, in fact, is the other way around. Context is a conceptual construct or an instance of a fiction. This fiction is used to conceptualize reality. For this reason, context is not just any kind of concept, but a metaconcept.

No metaconcept can be positively defined. In *fiction*, several metaconcepts are required to establish a metamodel. The metapattern *is* a metamodel. It only has three metaconcepts: context, object, and relationship. Context is then defined as a particular structure of object and relationship—there can never be positive proof that such a structure really exists. To look for such proof misses the point. Context, object, and relationship have axiomatic status in the metapattern. They are fictions in the service of understanding the rest of reality.

Remotely, the procedure of expressing context in terms of object and relationship might be compared to locating the middle point between two points on a straight line. Both original points are unambiguously located, and may be expressed by their distances to a fixed point on the same line. As measures of their location, this would yield d_1 and d_2 respectively. How can the halfway point (i.e., a particular context) be determined? The procedure assumes that such a middle point exists. It is given a variable name—m, for example. The vital property of m would be that its distance to d_1 is equal to the distance to d_2. Assuming that

$$d_1 < d_2$$

it follows that

$$(m - d_1) = (d_2 - m)$$

must hold. The location of the middle point is thus found as a function of both outside points. The general result is

$$m = (d_1 + d_2) / 2$$

Likewise, the metapattern offers a general procedure to express any context in terms of instances of its other metaconcept objects and relationships. This pervasive *functional* nature of context—its (meta)concept—makes the metapattern fundamentally different from other known metamodels for conceptual information modeling. Elsewhere, the fiction of context is not a function but a completely independent type of object/entity.

The metapattern's functional approach to context is the key to simplicity in conceptual modeling. This holds true even for information requirements of an extremely complex variety. The experience of KnitbITs shows that powerful tool construction technology may be derived from this functional concept of context, too.

1.6 Boundary

With its structuralist (as opposed to positivist) foundation, the metapattern offers great precision for conceptual modeling. Again, a distinction between reality and information is useful, this time to establish the boundary for context parsing. A *boundary* is defined by the complete set of information made up by information objects.

The whole set is called the *nil object*. This name might seem paradoxical at first, but we'll see that starting from zero helps formalize a principally open-ended progression into ever more detailed information objects. Keep in mind that the metapattern does not set any limit to establishing parts of a whole. No information object may claim atomic status.

Given the primary status of context in the metapattern, a specific object x minimally has a relationship with the nil object. This is depicted in Figure 1-9.

Suppose x_n is an object at inspection level n. It follows that its context consists of the chain of objects from x_{n-1} to and including x_0. This is illustrated in Figure 1-10.

The recursiveness can also be formally expressed, the context of x_n being an ordered collection.

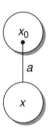

Figure 1-9 *The ultimate context is the nil object*

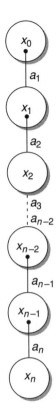

Figure 1-10 *Context decomposition yields a chain of objects*

$$\text{Context}(x_n) = \{a_n, x_{n-1}, \text{Context}(x_{n-1})\}$$

This holds for $n > 0$.

The exception is x_0, whose object does not have a context; that is, the nil object *is* its own context.

1.7 Relative Determination of Context and Object

Figure 1-10 clearly shows that *point of view* determines what counts as context and that one context can contain another.

As the set determining context grows, the context itself shrinks. When the whole information set (or information system) determines the widest possible context, for example $\{a_1, x_0\}$, it is more specific. That is the context of x_1. Consequently, the context of x_2 is the ordered collection $\{a_2, x_1, \{a_1, x_0\}\}$.

Again, what counts as a specific context depends on object choice. Such a point of view is variable. The same object can be either the point of view itself or an element of another object's context (the other object then shapes the point of view).

A third possibility also exists. Properties of some other objects are, in their turn, relationships and objects. The metapattern calls these properties *intext*. (Intext structure is discussed in Chapter 2.)

The objects constituting a context are fundamentally identical to the object that happens to be relevant for inspection. From a variable point of view, what deserves to be labeled as context or object appears to be relative (depending on the chosen point of view). This property of the metapattern is powerful, offering great flexibility and compactness. A single approach for conceptual information modeling can now cover a wide variety of problems and opportunities.

1.8 Characteristic Differences Between Approaches

What distinguishes the metapattern from so many other approaches to modeling is the ontological principle—the context having the privileged status in knowledge. Modelers unfamiliar with abandoning the object existence as the first principle in favor of context may be uncomfortable with this approach and with the lack of positive definitions. But it is precisely the assumption of contexts, objects, and relationships *defining each other* that is the metapattern's deciding quality. The absence of absolute definitions is not a problem; it is, instead, a powerful solution. The relative nature of metaconcepts is a precondition to arriving at the fiction of positive definitions of all other concepts.

In context orientation, the modeler should give priority to parsing contexts. This contrasts with traditional decomposition, which takes an independent object as its starting point. Precisely put, the assumption of an object's independence does not allow one or more contexts to enter the (conceptual) information model.

What happens is always the decomposition of an object *within* a specific context. Following this procedure, object properties are detailed corresponding to contexts. This explains how the metapattern adds freedom to conceptual information modeling.

1.9 Multiple Contexts

Emphasis is maintained on the object in its context. Let a single object, x, be involved in several contexts. The parsing of contexts need not result in an equal number of levels. Take **A** and **B** as two contexts. When x is Bill, context **A** might refer to a particular organization in which he works, whereas context **B** represents his favorite sports team (whose games he attends when they're played at home). Suppose that x, relative to its first context, is positioned at level m, relative to its second context at level n. This is shown in Figure 1-11.

A question that now arises is how the so-called connecting objects in the contexts **A** and **B** can be unambiguously identified. In a multiple setting, x_{m-1} and x_{n-1} are no longer sufficient. A suffix must be added to specify the relevant context. For example, $x_{A, m-1}$. A problem remains, however, because of the relative nature of context determination: x_{m-1}, not **A**, is the proper context, but what was indicated was **A'**. A logical mechanism consists of additionally indexing contexts on the basis of inspection levels. In Figure 1-11, as a boundary condition, A_0 and B_0 are defined as equal to x_0.

1.10 Unique Nodes

In Figure 1-12, only the object x is left undetermined with respect to both of its contexts. The solution is easily explained by starting with the nil object.

The object appearing on the first level in the context A_0 receives its unique identifier based on the specific relationship a_1. That means that this single node is unique. The node identification to process proceeds to higher numbered levels.

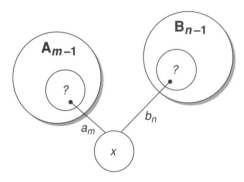

Figure 1-11 *Variable quantity of context decomposition levels*

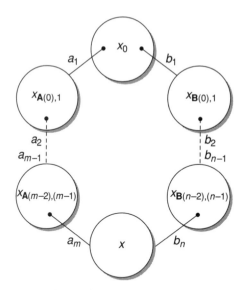

Figure 1-12 *Inspection level added for unambiguous identification of nodes*

The implication of this is important to understanding the metapattern. In fact, a certain object does not have a relationship with another object in general, but with that other object *in its capacity as a unique node*.

For this reason, Figure 1-12 still does not reflect the full variety of the metapattern. It only shows that a single object can be involved in multiple contexts. Unambiguous navigation, however, demands that the overall object be represented by a unique node *in every relevant context*. Every contextual node of x then also relates to a node that continues to represent the overall x. These are privileged relationships as they refer to the object's general identity. The letter i has been reserved for such identity relationships. This is what Figure 1-13 captures.

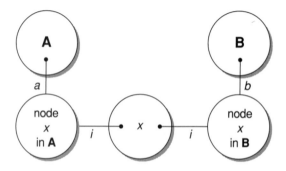

Figure 1-13 *Every node is unique*

1.11 Object Identity

Through multiple nodes, the radical context orientation changes the meaning of object identity. Actually, nodes provide an overall object with separate identities, that is, with one identity for every context. In terms of his diverse behaviors, therefore, the overall object of Bill is modeled as consisting of partial identities, exactly equal in number to his variety of behaviors.

Each overall object has one node with a special status as Figure 1-13 already explains. A mechanism is needed to bridge the separate identities of what is and should remain an overall object. All other object nodes point to the nil node, expressing the particular object's nil identity. A standardized identity relationship connects a "normal" node to the nil node. To keep the metapattern as structured as possible, even the nil nodes include a context (Figure 1-14). Each nil node maintains a nil relationship with the nil object. The acronym for the nil object is **No**.

Another notion that might appear counterintuitive is that the node representing the nil identity has hardly any need for properties. Some reflection will make this clear, since an overall object only "works" through its identities in (other) contexts.

Different behavioral Bills exist, each represented by a separate normal node reflecting a partial identity. The one overall Bill is exemplified by a single nil identity to which all behavioral Bills refer.

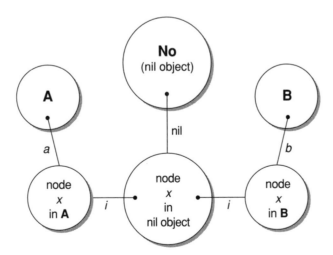

Figure 1-14 *Consistent application of concepts*

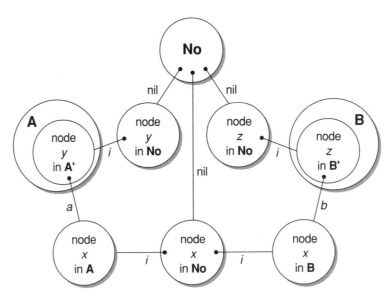

Figure 1-15 *The nil node at the root of the information set*

A specific object is, by definition, registered within a context. When registration is not based on a reference to an object in another context, it must be a completely new object and a nil node must be created. Reverse reasoning indicates that an object represented only by its nil node has lost any reason to exist in the information system.

All information objects (except nil nodes themselves) refer to a nil node. This is shown in Figure 1-15, an elaboration of Figure 1-14.

Even the nil object should have its nil node, clearly the case for a boundary condition that states that the nil object *is* its own nil node. It follows that the nil object and its own nil node have an implicit nil relationship.

1.12 Identity as a Network of Nodes

Traditional object orientation assigns identity at the level of overall objects. Context orientation replaces this view of singular objects with that of plurality within every object; the object always needs a context to uniquely identify the relevant part of an overall object, which is what identifying nodes regulate. When behaviors are identical, no distinction between contexts is necessary.

However, Bill-watching-his-favorite-sports-team will probably behave differently from Bill-at-his-regular-job. With such diverse behaviors, the overall Bill is differentiated into partial identities according to behavior-determining contexts.

As a consequence, an object no longer has a primary, singular identity. According to the metapattern paradigm, an object's overall identity *is* the collection of context-determined identities. By including the nil identity as a coordination mechanism, the overall identity can be expressed as an ordered collection of identity nodes.

$$\text{Identity}(x) = \{k_{x,0}, k_{x,1}, k_{x,2}, \ldots\ldots, k_{x,p-2}, k_{x,p-1}, k_{x,p}\}$$

where $p > 1$.

In the ordered collection of identity nodes, $k_{x,0}$ stands for the object's nil identity and nil node, respectively. The second suffix is meant to count contexts. As shown in Figure 1-16, the only order in the collection consists of the nil node as the center of a star-shaped network.

The unique nodes do not need their own inspection level explicitly indicated. Every node's context can now be recursively expressed. The formalization of § 1.6 serves as a model.

$$\text{Context}(k_{x,p}) = \{a, k_{y,q}, \text{Context}(k_{y,q})\}$$

Separate nodes allow the overall object to be modeled according to a corresponding number of contexts. Through networked nodes, the overall object is simultaneously kept together, continuing its existence as a whole.

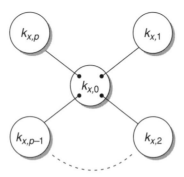

Figure 1-16 *An object's partial identities coordinated through its nil identity*

Chapter 2

Intexts

The emphasis in Chapter 1 was on context; an object's properties were never explicitly mentioned. Implicitly, however, context decomposition into a recursive alternation of object/relationship instances developed the structure for dealing with properties (attributes). By now it may be evident that an object's overall set of context-oriented identifiers constitutes just as many nodes for attaching relevant properties. By definition, properties are valid within a particular context; a set of properties that corresponds to a specific context is called *intext*.

2.1 Objects in Context

A minor change of perspective illustrates that metapattern properties follow the rules outlined for contexts. Whereas in § 1.1 the explanation started with one object having different contexts, the different objects here share the same context (Figure 2-1).

In more detail, the structure resembles Figure 2-2.

From this perspective, objects y and z are clearly shown as properties of object x. Again, the point of view gives specific meaning to roles of such information objects. Starting with object x, $\mathbf{A'}$ is its context, and y and z are its intext. When object y reflects the chosen point of view, its context is $\mathbf{A}$ (including object x) and there is no intext; that is, the particular intext set is empty. For example, Bill (x), as the employee of Case Study Corp. $(\mathbf{A})$, has been attributed a date of employment entry (y). In this particular context, no definition has been given for any breakdown of employment date into next-level properties.

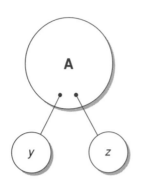

Figure 2-1 *Objects sharing context*

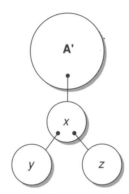

Figure 2-2 *First decomposition of context*

2.2 Intext in Context

Figure 2-2 is still misleading, however, because x indicates an overall object. This should be replaced by the node serving as the context-oriented identifier. Figure 2-3 is a major improvement.

This leaves no doubt about y and z being properties of x, within a specific context.

What holds for the context-orientedness of x and modeling of its partial identities, however, equally applies for *all* information objects in order to secure conceptual precision. Retaining y and z as general examples here, they must also be differentiated according to their relevant contexts. It is therefore specifically not as overall objects that y and z make up the intext of x in its capacity of $k_{x,p}$, but that y and z will be limited to contextual nodes, $k_{y,q}$ and $k_{z,r}$ (see Figure 2-4). The mechanism of context orientation can be repeated indefinitely.

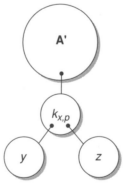

Figure 2-3 *Recognition of node uniqueness*

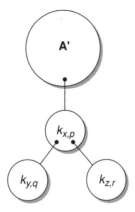

Figure 2-4 *Universal uniqueness of nodes*

In Figures 2-3 and 2-4, the relationship of the overall object with the nil node is not shown. It is presupposed where applicable.

2.3 Precision Versus Ambiguity

Starting at a particular node, the context is always an unambiguously ordered collection of relationships and (other) nodes. The intext, however, is often ambiguous. Each node usually has various other nodes as its "properties." Figure 2-5 presents a series in which the point of view changes with different nodes. Therefore, what constitutes the context and intext change, accordingly.

In this series, the nil object is not documented. Actually, the complete information set could be defined as the intext of the nil object.

Figure 2-5 really captures the central idea of the metapattern. Any view of information is dependent on a particular *point* of view. As the point of view changes, so do the contents of context and intext. The metapattern can therefore be considered an exhaustive procedure to assign a unique identity to every single point of view.

Since the metapattern is concerned with conceptual information modeling, "point of view" means how differently real-world object behaviors may be viewed. With every possible point of view uniquely accessible, precise behavior differentiation is optimized. The ways these conceptual models are translated onto construction specifications, however, are beyond the scope of the metapattern.

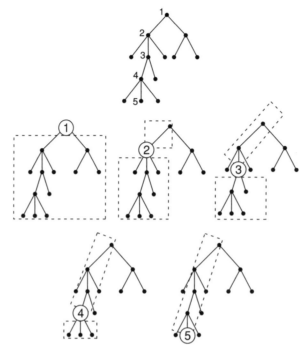

Figure 2-5 *Relative nature of context and intext*

The first priority of the metapattern is conceptual understanding with a life focus, a priority that serves as the best way to draw up effective construction models. The metapattern is not designed for digital construction modeling. Because it is aimed at realizing practical information systems, though, many of the metapattern's essential concepts are directly related to construction and implementation. However, for translation purposes, an approach specifically oriented to construction and implementation modeling must be aligned with the metapattern. An example is outlined in Appendix B, *An Alliance of Meta-models.*

2.4 Primitive Information Objects

The whole information set never solely consists of nodes and their context-oriented identifiers. Although this nodal network is in itself vital information,

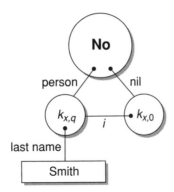

Figure 2-6 *Primitive information*

sooner or later properties must be made known through a primitive intext, in which all corresponding information objects are directly managed by their immediately superior node.

Suppose a person is newly registered. Suppose, too, that his or her last name must be entered *in the context of* person. In such a case, the last name is part of the primitive intext. The primitive information object is shown in Figure 2-6 as a rectangle.

The last name can be understood differently—as, for example, a component of the complete name. Another component would then be the first name. As we will see in Chapter 5, such a complete name is an example of a *composition,* an object in its own right. In the context of node-as-person, the composed name is represented by another node. Only through relationships for first name and last name are primitive information objects introduced.

The nil object in Figure 2-7 is abstracted into a solid, horizontal line from which all relationships and other information objects "hang down." The nil object is the preconditioned ground of any information model. For practical reasons, this ground is always drawn on top.

Whether or not a particular composition is useful or necessary depends on information requirements. In Figure 2-8 the complexities and possibilities are somewhat reduced.

An information object may act as part of a primitive intext. When this occurs, it always has a certain context, but never any intext. Its context minimally consists of one node identifying another object.

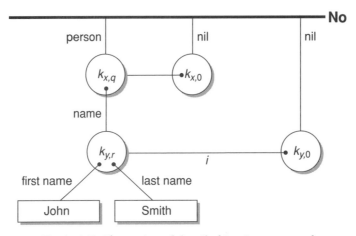

Figure 2-7 *Abstraction of the nil object into a ground*

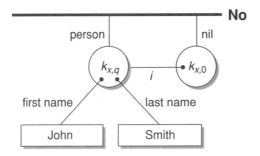

Figure 2-8 *A simpler alternative*

2.5 Pointer Information Objects

Now suppose that country of birth must also be registered. There are not that many countries; it is simpler to refer to, or in more direct terms, point at, an instance in the country set. Within the context of a particular person, country of birth does not appear as a primitive information object but as a pointer information object. The "value" of the reference is the "address" of the node in the relevant (other) context. In all figures beginning with Figure 2-9, a circle projecting over a rectangle is used as the symbol for a pointer information object. Do not confuse this mention of pointers with implementation, as in computer programming. Pointers here are purely conceptual devices. The meta-

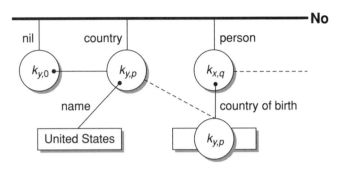

Figure 2-9 *Pointer information for reference*

pattern uses such a reference explicitly as an object-in-intext, even though a mere relationship would convey the same information. The overview is simplified by objectifying the reference/pointer. It also makes it easier to shift from a pointer information object to an intermediary information object (see § 2.6) and vice versa.

Having a pointer information object in the intext amounts to a direct relationship, shown in Figure 2-9 with a dotted line, between two identifier nodes of the same overall object. They already maintain an indirect relationship, by definition, through their mutual nil identity. The circle within the rectangle symbolizes the relational aspect on which a pointer is based.

Like the primitive information objects, pointer information objects do not contain intext. The rectangle indicates that such pointers simultaneously reflect a primitive aspect.

2.6 Intermediary Information Objects

The power of the context-oriented approach to information modeling lies in the assignment to an object, that is, an object's part, of a specific-but-rounded identity corresponding to a specific context. This requires a third kind of building block, the intermediary information objects.

Let's say a company specifies a person as its customer and registers additional information about the person *as a customer*. For this purpose, an unambiguous node is created (Figure 2-10).

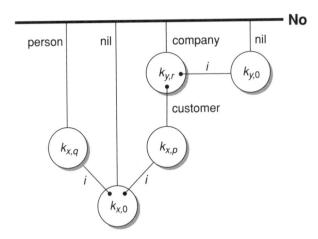

Figure 2-10 *Reference at intermediary node; coordination through nil identity*

The customer's intext, with the customer identified by the node $k_{x,p}$, may consist of primitive, pointer, and/or intermediary information objects.

Let's assume that, despite the specific customer context, we need direct information covered by the person context. Under such requirements, the node $k_{x,p}$ should be supplied in its intext with a pointer information object. In addition to their indirect relationship (through a joint nil identity), a direct relationship exists between the object-as-person and the object-as-customer-of-company-y. This is convenient for presenting general information about the customer; such information is taken from the general information about the corresponding person, shown in Figure 2-11, which leaves out some details contained in Figure 2-10.

2.7 Intermediary Character of Context

Recall that from the point of view of a certain node, its intext has a multifaceted character. Information objects in a node's intext may be primitive, pointers, and/or intermediary.

The context, however, is of a uniform nature—a consequence of the rule that primitive and pointer information objects do not themselves have any intext; they are not so much nodes as final destinations. It follows that only an intermediary information object can lead to another intermediary information

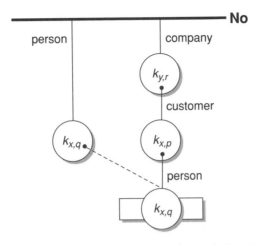

Figure 2-11 *Direct coordination of partial identities*

object. Therefore, the uniform, all-intermediary character of the context of *any* information object amounts to a series of unique nodes. Chapter 1 gives the clearest description of this character, treating all objects purely within their respective contexts.

2.8 Range for Object Identity

The nil identity, as related through the nil relationship with the nil object, leads to a radical conclusion. It is now possible, apart from the nil object, to model the complete information set on the basis of a single overall object. With specific contexts, the meaning of specific behavior is always guaranteed, as shown in Figure 2-12.

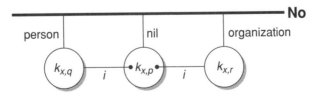

Figure 2-12 *Radical differentiation through contexts alone*

This seems like the wrong idea for most practical information sets. Traditional object orientation poses opposite problems because a certain object type is often too limited. When more detailed types no longer conform to a neat, manageable hierarchy, the classification fails to function properly. Against the background of the metapattern, the cause of such failure becomes evident: contexts with no modeling or contexts that are only minimally modeled.

The metapattern forces no such limitation on the modeler and the modeling approach. Contexts are always explicit and juxtaposed. (In Chapters 3 and 7, the difference between OO subtyping and metapattern *juxtatyping* is explained.) Only the context consisting of the nil relationship to the nil object separately is defined as a boundary condition. Being typeless has now been given a (positive) value.

The metapattern allows a wide range of model alternatives. At one end is the radical possibility of a single overall object; at the other, as many overall objects may be modeled as there are separately identifiable contexts. Within these extremes, the proper balance must be modeled in light of prevailing information requirements.

Being aware of what the context-oriented approach tries to accomplish is helpful. Its goal is the simultaneous treatment of differentiation *and* integration. An object is split according to contexts but, at the same time, the overall object continues to exist comprehensively. A balanced distinction into an overall object is achieved when behaviors can be both meaningfully differentiated (through contexts) and meaningfully integrated (through the joint nil identity). Given this criterion, the modeler must base choices for overall objects on their integrated responsibility and accountability. Differences exist, for example, among behaviors as family member, customer, citizen, taxpayer, voter, and employee. At the same time, those qualities are appearances of an encompassing unit. In our society, at least, their respective responsibilities are contained by what is called a person. It is thus meaningful to specify each appearance as a node in a corresponding context.

Although in real life, the person context has a special status, such background information, needn't be maintained in the system. In the system a person can (and with the metapattern available, *should*) be treated as one of many juxtaposed contexts; nil identity provides the generic mechanism for coordination among all parts of an overall object.

In social life, responsibilities are not always similarly ordered. An organization, for example, is held accountable on equal *as well as* on different terms as a person. Another overall object could then be contextualized after organization, taxpayer, supplier, employer, customer, and so on.

2.9 Context-Oriented Normalization

For relational information models, a well-known method exists for avoiding unwanted duplications. This heuristic is called *normalization*. The metapattern offers similar opportunities. A primitive information object is registered only once, by definition, but another primitive information object could hold an identical value at the same time. This does not count as duplication because each object follows its own unique life cycle.

Pointer information objects are also unique, by definition. The same holds for intermediary information objects (that is, nodes for object identification). What makes them unique is the specific context. Both pointer and intermediary information objects contribute fundamentally to constraining, and even eliminating, information duplication.

Please note that these are strictly conceptual considerations. Such terms often reappear at the construction modeling stage, but they carry different meanings and consequences in that context.

Chapter 3

Types

To provide a sharp outline of concepts for context and intext, we have restricted our discussion of the metapattern to specific relationships and objects. To support a somewhat more complex specific structure, we need another structure on a higher level of abstraction. This chapter, which sketches that addition by referring to types, takes an inverse approach, highlighting the metapattern's characteristics. Traditional object orientation uses the class or type as the starting point; a specific object is then exclusively regarded as a member of the type-defined set or class. For the metapattern, however, the various contexts of objects occupy place of principle.

3.1 Node as Type

The concept of *type* pertains to conditions ruling one or more instances. An instance belongs to a certain type when the latter's conditions apply. With Bill exhibiting all the relevant properties of what it means to be a person, he is considered to belong to the person type. In short, he *is* a person. A specific object in a specific context may behave in a way that is uniquely specific. Within the complete information set, this level of behavioral specification reflects one extreme of the range for typing. The other extreme reflects identical behavior for all objects, all objects being identical. In the first-mentioned extreme possibility, the indicator of the specific type *is* the specific node as a unique identifier:

$$\text{Type}(k_{x,p}) = k_{x,p}$$

Thus the node $k_{x,p}$ is uniquely typed. Such a type is described not only by the relationships in the particular context but also by the particular nodes higher up the hierarchy of inspection levels. Figure 3-1 shows a case in which the same person x is an employee within two different organizations.

Indeed, when the node itself is also considered a type, the behavior of employee x in company y can be "typed" differently from the same person x's behavior in company z. There are, in fact, two different employees, both of them "grounded"

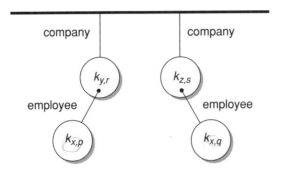

Figure 3-1 *Unique behavior at node*

in the same person. Since each node is a completely singular type, their existence as employees has no consequence for behavior.

3.2 Context as Type

It is already less extreme to consider the context of a node—not the node itself—as the relevant type, since several nodes may share the same context. In this case, the type is indicated just like the context (see § 1.11). From

$$\text{Context}(k_{x,p}) = \{a, k_{y,q}, \text{Context}(k_{y,q})\}$$

it follows that

$$\text{Type}(k_{x,p}) = \{a, k_{y,q}, \text{Type}(k_{y,q})\}$$

This agrees with the remark made in § 1.5 that the context is an ordered collection of relationships and objects (nodes). As such, context orientation is equivalent to a hierarchical classification structure.

At this point, perhaps we should stress once again one of the main differences between the metapattern and most traditional approaches to conceptual modeling. When other approaches apply the concept of context, they appear to do so from a macro perspective in which any context itself is left unspecified. This serves as a single framing device. Within such a macro context, a complete (but now relative) information model develops. This macro perspective offers little precision—often too little for differentiating behavior.

In contrast, the metapattern's micro perspective allows real-world differences in behavior to be specified with ultimate precision. After all, a particular context does not remain outside an information model (which, by applying such a procedure, is always relative as a whole). Context according to the metapattern is a variable to be *valued within* conceptual information models. It means the same information model can support a great variety of contexts or, rather, context instances. As we just discussed, behavior may even be typed at the extreme of singular nodes, the equivalent of each node having a singular context. More precision in differentiating behavior cannot possibly be supported.

Everything depends, then, on how contexts are *developed* using object-and-relationship pairs to describe them. What is optimal should reflect relevant information requirements and their underlying problem. At the conceptual modeling stage, the life as opposed to tool focus needs to be applied. Because new problems occur regularly, developing conceptual models is very much a creative process. No definitive recipe can arrive at the overall modeling result. Most of life's problems cannot be solved mechanically. But the modeler may already feel familiar with some parts of the problem, seeing opportunities for reuse of conceptual models. A more or less stable conceptual solution may then be called a pattern, but even then a modeler should always question its stability (perhaps an established pattern does not really serve a particular new requirement). With microscopic possibilities for contexts, it is easy to modify existing patterns or develop entirely new ones.

3.3 Typical Generalization

The first extreme in typing—that of the individual node itself (see § 3.1)—should not be considered a purely theoretical boundary case (that is, a rarity). Sometimes a real, practical need exists for such variety.

Of course, the relevant types are often more general in nature. Take again the example given in Figure 3-1. Suppose it matters which employee and which company are involved; an employee's behavior follows the same model everywhere. The type then is still determined by both relationships; that is, by the ordered set {employee, company}. When the upper node is also irrelevant (that is, it doesn't matter whether the employee works for a company, a foundation, or a government agency), the type is further generalized to employee.

Through subsets of a context, the metapattern offers the opportunity for highly differentiated typing. In § 3.4, the generalization is restricted to the discrete relationships, resulting in fairly abstract types. However, this already represents an extension of traditional object orientation. An even more elaborate typing schema would include individual nodes. In § 3.5, we offer a concise explanation on dealing with nodes in typing, resulting in correspondingly differentiated behavior. Even more concisely, § 3.6 states that a relationship can also serve to localize a type (not as a discrete unit). As such, a relationship does not act as a discrete unit but supports selection on the basis of certain criteria.

3.4 Relational Typing

Relationships among objects in any information set should, at a more basic level, also be counted as information objects. This makes it possible to position them in a relevant context which is, in turn, oriented toward relational typing.

In Figure 3-1, three possibilities exist for *relationally* typing the behavior of employees in companies. First, both relationships can matter. Note that their order in the context is important; type indicators are gathered from the original information objects in their contextual and intextual structure.

In Figure 3-2, nodes are no longer recognizable as instances. For intermediary information objects, the "aggregated" node is supplied with a short description

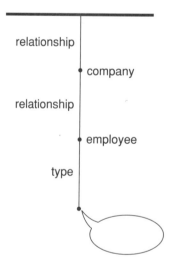

Figure 3-2 *All relationships that determine type*

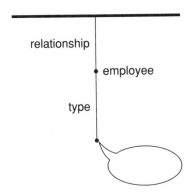

Figure 3-3 *Type determined by subset of relationships from context*

to its right or left. The nil object, introduced earlier as a schematic device, is no longer shown as a separate (boundary) node; instead, it appears as a thick, solid line at the top of the illustration. Type details are not specified in illustrations; the idea is to present a fundamental description of the metapattern. At the other extreme of the type relationship, primitive, pointer, and/or intermediary information objects may be used to specify a certain type. A text balloon indicates instances of unspecified intext; a dotted line suggests the existence of intext. No indicators are used if the possibility of confusion doesn't exist.

A second alternative for a type (still assuming the concrete information structure of Figure 3-1), shows that only the "lowest" relationship may be needed to differentiate the object's behavior. This is shown in Figure 3-3.

The third alternative to typing takes the other extreme. Assume a general type for *all* objects; it is relationshipless—that is, it has no reference to relationships in the structure of original information objects. Figure 3-4 depicts this ultimate abstraction.

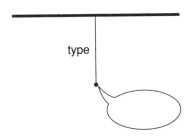

Figure 3-4 *Ultimate abstraction in typing*

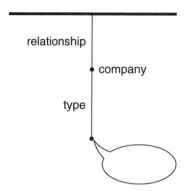

Figure 3-5 *Company type*

A general type such as this can also be used for company behavior. If a more specific type for the company is needed, there is only one other possibility. Shown in Figure 3-5, it is based on Figure 3-1.

Because the types for company and employee are split, Figures 3-2 and 3-5 may be brought together in Figure 3-6.

When relationships themselves are related, as in Figures 3-2 and 3-6, some information about types is revealed. The interpretation, according to strictly relational typing, is that all nodes occupying a relationship with the nil object (in a context capacity) may entertain in their intexts an employee relationship

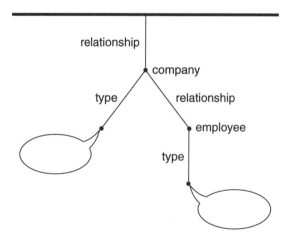

Figure 3-6 *Integrating relationship-based types into an overall model*

with information objects. The more detailed behavioral rules for such information objects are then specified under the type for relationship.

To retrieve applicable behavior rules from the context, as many relationships as possible should match the relational pattern that serves as a type context. To obtain a straightforward matching procedure, it's reasonable to proceed from the bottom up—the "direction" in the illustrations. The type in Figure 3-3 applies only when the type in Figure 3-2 does not exist.

Care must be taken not to interpret the suggestions for type retrieval as direct construction specifications. They are supplied here to support unambiguous interpretation at the stage of *conceptual* modeling. Of course, not only separate information systems but even a tool technology may be developed to incorporate the metapattern perspective in reality. The concepts in this chapter may then be taken as general hints in how to deal technologically with digital information objects at the (first) abstraction level of typing.

3.5 Node Selection

Relational typing may be extended by adding nodes that govern selection. Such nodes contain a prescription for defining a subset holding elements with similar behavior. Not all companies, for example, are required to make their annual accounts public; only companies with statutory limited liability are. In this way, relational typing may be enhanced, yielding a larger number of types. Please note that those are not exactly subtypes as in traditional object orientation; more variety is supported.

These prescriptive nodes for type determination (see Figure 3-7) must be placed between two other nodes representing a contextual relationship in a specific structure—a structure of instances, not types. A number of nodes and selection procedure outcomes must be included to reflect the type-based behavioral variety to be modeled. Each selection node has an intext where criteria are stated. If the node—that is, the node elsewhere in the specific information structure— complies with a given set of criteria, the next step in assigning type is determined. Without sufficient validation at the time of type definition there is always a risk that matching context with type does not yield disjunctive results. In such a case, a specific information object's type is indeterminate.

At this point, matching concerns comparing the original node together with its complete context on the one side, and something that can be called a type intext

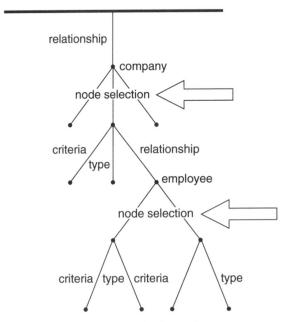

Figure 3-7 *Typing beyond relationships in context*

on the other. As suggested earlier, type intext contains matching rules from the bottom to the top of the node-plus-context. However, that context was originally specified top-down. The ordered collection that *is* the context must thus be adjusted for the matching procedure to work properly.

Suppose, as in Figure 3-7, five relevant subsets exist; three refer to companies, the others to employees. The mechanism for node selection can be structured as shown in the figure. For the sake of simplicity, the information object for the company relationship is given only one more detailed intext for node selection.

Figure 3-7 should only be considered as an example, because differences often exist between what is relevant to the typing of company and employee behavior. The behavior of employees might need a different classification of companies than the behavior of the companies themselves. When this occurs, node selections must be differentiated accordingly.

A special case of node selection consists of the complete absence of any criterion. Every node in the specific, original information structure complies. This most general type can be used as a default to implement the more specific approach of relational typing. The same holds for node-specific types and for any combination.

On the other hand, a specific node may define its own unique type. In such cases, it would be cumbersome to create a parallel structure for the type. It is more efficient to place the typing information directly in the intext of the particular node. But such an implementation requires an additional mechanism to include such uniquely localized typing information in general reports on types.

3.6 Relationship Selection

In § 3.4, we considered the relationships for relational typing as discrete instances. Additional differentiation is possible (top to bottom, operating like node selection) by applying relationship selection in order to arrive at the generalized type of a specific node. This mechanism also allows all types to be accounted for in a general structure. In this type-oriented intext of the nil object, information about relationship and node selections is interchanged until a match is reached with (part of) the original node and its intext.

3.7 Tailor-Made Typing

A central assumption of the metapattern is that contexts must be modeled, each context having a structure consisting of relationships among objects. As this chapter explains, context-equals-classification offers a confusing array of opportunities for type variety. The simplest option is to consider the bottommost relationship of a context as the node type. This amounts to the typing paradigm of traditional object orientation.

By contrast, the metapattern offers a wide range of typing possibilities, up to defining a specific node as its own, unique type. This variety is supported because types, modeled after the metapattern approach, are both integral and integrating elements of the complete information set. In its turn, each specific type is also modeled as an object-in-context containing a correspondingly specific intext. At such a "typical" node, the intext describes and prescribes, among other aspects, the other objects-in-context for which it acts as type.

The typing information is actually limited to the highest level of that other node's intext. No more is required, since all intermediary information objects at the highest intext level are typed themselves. This continues until the lowest-level nodes are reached. The metapattern implies recurrence of typing at all inspection levels of the information structure.

The way in which types are described in technological detail is not within the scope of this book. Such details would only detract from an understanding of how the metapattern functions in conceptual information modeling, this book's main focus.

3.8 A Different Inheritance

The context-oriented approach eliminates the need for inheritance of behavioral rules for the different appearances (or identities) that constitute an overall object. In various contexts, the same overall object "owns" a corresponding number of partial identities; each has been developed on the basis of a disjunct type, and takes its behavior from those contextual types—Bill at work, Bill at the gym, and so forth—so a certain type is *not* a subtype of any other. Types for different identities within a single overall object are fundamentally juxtaposed, as are their contexts (see Figure 3-8). Or, similar to subtyping, one context can be part of another, as shown in Figure 3-9.

Which model is right depends on the particular information requirements. For instance, car behavior is additional but *completely disjunct* to vehicle behavior.

The metapattern does provide for some sort of inheritance. It generally understands "inheritance" to mean that a particular node may use any intext properties of any node from its context; that is, from nodes at higher levels in the modeled hierarchy. Suppose that (1) an information object exists within a context; (2) another information object is part of that context; and (3) an address is

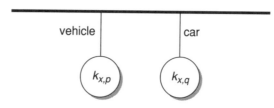

Figure 3-8 *Juxtaposed types*

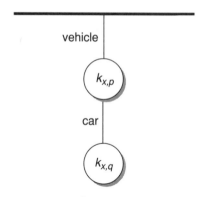

Figure 3-9 *Types through recursion of context*

specified in the intext of that other information object. That address could be declared applicable for all information objects emanating at all lower levels from the information object that actually contains it as a distinct property. For example, although all employees inherit the address from the respective organizations of which they are a "property," the possibility that an employee has a different address is maintained. An instance at a lower level blocks the procedure of looking at a higher level for an address to inherit, a mechanism underlying Figure 3-10.

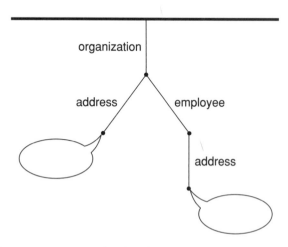

Figure 3-10 *Instance-level, rather than type-level inheritance*

Each hierarchy invites such a mechanism to aggregate its domain of applicability (not the information itself). Inheritance is a powerful mechanism for avoiding, and sometimes even eliminating, duplicate information. Through context orientation, the metapattern offers an intuitively natural aggregation strategy.

In Chapter 5, *Compositions*, we introduce Cartesian products, which contain something like a hidden hierarchy. Awareness of their structure helps drive out duplication even more; using those information objects can be considered a special case of inheritance.

Because types are also modeled using the metapattern, a certain kind of subtype is reintroduced. The difference is a consequence of the disjunct character of contexts. Where types are layered, their structure reflects the layering of the original, specific information (with information objects at different inspection levels). This is equivalent to context (or parts of contexts) with types. For example, because both organization and employee reserve a place for address in their respective intexts, *in that sense* an employee may be considered a subtype of organization.

What type *a* inherits as a property (or behavior) from type *b*, an information object of type *a* inherits as behavioral rules (or properties) from the related information object of type *b*.

As mentioned earlier, types are represented by discrete information objects. Those type objects also have types, as the metapattern allows for explicit metatyping—an additional reason to call the modeling approach *meta*pattern. A single approach is supposed to encompass all semantic levels at which information is structured. For practical purposes, we assume a difference between (1) specific information and (2) information controlling the behavior of that (other) specific information. It is customary to classify the former as instances and the latter as types. Another familiar term indicating the latter is *metainformation*. But the concrete expression of a particular type is also grounded in specific information. The next level type is then called the *metatype*. Though such abstraction can proceed indefinitely, it invites confusion to address several typing levels without professional overview.

By always starting from specific information, whatever it may represent, the metapattern only recognizes its metainformation directly as a type. But in its own right, every type can also be seen *as specific information*, leading to its own particular metainformation. By changing the point of view, any abstraction or aggregation of behavioral structure can be achieved as a chain of interchanging information and metainformation.

3.9 Strong Polymorphism

Context orientation makes type inheritance almost disappear. As a result, polymorphism greatly increases. The individual contexts, and consequently the contextual types, assure precision within the variety. What is known by a general name always follows the rules specified within the relevant context. Bill may, for example, write both at home and at work, but there are most likely very different behaviors involved.

We'd like to emphasize again that an overall object does *not* have a single, overall type. Types are "limited" to the overall object's contextual identities; that is, to its parts, which own a unique identity within a particular context. As a corollary, parts of otherwise different overall objects can share a type. Their equally typical differences show up in the types they do not share for their other identities or parts.

Suppose it does not matter whether a customer is a person or an organization. That is, the required properties are always similar—the structure of all customer intexts is identical. Under those circumstances, person and organization share the customer type for one of their partial identities. Those nodes lead to their respective nil identities and to identities belonging to different types. This flexibility represents a major benefit of the metapattern. Figure 3-11 sketches an example of this, with nodes as instances of specific information objects.

3.10 Behavioral Forms and Encapsulation

The author presented the context-oriented approach to information modeling in an earlier publication. In it, he developed behavioral forms, which are analogous to normal forms in relational information sets, at least in terminology.

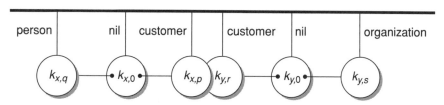

Figure 3-11 *Mixing partial identities across contexts*

Those behavioral forms mainly control the extent of encapsulation. Like the normal forms that inspired the concept of behavioral forms, even the latter show an implementation bias. The metapattern is the next step in the development toward decreasing that bias, emphasizing even more the conceptual treatment of information requirements.

The definitions for the five identified behavioral forms, as stated in the original publication, follow. See also the English-language monograph titled "Multicontextual paradigm for object orientation: a development of information modeling toward the fifth behavioral form." (This text was published in the book *Informatiekundige ontwerpleer: strategieën in objectgerichtheid,* of which the other contents are in Dutch.)

> I formally consider information to be in *first behavioral form* when the pertaining object has the opportunity for unique behavior. Every object, therefore, is uniquely . . . itself. Or, put in another way, every object always defines itself as one class, for it is always a class in itself. This uniqueness condition is necessary to support diversity of behavior.
>
> Every higher behavioral form presupposes all lower forms. Information in second behavioral form is, therefore, also in first behavioral form.
>
> Beyond first behavioral form, *second behavioral form* stipulates that the object's unique identification is totally independent of any external information requirements. In other words, the object's key is entirely nonvalue based.
>
> Every object, except the complete information base, is positioned within a context. And that determines *third behavioral form.*
>
> By turning the words around that I used to typify third behavioral form, the fourth behavioral form comes into focus. Of course, first of all, the fourth presupposes the third behavioral form. Then, in addition, an object is not only familiar with all its contexts but also encapsulates them. All relevant contexts are contained within an object in *fourth behavioral form.*

Remark added here from the subsequently developed encompassing perspective of the metapattern: The corresponding mechanism is the unique node allowing part of an overall object to "own" an identity *within* a particular context. All other nodes belonging to the same overall object maintain an identity relationship with its nil identity. The nil identity is not yet explicitly specified by the fourth behavioral form.

Any object that is in fourth behavioral form and, in addition, limits encapsulation of intext to the next lower order is in what I define as *fifth behavioral form.*

Chapter 4

Time

Context, in an ontological sense, precedes object. This idea—the main tenet of the metapattern—determines how a modeler who follows the metapattern approach presumes that reality is fundamentally structured.

Practically, context provides an overall object with different identities for its contextual parts (also called partial identities). Indeed, the number of its separate partial identities equals the number of contexts in which an overall object appears or becomes manifest through its corresponding parts. Every contextual identity of a real-world, overall object is conceptually *represented* by an information object. In conceptual information models, an information object in its capacity of individual identity equals a unique (intermediary) node.

The contextual differentiation also supplies an excellent starting point to deal fundamentally with the aspect of time in conceptual information models. A uniform, compact treatment rests on the recognition of the variable nature of real-world objects, and thus on the variability of their corresponding information objects. For the metapattern, change rather than continuity guides the life of information. Change, however, always implies the possibility of continuity—defined as the absence of change during a particular period of time. Continuity is change with zero value (which is nonetheless a value). In general, practical success with the metapattern can be significantly and consistently improved by abstractions such as those applied here to modeling pervasive time management of information.

4.1 Time-Based Relationships

Suppose nodes $k_{y,q}$ and $k_{x,p}$ are connected (Figure 4-1) through relationship *a*, with $k_{y,q}$ an element of the context of $k_{x,p}$.

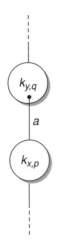

Figure 4-1 *A relationship of nodes*

A consistent management of time first requires that the existence of a relationship between nodes, whatever its nature, has been established. Figure 4-2 shows how an upper and lower node together constitute a unique relationship.

As properties of such a relationship, one or more existence states must be included. Their importance is specified alongside the node representing the set of states within the relationship context.

A single existence state contains a value for the existence mode and a time value (including date) for which the given existence value holds (Figure 4-3). Figure 4-3 integrates Figure 4-2, but does not repeat its details. Actually, the choice of *starting* times is not fundamental. Consistent application of final times delivers the same effect.

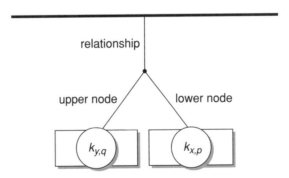

Figure 4-2 *Relationship defined through nodes*

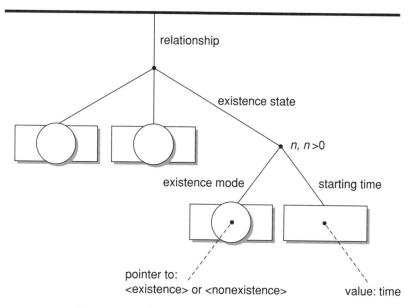

Figure 4-3 *Information on relationship existence*

4.2 Starting Time of Effect

When every change is registered as a state, including the time from which that state takes effect, then state at *any* time can be derived. Suppose that t_1 is the starting time for the state of existence. When the existence mode is changed at time t_2 to the state of nonexistence, the state of existence is limited to the period between t_1 and t_2. Implicitly, the state of nonexistence holds for the whole period preceding t_1. Figure 4-4 summarizes this time-based mechanism.

As a benefit, this approach allows an interchange between states of existence and nonexistence. The state of existence is no longer restrained to a single, uninterrupted time period enclosed by two periods for which the state of nonexistence is valid.

A consequence of reading time (or information about time) in the proposed direction is that the state of nonexistence is not explicitly registered. It must be derived from the earliest starting time to appear in an existence state holding the value existence.

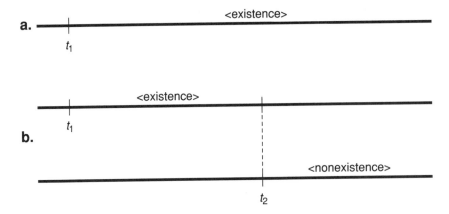

Figure 4-4 Succession of states

4.3 From Existence to Value

Whenever *any* relationship exists it is necessary to focus on its *value*, which is at least an information object in the intext of the node representing the relationship itself.

There are many ways to model that part of its intext. Here, priority is given to changes in value; that is, to value entries. In its turn, each value entry has an intext consisting of a pointer to the value of the relationship and, again, to one or more existence entries. Figure 4-5 concentrates on this mechanism by leaving out details from Figure 4-3.

Using this model, or any similar model (see § 4.1), the relationship between $k_{y,q}$ and $k_{x,p}$ can hold value *a* from time t_1, value *b* from time t_2, possibly value *a* from time t_3 again, and so on.

Actually, the registration of relationship values and their nonexistence is not dependent on registration of the relationship itself, regardless of its value. This poses no problem as long as the validity check on the relationship is given priority over checking the state of value.

Changing the value of the relationship changes context (context of $k_{x,p}$ in the example). This raises the question of whether, at the same time, type $k_{x,p}$ changes. Indeed, this *could* happen and would then be an example of dynamic typing.

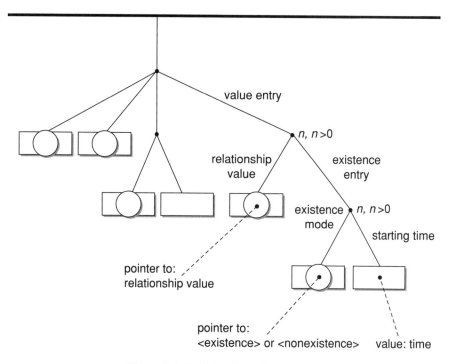

Figure 4-5 *Relationship values in time*

4.4 Time-Based Information Objects

Any intermediary information object—a habitual node in a conceptual model—needs only one or more existence entries to establish its position along the time dimension. Such nodes, as shown in Figure 4-6, do not "contain" any value themselves, but may "lead" directly to such a value, either in its own intext or in an intermediary manner, through a pointer information object in its intext or indirectly via its nil identity.

Chapter 2 defines primitive and pointer information objects as having no intext. An exception is existence entries. Figure 4-6 illustrates this situation, substituting a primitive or a pointer information object for the node (that is, the intermediary information object).

The rule stating that primitive and pointer information objects *do* have existence entries for their intexts is cancelled, for practicality, for information

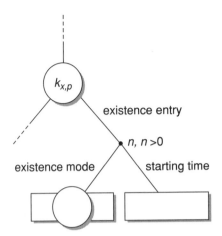

Figure 4-6 *Intermediary nodes are essentially valueless*

objects constituting those existence entries themselves. These are (1) the pointer information object referring to the value existence or nonexistence and (2) the primitive information object containing a value for starting time. This new rule for the presence or absence of intext is necessary; the previous rule, applied to existence objects, would lead to an infinite regression.

One might erroneously conclude from this an inconsistent metapattern application and a focus switch from life to tool. Indeed, an important part of the reality being conceptually modeled is now the information set to be constructed and operationally used, rather than the reality outside it. But there really is no conflict with the essential life focus of conceptual modeling. The tool, too, will eventually be integrated into life. It is thus logical that operational aspects need conceptual integration. A conceptual model that does not take into consideration all relevant reality would lack precision. It would be a mistake to view time management of information objects as a predominantly technological issue. It needs a strong conceptual foundation.

4.5 Variations in Time

All changes in the information set can be reduced to procedures outlined in the previous sections. Suppose that, starting from time t_2, node $k_{x,p}$ is no longer connected to $k_{y,q}$ through relationship a but to $k_{z,r}$ through relationship b. This amounts, first, to an existence entry against the relationship between $k_{y,q}$ and $k_{x,p}$. This new entry contains a pointer to nonexistence as the value for existence mode and the value t_2 as starting time. The relationship value a no longer deserves attention, since such values depend on the existence of the relationship itself.

Second, a relationship between $k_{z,r}$ and $k_{x,p}$ must be established (assuming it does not exist). An existence entry is immediately added with a pointer to existence as the value of existence mode and t_2 as the starting time. To the intext of the new relationship, we add a value entry specifying that from time t_2 the relationship value is b.

If the relationship between $k_{z,r}$ and $k_{x,p}$ is already available in the information set, an additional existence entry is sufficient (assuming that the value of the relationship was previously also b).

Operations that change the structure of information are especially type sensitive. As shown in § 4.3, however, there is no fundamental problem with the metapattern. Specifying types reflects the additional variety that can be controlled.

Finely tuned time management guarantees that normalization remains valid along the time dimension. A pointer information object, for example, uses a particular, user-defined *time of relevance* to direct its follow-up. The object pointed to "answers" by supplying the value of the primitive information object as valid at the requested time of relevance.

Another feature of the metapattern allows a node to be moved from one context to another—an extremely powerful ability because the move does not affect the node's intext.

Suppose the subsidiary relationship is changed for company x. It reports to division 2 instead of division 1. The changes in the information set are limited to that particular operation. From the given starting time—assuming that all company x employees were originally registered in the intext of x-in-the-context-of-division-1—all employees are members of division 2, not division 1. By specifying a time of relevance before the time of reorganization, we can still see the original picture (see Figure 4-7).

To guarantee precision at each intermediary node, the metapattern rules that at any point in time, one context—and only one—is valid.

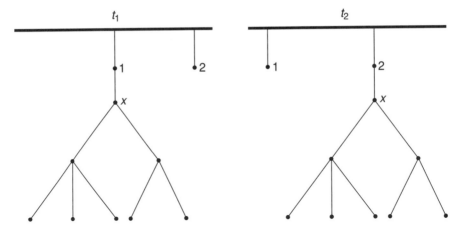

Figure 4-7 *The power of a single relationship change*

4.6 A Change of Nil Identity

It is also intriguingly powerful that a particular node can, in the course of time, change its relationship to a nil identity. By exchanging nil identities, *its* nil identity may be different from a certain time. Because the node always reflects an identity of an overall object in a particular context, changing its nil identity means that the contextual identity has become part of *another* overall object. Figure 4-8 shows the mechanism of this highly adaptive feature.

The ability of a node to change nil identity reveals that even the nodal suffixes x and y could be misleading. In the example shown in Figure 4-8, from time t_1, node $k_{x,p}$ does not belong to the overall object x but to the overall object y. Thus, all common nodes should be counted using only a single suffix, as shown in Figure 4-9. Only the special nodes for nil identities are supplied with a second suffix fitted with the constant value of zero.

Changing a contextual identity from one overall object to another need not be limited to overall objects that share type for all identities. The new overall object may just as well count organization instead of person as type for one of its partial identities. Particularly when corrections are necessary, changing a nil identity offers a powerful mechanism for keeping the information set realistic. An unambiguous audit trail needs additional entries available to specify which information object is valid or nonvalid and from which time. (Note: Validity mode is closely related to, but still different than, existence mode.)

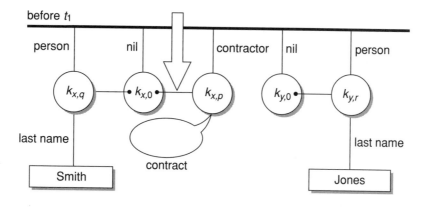

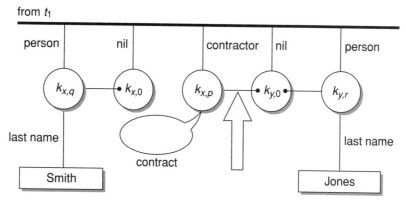

Figure 4-8 *A partial identity may change to another overall object*

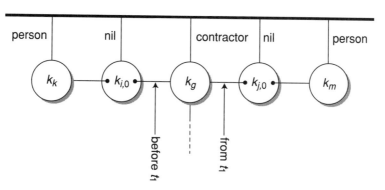

Figure 4-9 *Uniqueness over time requires abstraction from a particular overall object*

4.7 Audit Trail

Strategies guaranteeing all possible support for accountability are based on the integration of the time dimension into information models. A life focus is a strong reason for adding fundamental mechanisms to provide easily accessible, transparent audit trails.

The information set requires, as a structural facility, the option to reconstruct its user state at any point in time. By taking change as the rule rather than the exception, we have already laid a firm foundation for accountability. We still need an operation to report that certain information once considered valid has been subsequently declared nonvalid (for whatever reason) and corrected.

However, when new information replaces old, thereby making the old information disappear, we compromise accountability. The radical but only viable solution is to keep all information available as a matter of principle. To introduce exactness and completeness into the audit trail, the once-valid-now-nonvalid information must be labeled as such and maintained.

Just as a particular relationship or information object exists or nonexists, a difference can be made between states of validity and nonvalidity, as shown in Figure 4-10.

Because we perceive the state of validity as a change applicable from a particular point in time, those periods during which information is either valid or nonvalid

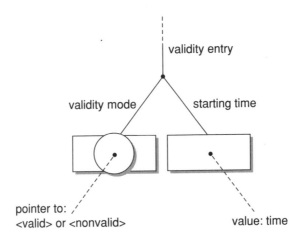

Figure 4-10 *Support of comprehensive audit trail*

can be interchangeable. For information to be reconstructed from the perspective of validity, the registration of original information must include a validity entry (analogous to the required existence entry). Any validity entry must contain its time of registration. The validity mode of entry with the last time of registration determines the operational user state of the information set at the requested time of relevance.

All information objects have, as part of their intext, one or more validity entries, with one exception. Only information objects in the intext of a validity entry do not themselves include validity entries. Otherwise, an infinite regression would result. Instead, when necessary, one entry succeeds the next. Through registration times, the audit trail is always precise and unambiguous.

A useful audit trail also leads to the person responsible for registered information. For that reason, each entry, and especially the entries for existence and validity, are "intexted" with a specific pointer information object. The pointer leads to additional information about the person handling the registration. Whether the actual user *really* was the person indicated cannot be completely guaranteed by the information system, but the pointer provides an important clue to accountability.

Besides pointing to the person involved in and/or responsible for the information change, the metapattern assumes a pointer to the specific user interaction (that is, administrative procedure) that controlled the operations effecting the change. Such procedures must be formally typed and implemented, and users should interact with their information system on the basis of such interaction types. Each information change or addition can then be addressed to an interaction instance, providing use and accountability integration. Such natural integration is always the best guarantee for a successful audit trail.

4.8 Metapattern as Infrastructure

By supplying contexts with finely tuned integrations of the time dimension and accountability, the metapattern holds a rich store of standardized facilities. As such, it greatly extends earlier approaches to modeling infrastructure for information processing. Since infrastructure can also be viewed as all-that-is-standard, the metapattern literally defines a higher, more encompassing standard. Increasing variety in the infrastructure helps minimize the effort needed for customizing information processing. Even more interesting is that through customizing, qualitatively different, more powerful information systems can be developed and kept dynamically operational.

4.9 Past and Future

Because all information objects explicitly include the time at which both their existence proper and their property values (intext) take effect, the time orientation of the information set is no longer limited to the present (that is, time of registration). Factoring time into periods during which a particular existence mode and validity mode hold allows information to be entered both retrospectively and prospectively. As long as the present time has not caught up with a time indication once viewed as future, the information involved counts as planning. And all information with past starting times are (partly, at least) in an archival state.

All information about past, present, and future is retained in the information set. To really guarantee an audit trail, such a policy is mandatory. Equally for wide- and deep-ranging analyses, time-series information must be available. Data mining considers such analysis as a separate subject. The metapattern favors an integrated perspective.

The principle is to maintain all information, properly labeled, in the set. It should also be possible to remove the information. The metapattern makes a clear distinction between such removal on the one (exceptional) side, and the modes of nonexistence and nonvalidity on the other (normal) side. The latter are automatically accounted for when applying the metapattern. Removal must always be a separate activity, with special attention paid to minimal requirements—not only for an audit trail, but also for operational analyses.

Chapter 5

Compositions

Information objects may be combined according to preestablished rules. Such an assembly or configuration of instances is another instance itself. It is a whole consisting of parts. Here they are called *compositions*. The introduction of compositions increases the infrastructural scope of metapattern applications. Actually, a composition type is already a pattern in its own right. As such, it can be used and reused for further information modeling.

Each composition consists of various relationships and information objects. What previous chapters have prescribed for contexts, intexts, types, and time also applies to these aggregate building blocks for conceptual modeling.

5.1 Homogeneous Classification Hierarchy

There is often a need to connect similar information objects through similar relationships. Take, for example, an articulated organization that consists of units in a hierarchical structure as shown in Figure 5-1.

The metapattern follows general practice in defining such a structure of instances as an inverted tree. The node representing the highest-level unit maintains an organizational relationship to the nil object. Every lower node connects to a higher node through an organizational relationship, too. In Figure 5-2, the letter *o* is used as an abbreviation.

On the basis of its regular structure, the tree may be represented in shorthand notation with just a single relationship and a single node. The recursion is symbolized by the node being drawn as a circle with a dot as its center. The recurring relationship is only shown once, since the different symbol for the node makes the compositional character clear enough. In fact, as far as the relationships and nodes are concerned, Figure 5-3 now shows them at their type level of semantics.

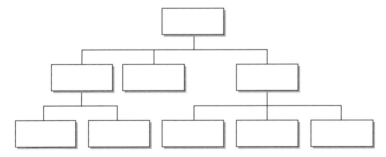

Figure 5-1 *An example of a hierarchy*

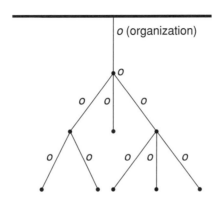

Figure 5-2 *Organizational units "organized" as a tree*

The simplicity of this composition invites broad application. It often fits a wide variety of information requirements, since a hierarchy offers a richer variety of meanings than a one-dimensional list does. Whenever the least doubt exists about how a list would perform conceptually, for flexibility's sake it's a good idea to

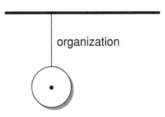

Figure 5-3 *Shorthand notation for homogeneous tree*

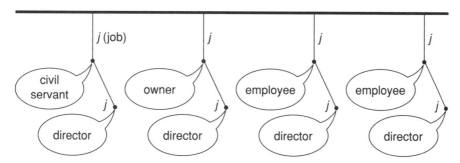

Figure 5-4 *What's in a name?*

start with a list of elements for later assembly into a homogeneous hierarchy. The nodes in the hierarchical structure become the effective information objects.

Take, for example, jobs within an organization. A civil servant may hold the title of director, but his or her duties, responsibilities, and rights differ greatly from a company manager with the same title. A company owner may also be called a director; a foundation or agency may employ directors; and then, of course, there is the movie director.

A one-dimensional list cannot escape artificial treatment of such different jobs with identical names. A hierarchical classification, on the other hand, maintains perfect overview. Figure 5-4 shows a variety of jobs with the title "director." That all directors appear at the second level of the job hierarchy is a coincidence.

Analogous to Figure 5-3, job variety can be succinctly pictured as a composition; that is, as a particular homogeneous classification hierarchy. Figure 5-5 is identical to Figure 5-3 except for the difference in context-building relationship.

These compositions can be applied most naturally when the original name—organization or job, say—is no longer reserved for the constituting elements but for the resulting compositional nodes. This means that the composition civil

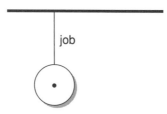

Figure 5-5 *Homogeneous hierarchies are ubiquitous*

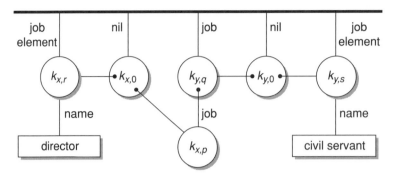

Figure 5-6 *From elements to composition*

servant/director is a job instance. And the composition employer/director is another.

As we suggested earlier, the constituting parts—civil servant, employee, director, and so on—should then be called something like job elements, job units, or job terminology.

Let's assume that the job civil servant/director must be reported. To do so, correct names for elements must be used as well as detailed relationships known to exist among instances of job, job elements, and job element names. Figure 5-6 shows this mechanism at the instance level of nodes.

5.2 Cartesian Product

The idea of applying a Cartesian product to a conceptual information model can be introduced by explaining its geometric origin. For example, to unambiguously describe all points in a two-dimensional space, two base lines (nonoverlapping) are necessary and sufficient. Together, they constitute an axial system. An individual, two-dimensional point is represented by the ordered set of one-dimensional points, one on each axis. Convention places the value on the *x*-axis before the value on the *y*-axis. A three-dimensional space requires a system of three axes in order for every point to be located with complete precision, and so on.

Conversely, it's possible to start with the axes and give a nongeometrical meaning to values. Suppose that ten people, ten organizations, and ten jobs exist. The number of combinations, their Cartesian product, is $10 \times 10 \times 10 = 1,000$.

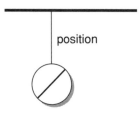

Figure 5-7 *Shorthand notation for Cartesian product*

Thus, 30 original information objects (10 + 10 + 10) may be combined to create 1,000 different compositions. The explosion into a wide space by starting with axes that in preparation are more easily managed separately makes the Cartesian product an interesting composition.

We advise giving every Cartesian product at the type level a name in its own right. Here, *position* is the name of combinations (instances) of person, organization, and job.

As Figure 5-7 indicates, the composition that arises out of the juxtaposition of other information objects carries as its symbol a circle with a slanted diameter. When more details are supplied, the pattern for position resembles Figure 5-8.

The *position* is not just any example of a Cartesian product. As we'll see in Parts III and IV, the particular combination of information objects it represents is made relevant for all sorts of information requirements.

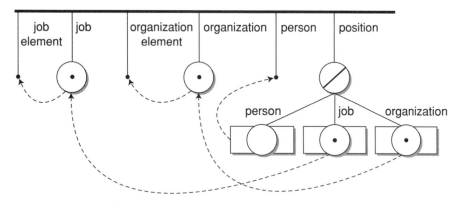

Figure 5-8 *The anatomy of an information object as a Cartesian product*

Let's consider a certain person. He or she may be part of several positions. It seems logical, at first, for the organization element in those positions always to be played by the organization that maintains the information set. Doesn't the employer *own* the information system, and use it for its own, internal personnel management?

After further consideration, however, this condition is clearly an unnecessary obstacle to a variety of opportunities. Because the organization is *an explicit element*, internally and externally oriented sets can be joined. The same idea is valid for jobs. By bringing all varieties together in the single concept of position, we can greatly enhance overview.

In a multidimensional space, points exist that have zero as their value along one or more (or even all) axes. Similarly, the Cartesian product composition is even more powerful when one or more of its constituting elements is left with its value "nonvalued." The advantage is that a single construction—position, for example—incorporates an even wider space. Let the equivalent for the number zero be the value [undetermined]. Then, a position that leaves the person [undetermined], but has determined values for organization and job, provides the logical node to attach the requirements for that particular job in that particular organization. When a person is evaluated against such requirements, the results must become attached to another position—to the position instance specifying the same organization and job, but with that person now added as a constituting element.

Positions are also convenient building blocks in models for work procedures, authorization, and marketing relations (just a few examples). Integrating such varied applications opens many new opportunities. The position composition offers a controllable mechanism—for example, to provide external contacts (marketing relations) with access to well-defined interactions (authorization) using the information system.

5.3 Double Compositions

With the metapattern, an instance of a Cartesian product envelops several pointer information objects from a single node. As a single node in its own right, it then becomes simple to arrive at a homogeneous classification hierarchy with positions. It is exactly the same principe we applied earlier to compose an organization from organization elements, or a job from job elements.

The new composition should preferably be given the most common name. In this case, the name is *position*. As a consequence, the composition presented in § 5.2 is renamed *position element*.

A Cartesian composition in a homogeneous classification hierarchy is shown as two concentric circles wherein the inner circle contains a slanted diameter (see Figure 5-9).

With such multilevel compositions, even greater information requirements can be met elegantly. For instance, a common occurrence is for somebody to hold a job not in a personal capacity, but on the basis of a different position. An example might be a member of a committee of employee representatives; only as an employee of the specific company is that person qualified for the committee position. When this perspective is explicitly available, it appears that many positions are of this recursive nature.

Such formal postings may be repeated indefinitely due to the redefinition of position as a homogeneous classification hierarchy. Perhaps that particular employee representative is also treasurer of the labor union committee. And who knows what positions he or she may undertake as a result of that posting? Figure 5-10 offers such an example.

There should be no strict rule that the same person appears in all position elements in a hierarchy. Where a different person is included, the meaning of the composition changes. In this way, the same compositional idea can be used to manage temporary replacements. The interpretation is that the person holding a certain job in a particular organization *takes the position* of the other person with the other job in the other organization. Because the hierarchy is indefinite, he or she can replace someone else in yet another capacity.

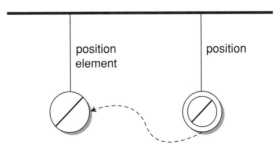

Figure 5-9 *Cartesian product as element of a homogeneous tree*

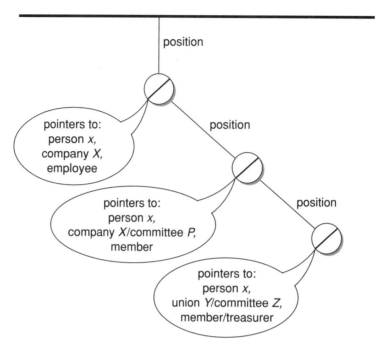

Figure 5-10 *Dependencies between positions as a hierarchy*

5.4 Inheritance Through Composition

In Chapter 3, *Types*, we learned that a composition includes a hidden hierarchy. The mechanism becomes clear with two instances of a composition, as shown in Figure 5-11.

Let's assume that a constituting element of one instance is "valued" and that same element of the other is "nonvalued." Other elements all have equal values.

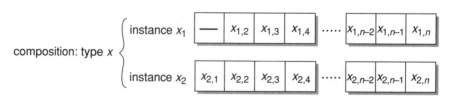

Figure 5-11 *Implicit inheritance through component values*

The second instance may be viewed as more abstract; that is, as resting on a higher hierarchical level. Conversely, the first instance may be considered to *inherit* from the second.

Let $x_{1,1}$ be [undetermined] and $x_{2,1}$ not be [undetermined],

and let $x_{1,i} = x_{2,i}$ for $i > 1$.

Then x_1 represents an abstraction over x_2.

The scope of abstraction and thus inheritance may increase as more and more constituting elements of the second composition instance contain a more general value (as compared to constituting elements of the first composition instance). The ultimate in value abstraction of a single constituting element is its "nonvalue" value. We call this unquantified equivalent of zero [undetermined]. The ultimate in composition-based abstraction is reached with the instance that has all of its constituting element values set to [undetermined].

This theme allows many variations. Let the "valued" constituting element be a node in a separate homogeneous classification hierarchy. An organization provides a good example. The search for appropriate behavior can move up that hierarchy, abstracting from the next node at each step. Or let there be another composition, with values for its constituting elements obtained through moving up the hierarchies of one or more of elements. The properties of that derived composition instance may be declared applicable to the original instance.

Because a composition has by definition (defined according to the metapattern) more than one constituting element, indeterminacy deserves special attention. The description for composition type must include the order in which values for its constituting parts are abstracted when searching for another composition instance that provides the relevant properties as intext.

In its own right (not as a constituting element in yet another composition), a homogeneous classification hierarchy offers a powerful mechanism for inheritance. Most often, what is inherited is not so much behavioral *rules* (being equal for all nodes), but specific behavior (intext; that is, static and dynamic properties). If the concept of organization is modeled as such a homogeneous hierarchy, then the holding's address (or bank account number, etc.) also applies to the division—that is, when a division does not contain its own intext on these properties. A property-like address can be inherited, down all levels of inspection.

As mentioned in Chapter 3, the same inheritance mechanism can be used for all hierarchies, including heterogeneous hierarchies. What separates heterogeneous from homogeneous hierarchies is that the latter can be typed and thus more simply conceptually modeled.

5.5 Conclusion on Design

With these remarks on inheritance through compositions, the general explanation of the metapattern and its own design ends. Though compositions are not really fundamental to the metapattern—they are, instead, specific applications—their general description has nonetheless been included in Part I because compositions are powerful building blocks in modeling. Successful conceptual modeling with the metapattern is greatly enhanced when compositions such as the homogeneous classification hierarchy and the Cartesian product are fundamentally understood.

In the first of five hypotheses guiding the composition of this book (see *The Book and Its Parts* in the Preface) we stated that the metapattern offers a powerful approach to conceptual information modeling. Part I has concentrated on the metapattern's major structural aspects. With few specific examples and nothing comprehensive yet presented, you may be unsure about the metapattern's advantages and disadvantages. Still, even from this largely theoretical perspective it should be clear that the metapattern appears to have no limitations compared to the traditional object orientation to information modeling. This follows directly from context orientation. Contexts offer an extra degree of freedom in determining behavior of (information) objects. That is, their static and dynamic behavior can be specified with an extra order of differentiation.

We'll evaluate the metapattern further in Part II with a series of conceptual modeling problems that are difficult (often impossible) to solve properly with traditional object orientation. By studying the metapattern's practical solutions, we hope you will gain a more thorough theoretical understanding. After all, without a proper theory, no relevant practice can ever be established.

Part II

Conceptual Solutions

Chapter 6

Encounter

After reading Part I, which established the basic theory of the metapattern, you should find it easier to recognize opportunities for its use in solving practical problems. We now invite you to consider a case with which you may be familiar, perhaps from the literature. If you don't know of the original case, perhaps you're familiar with other paradigms having an entity/relationship and traditional object orientation.

Often referred to by other names (for example, reference models or analysis patterns), conceptual information modeling has received little attention. In Parts II and III of this book, we review four other books that deserve study—little else, unfortunately, is currently available to professional conceptual modelers. The few existing publications, however, offer valuable and perhaps familiar case material. We review portions of their contents to provide a background against which to explain more practically the metapattern and its paradigm shift in modeling.

Most problems discussed in Part II are inspired by J. J. Odell who, throughout his work, emphasizes conceptual modeling. In his excellent and stimulating book, *Advanced Object-Oriented Analysis & Design Using UML*, Odell collected 22 previously published essays. Because he addresses advanced topics in object orientation by presenting theoretical frameworks, Part II, which comments on his treatment, is largely theoretical. It has been explicitly designed to bridge the metapattern theory of Part I with a variety of practical applications of the metapattern. Many specific patterns offering operational value therefore appear in Parts III and IV.

In this chapter, as a sweeping encounter with his thoughts on conceptual modelings, we analyze only Odell's first essay. Later chapters deal selectively with other essays.

6.1 Conceptual Model and Implementation Considerations

In his essay, "Modeling Objects: Using Binary- and Entity-Relationship Approaches," Odell's main argument concerns the decision to model information as an object class. He maintains that only what has been conceptually specified as an object type leads to implementation as an object class. He notes that "the class acts as an index for both structure and operation in the OO world." Clearly, his objection to traditional entity-attribute-relationship (EAR) models is that EAR attribute types are unclear as to whether an object type has been modeled. He suggests that, when applicable, an attribute type be enhanced to include an explicit description of an object type.[1] Indeed, this is an adequate solution to the problem he has identified.

Odell does not pursue another issue: With binary-relationship (BR) models, anything indicated on each side of a relationship may be considered an object type. This could lead to overspecification (instead of the possibility of underspecification with EAR). The solution is the inverse of what Odell suggested for attribute types in EAR; a BR object, when applicable, is to be disabled as an OO object.

In his essay, day, location, and color are the contested information objects. Must a corresponding type, and thereby class, be attributed to, say, day? In this context, Odell states somewhat remarkably that "implementation is not the issue in OO analysis [for t]he primary goal of analysis is to model the end-user's concepts and leave the concept implementation to the designers." This contrasts with the problem he raises about whether to specify a class for information of a particular type. He writes: "To properly assist the OO designer in making correct implementation decisions, the OO analyst must clearly specify *all* object types." This is the balanced view. As the conceptual model controls many decisions about implementation, it also contains transformation concepts. That a type may become a class is just an example. The conceptual modeler must handle such transformation concepts with awareness and care.

---

1. The essay as published in *Advanced Object-Oriented Analysis & Design Using UML* does not clearly present the suggestion. No doubt by accident, Figure 1.4(a) has been copied from Figure 1.2(a). In *Object-Oriented Methods: A Foundation*, Martin and Odell treat the same problem. There, Figure 24.4(a) makes clear what Odell's suggestion entails.

The metapattern makes a distinction between primitive and pointer information objects. A primitive information object corresponds to a normal entity attribute. In Chapter 4, *Time*, particular points in time are presented as primitive information objects. Apart from its context, this means that every point in time is completely independent of others.

As an alternative, the relationship for starting time could have been conceived as a pointer information object, making that object part of a time management system beyond its own immediate context. The information set may contain several identical pointer objects that effectively and even *systematically* pertain to the same time point.

The cohesive mechanism offered by pointers has a price. By definition, a pointer never provides direct access to information; one or more relationships must be navigated to arrive at the information itself. How this functions is shown in Figure 6-1, taking elements from the case Odell explains in his essay. Alternative b stresses that somewhere in the information set a particular date must be "primitively" available.

Actually, these alternatives do not reflect "the end-user's concepts," at all—certainly not at first. Users do not perceive how conceptual specifications influence implementation. Therefore, the conceptual modeler (whom Odell calls an analyst) must inform future users and enhance their decision-making quality by presenting alternatives. Playing the role of change agent, the modeler helps users gain trust in what is essentially a *design process* toward an information model. That is, when a model is created, it is designed, not analyzed.

But users often lack the capacity for positive verification, which explains why modeling for complex information requirements is a separate profession. A user

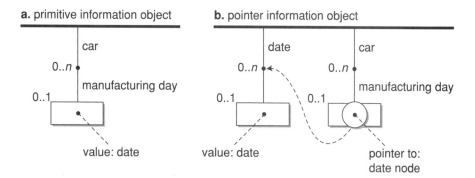

Figure 6-1 *Choice between primitive and reference*

must have sufficient ground for trust in the professional. And the professional must appear to make complex decisions about information *on behalf of* the user.

Figure 6-1 shows the cardinality of information objects beside their nodes. In some cases, the minimal value of zero for the number of instances might appear unorthodox, but information really could be unavailable.

On the other hand, in the course of time and/or through corrections, a multitude of information objects may exist. As time is universally managed in the metapattern at the lowest level of aggregation, the additional cardinality of existence and validity entries is nowhere stated explicitly.

6.2 Navigational Guidelines

Figure 6-2 presents an information model in terms of the metapattern of Odell's case in his essay, "Modeling Objects: Using Binary- and Entity-Relationship Approaches." This is, however, only one of many alternatives. For simplicity, we have left out details, such as at which information objects pointers are directed.

Compared to Odell's original model, the metapattern's interpretation already provides more opportunities. Location, for example, is explicitly modeled in two different contexts, allowing for corresponding differentiation between intexts.

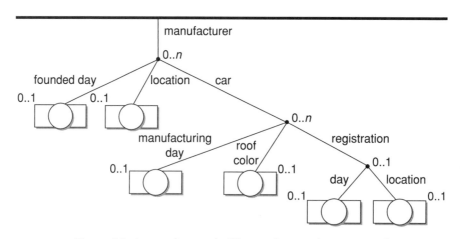

Figure 6-2 *A manufacturer builds cars that are then registered*

At the location level, such flexibility is impossible with BR or EAR models; derived entity types would have to be introduced.

It is especially illuminating that date appears in many different contexts.

Based on the concept of context, and in particular on the nil object, the conceptual model can take navigation into account. Of course, an OO class is already fitted for navigation with mechanisms to control access to its instances. The metapattern invites development of conceptually equivalent models; they are simultaneously highly differentiated with respect to implementation as concrete information sets. As such, the metapattern is also a tool for bridging the gap between conceptual and implementation models. As stated earlier, some important implementation issues can already be "prepared" in the conceptual model by using transformation concepts.

The metapattern tries to incorporate a positive legacy of hierarchical and network data modeling. On the negative side, those traditional modeling approaches are almost completely biased toward implementation. Though implementation issues may indeed be prepared, the focus remains firmly on life rather than on tool. (See the *Introduction* for an understanding of life and tool focuses in the context of information system development.)

Figure 6-3 contains an alternative to the model sketched in Figure 6-2. Car, not manufacturer, is taken as a starting point.

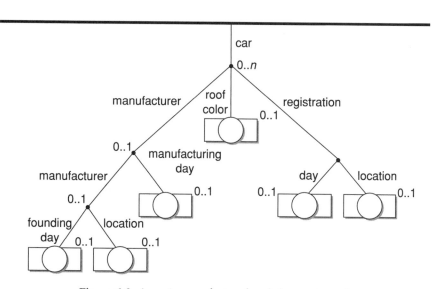

Figure 6-3 *A car is manufactured and then registered*

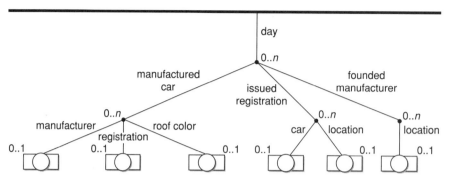

Figure 6-4 *A day with different events*

It is also feasible to take day as a starting point for modeling (Figure 6-4).

This last alternative is particularly artificial. This should come as no surprise, since day is one of the attribute types Odell uses to support the case for extending EAR models. Following Odell, it seems logical to develop the model from three points of view, not just one. So, in Figure 6-5, the "normal" entities—entity types, actually—of manufacturer, car, and (car) registration are all given a minimal context.

As needs arise, dotted lines are used to connect information objects. They help clarify which navigation is supported by pointer information objects. In Figure 6-5, one such line has been added for "jumping" from the registration-of-car to the (car) registration itself.

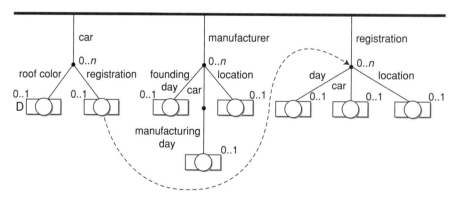

Figure 6-5 *From a single, implicit context to multiple contexts*

Figure 6-5 reflects only one of many alternatives. The choice of which information model is best can be judged against the advantages or disadvantages of context designs (traditionally: types and classes, respectively) and navigational options, among other criteria. An EAR or BR model does not use the concept of context, at least as a metaconcept, so it cannot provide insight. In particular, something like the nil object is completely absent. EAR and BR, therefore, lack even the base from which to integrate suggestions for navigation into a conceptual model.

It is possible to make more elaborate preparations for navigation at the stage of conceptual modeling. When an information object is indicated by a capital letter D, as in Figure 6-5 (the roof color of a car), access should be as direct as possible. The mechanism for doing so—through an index, for example—is and should remain a matter for implementation.

6.3 Type-on-Context

What should be apparent with EAR and BR models is their redundancy. A relationship's name is often identical to an involved entity's name. This occurs with relationships in all directions.

An information model designed with the metapattern is less troubled by such redundancy because intermediary and pointer information objects are not complete objects. Rather, they perform the service of establishing a partial identity for what constitutes an overall object. It is particularly difficult to come up with additional names for all partial identities; the preference is thus to leave out names for nodes altogether.

By *not* assigning names to nodes, the fundamental nature of the metapattern's differences stands out even more clearly, since relationships provide the most important elements in typing. Although specific information objects may contribute to establishment of a type, relationships usually suffice. EAR/BR modeling is radically different; the concept of entity has priority, leading to type-on-entity, and the axiom of traditional object orientation is type-on-object.

In the metapattern, priority is squarely given to context, not object. In general, the type is "on" the (whole) context. In usual practice, only type-on-relationship is actively used from this wide range.

But the possibility does exist for a concrete information object to participate in determining the type of an (other) information object. When used, this typing mode must be expressed in the model, explaining why instances and types are sometimes mixed in the same model. Rather than being a shortcoming of the metapattern, this exemplifies its powerful variety.

Another interesting metapattern feature is that no inverse relationships, which traditionally point out the need for a navigational path, appear. They are indicated explicitly, with complete precision and in a positive way. This happens where (partial) identities of an overall object are specified in various contexts. The (car) registration in Figure 6-5 is a good example, because it exists more or less in its own right (on the figure's right) and as a property of a particular car (on the figure's left).

6.4 The Relative Nature of Unification

To conclude our first encounter with Odell, we'll discuss the unified modeling language (UML) which he revised his original essays to comply with. He even mentions UML in the title of the book reviewed here.

One aim of UML is to reach a standardized notation. The metapattern, however, takes a different course for notation. Why? First of all, the metapattern is not object- but context-oriented. Its concept of context helps us see that UML's extent of unification is limited to traditional object orientation. The lack of support for multiple contexts, as they appear through the metapattern, is reflected in the proposed notation of UML. The metapattern cannot comply with what does not exist.

Second, the metapattern is limited to and explicitly stresses conceptual information modeling, including some necessary transformation concepts to prepare for other activities in constructing and using an information system. UML, on the other hand, is intended to cover all aspects and stages of modeling during the design and construction process. Is such a wide claim realistic?

A tenet underlying the metapattern reads that no uniform focus suffices to develop high-quality tools for a life of high quality (see the *Introduction*). Of course, it is possible throughout to design life with a tool focus, which frequently happens. Regretfully, however, a tool focus does not fully respect life; only a life focus does. What a tool focus does and should respect is tools. At its extremes, a development process should consist of two essentially different focuses: one on life, the other on tool. UML is thus viewed here as a strong attempt, originating from software engineering, to extend the tool focus forward along the development path so that it can also control life.

Ideas behind the metapattern oppose any single metamodel for the full development process (except for the one stating that focused metamodels should be used). Instead, at least two metamodels should coexist. What is at stake is alliance rather than compliance. Appendix B presents an example of coexistence between the metapattern and the reference model for open distributed processing (RM-ODP). In general, each metamodel should only be applied as the relevant focus determines. Within its proper context, the initiative of UML has great merit.

Success with the metapattern lies in understanding its own proper context, too. It is precisely the invitation to accept, through different life object contexts, the predominantly relative nature of real behavior. It is this behavior that makes the metapattern suited to supporting conceptual information modeling with the focus on information tools for life in all its variety.

Chapter 7

Discussion

Most of Odell's essays remain valid for context-oriented information modeling. Our selection from his work is deliberately one-sided, with an emphasis on provoking discussion. Of particular interest are problems that help illuminate (1) how the metapattern differs from traditional object orientation and (2) how it enables a modeler to accomplish better solutions. In this chapter we review the remaining four essays in the Structural Issues section of Odell's *Advanced Object-Oriented Analysis & Design Using UML,* which we urge you to consult in its entirety.

7.1 Context-Oriented, Multilayered Typing

In "Object Types as Objects and Vice Versa," Odell discusses some fundamental aspects of object orientation. He uses a case about audio equipment as an example. To a salesperson, product types are relevant. A sale to a customer concerns any cassette player of type X or any compact disk player of type Y. Whichever instance of one product type or another changes hands is not yet important.

However, in the world view of the inventory clerk, individual products figure prominently. *Instances* to the salesperson are only *types* to the clerk, who must know that he is dealing with the instance x of type X or the instance y of type Y.

Odell illustrates that object-oriented tools often lack important qualities. A major limitation is that the number of modeling levels is already fixed. Another is that the metamodel—Odell's term—can almost never be adapted. The only available possibility is defining different types that can be instantiated (that is, instances may be derived from them). But due to the lack of flexibility, problems may emerge on two sides, as Odell indicates. First, an instance of some type can be a type itself. Second, the "fixed" metamodel may block further aggregation and abstraction.

To overcome such obstacles, Odell favors a universal modeling framework, one with no fixed rules and with strictly independent levels. In summarizing the advantages he writes: "An approach of this kind can both describe different models and provide a common framework for expressing and comparing models."

The metapattern supports Odell's important ideas, even allowing elaboration of his problem statement. He starts by distinguishing between two appearances of a particular object: one constitutes an instance, the other a type giving rise to instances.

From a context-oriented viewpoint, something like sales and inventory contexts seem to exist. An important question might be: "Is the type of audio equipment relevant to the inventory clerk who deals with specific products?" Or, perhaps, "Is the clerk adequately informed when the products are uniquely identified?"

Although it will always be necessary to await the answer for a particular context, product types are fundamentally different enough to be of interest. The conclusion is that (product) type should be part of the inventory context. How that context is exactly modeled—by specifying relationships and/or nodes, for example—is irrelevant at this stage. The issue here is that product type determines the behavior of its product instances.

But this does not make product type the sole determinator of the type of the product instances. Within the complete context, several relationships and/or information objects may exist, all contributing to the type for underlying node instances. Perhaps audio equipment is only one of many product categories in the whole information set. Such an additional differentiation of context annex type is shown in Figure 7-1.

Figure 7-1 opens the possibility of entering an expression about specialization versus generalization into the relationship between an information object and its context. It agrees with Odell's intention of the (more) general information object constituting a type for the (more) specific object. But an information object may be like a part, with the context acting as its whole.

Along these lines, Odell's case can be generalized, beginning with product elements. From them the concept of product as a homogeneous classification hierarchy is formed, with each node representing a separate product. All nodes likely share the same type, leaving out generalization and specialization. But products in the context of another product could be considered its parts, and when different behavioral meanings are required in sales and inventory contexts, corresponding partial identities or contexts should be modeled (Figure 7-2).

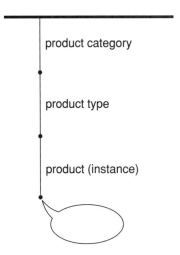

Figure 7-1 *Necessary and sufficient detail in typing*

The route following generalization/specialization in the context of the information object circumvents Odell's problem. Why? Because now hierarchical types are given a correspondingly hierarchical place on what he calls the data and process level (refer back to Figure 7-1). Another route eliminates a hierarchy of types altogether, thereby making the whole problem disappear (Figure 7-2).

Typing is, generally speaking, a matter of hierarchical classification, combining strategies of generalization/specialization and whole/part. A particular combination, considering relevant hierarchical levels, amounts to a particular type.

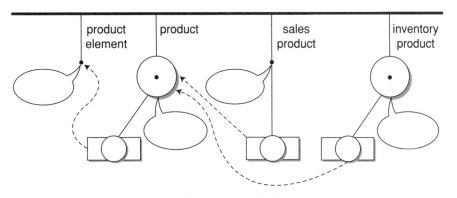

Figure 7-2 *Differentiation of product behaviors*

Odell does not start from such a general view. His framework appears to be a special case of two levels; the relationship between instances at those levels is determined by generalization/specialization. However, it is almost impossible to recognize the general view from such a special case. The other way around is straightforward.

Odell raises two problems. The first is the double appearance of an object, that is, as an instance and as a type of (other) instances. His second problem concerns the opposite end of the range—not differentiation but aggregation of types. His objection against limiting the number of metalevels is practically removed by the metapattern because the expression of meta-information (or type) equally follows the metapattern. Meta-information may also contain a reference to a particular type. In this way, types may be connected along a chain of increasing abstraction.

In "Object Types as Objects and Vice Versa," Odell suggests that the end of such a chain is controlled by modeling approach types. Again, this constraint is not shared by the metapattern, because types do not own an established status, with instances being the consequence. Rather, the inverse applies. Primary status is accorded to context, with instances-in-context coming second. Types, including the number of abstraction levels used for their determination, are tertiary. This makes the metapattern's concepts relating to types constitute a different order. They are not, as with traditional object orientation, of the highest order within the information set.

7.2 From Power Type to Type-on-Context

The problem Odell presents in "Power Types" concerns multiple levels in the types of properties. His case deals with trees; with tree species like sugar maple, American elm, and apricot; with properties of tree species; and with properties of individual trees.

An individual tree (an instance) has a particular location in space. All trees have that kind of property. Another kind of property trees share is their species, sugar maple, for example. To avoid duplication, the "typical" leaf pattern should be a property of tree species, not of tree. The problem narrows down the requirement that, apart from a general property such as location, one or more properties of tree instances depend on the tree species involved. Thus, every tree species determines, at least partly, a corresponding tree type.

Odell proceeds by defining all tree species as subtypes of tree. At the same time, each tree species is an instance of the type tree species; in its capacity of such an instance, a tree species has, for example, a particular leaf pattern as a property (value).

The double capacity in which tree species act requires unambiguous control, which is probably the reason why Odell chose to identify tree species as a power type. His definition of a power type is "an object type whose instances are subtypes of another object type."

Odell states that "a particularly complex expression of categorization called power types is not addressed by traditional object structure approaches." The metapattern, however, offers a transparent solution. The differentiation is required for properties of trees. Precision in placing properties succeeds through applying corresponding contexts. As a full context may determine a type, the resulting information model remains compact.

The intext of a tree *in the context of* a tree species may be modeled with all its details elsewhere in the information model. Figure 7-3 shows the relationships of location and geographical area (expressed identically as location). Both lead toward partial identities of the same overall object. What the metapattern recognizes as an overall object, working through various contexts, Odell can only use as a single symbol. The metapattern opens the possibility of pointing, from within different contexts, to the same (partial) identity of an overall object. Whenever necessary, all its other partial identities may be reached from one of its partial identities. This is guaranteed by pointers to the same shared nil identity.

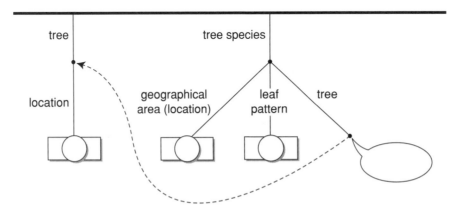

Figure 7-3 *Distributing behavior to appropriate contexts*

In addition, for direct navigation (a conceptual direction), an explicit pointer object may be included.

The information model of Odell's case can easily be upgraded by considering tree species as a homogeneous classification hierarchy (instead of being modeled as a singular information object). Again, concept meanings should be changed accordingly. To construct a hierarchy, we must first define its constituting classification elements (Figure 7-4).

Odell untangles the logical knot by explicitly specifying the upper boundary of the tree classification as constituting the *general* type. This makes all tree instances conform to this type. Including boundary values in the structural model renders the model even more compact. In Figure 7-5, the "general" classification value is implicitly present.

For conceptual modeling, this serves as another example that an established boundary between information structure and information values does not exist. At this point it's interesting to discuss why mathematicians choose to call some values "boundary values." What boundary values really do is "fix" applicability of a more general structure. A higher-level structure can contain, as values, information that would otherwise be incorporated into the lower-level structure. Information is more definite in a structural than in a value form. Since it's easier to change values than structure, a higher-level structure is often an important improvement in flexibility.

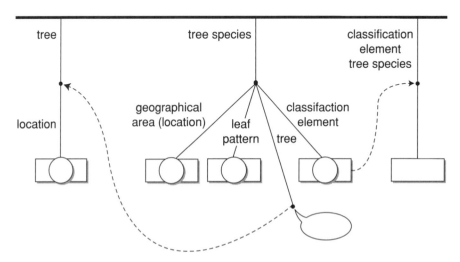

Figure 7-4 *Upgrading possibilities through compositions*

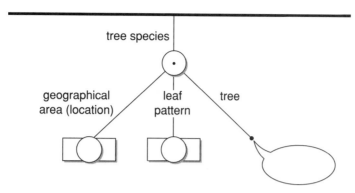

Figure 7-5 *Abstraction through object instance with boundary value*

Without an appropriate boundary value, tree type classification would not suffice as a structure. Additionally, a typeless type (or a general type) would be necessary. Essentially, this procedure is identical to including zero in the number system. Zero is the quintessential example of a boundary value; it is the numberless number.

A conceptual information model should reflect the optimal level of abstraction. Its measure is relative—it is dependent—on actual, predicted information requirements. The professional modeler strives to *invent* more and more abstract concepts. However, when the structure (in regard to the life problem the tool must solve) can no longer be fixed by assuming one or more boundary values, the abstraction has obviously been pursued too far or in the wrong direction. The modeler must then decrease abstraction or change direction. A conceptual information model without boundary value definitions indicates that concepts at a still higher level of abstraction may be discovered.

The heuristics of finding an optimal conceptual model/structure are practically limited by the modeling time available, as well as by the knowledge and imagination the modeler brings to the task and can inspire in other stakeholders. Most principals, alas, still don't fully understand that time (that is, money) spent on conceptual modeling is the single best guarantee of success. A well-orchestrated effort of conceptual modeling serves to involve stakeholders and gain their support.

Finding a balance between structure and values must be taken seriously with every modeling approach. The metapattern softens such design decisions somewhat, because structures, too, may be changed (see Chapter 3, *Types*). This should not detract the modeler from introducing abstraction into models but, rather, inspire their continuous improvement.

Take the model shown in Figure 7-5. Due to type-on-context, each tree node placed under the node for tree species corresponding to the value general is, at that point, supplied with the location property. Other nodes in the hierarchy may appear to serve as (partial) identities of the same overall tree object instance. Intext for each tree instance node is also determined or differentiated by the (other) specific tree species nodes that are part of its context.

The metapattern has no need for power types. The context orientation is already a sufficient mechanism for precision in differentiation and coordination. The only objective of classification is to create *necessary and sufficient* differences. Because its context is the complete classification of any information object, its type is immediately and fully defined by that very context.

The elimination of power types must be considered a major advantage; they can easily lead to confusion, as the typing of types is at stake. It takes a highly disciplined approach to consistently make proper distinctions between one type of type and another.

From a logical point of view, tree species are not subtypes of tree, because tree is associated with instances. One tree species can only be a subtype of another tree species. Where Odell introduces super types, he does not make the double role (or interpretations) of tree apparent. Figure 7-5 does acknowledge the distinction between types of types. Indeed, a more logical overview is guaranteed, since a tree species is always placed "above" a tree instance. An important consideration in modeling is to keep decomposition as straightforward as possible. Thus the decomposed tree species belongs to the context of a tree instance, not its intext.

Among the cases Odell presents in his essay "Power Types," the insurance policy deserves to be mentioned, too. His point is that the properties of a policy should be differentiated according to several perspectives. He again defines as many power types as there are relevant perspectives, and some are further subdivided.

Basically, the metapattern offers two alternative solutions. The first corresponds to Figure 7-4, in which different perspectives are translated into juxtaposed contexts for different (partial) identities of an overall insurance policy.

The second alternative is sketched in Figure 7-5, in which all perspectives are represented in a single homogeneous classification hierarchy. Based on such a hierarchy, an overall policy is registered with as many nodes to annex (partial) identities as are required to accommodate relevant intexts.

7.3 Structural Operations

The metapattern offers many modeling options. It may sound paradoxical, but certain limitations are necessary: by *realistically* limiting behavior, an unambiguous orientation is offered.

In "Specifying Structural Constraints," Odell supplies a clear introduction to various limitations relevant to the relationships between a particular object and other objects. He includes reflexive relationships in which an object relates to itself. He also discusses a range of relationship options, from simple conditions for the number of instances (cardinality) to complex rules of governance.

Structurally, the metapattern does not depart much from traditional object orientation. It also needs operations to establish and maintain structure in an information set. A type's description must allow for the proper elaboration of necessary and sufficient structural operations.

Only the essay's opening sentence invites a discussion with the metapattern (all but that sentence are strongly recommended). It reads: "We know that objects exist in our world, that objects relate to one another, and that these objects and their associations can be changed."

The metapattern has left behind this principle of treating each object as an absolute unit, and that is not a matter of software engineering. The paradigm shift is grounded in the epistemological attitude of the modeler, in how he or she knows the world.

The metapattern replaces the traditional object principle with the context principle, giving context a privileged ontological status. Only within a particular context is an object supposed to exist. Since the same object may exist in a multitude of contexts, its appearances are limited to contextual, that is, partial, identities. Only within those identities and their context-bound intexts do they make *sense* from an information point of view.

Odell seems to express an opinion about the whole world. The metapattern makes no such claims about all of reality. Its structural definitions are limited to how people perceive their world, so what is defined "only" refers to a model of information objects and their relationships. All the metapattern assumes about objects and how they relate to the world is that it's *as if* the information set is the world's representation—or at least, that it represents a relevant part of the world.

7.4 Contextual Principle

A formal (that is, strict or mathematical) notation supports precise communication and understanding. That is why Odell and his coauthor G. Ramackers in their essay, "Toward a Formalization of OO Analysis," provide "an initial attempt to produce such a formalism for those notions used to represent the results of OO analysis." The authors favor the language of set theory. Because an information model always specifies objects-in-structure, the formalization of object relationships deserves special attention.

Entering into detailed comments on the text of Odell and Ramackers would lead us astray. Their principle is already fundamentally different from the metapattern; their tenet is that a concept serves "to classify those things around us." As far as its formal aspects are concerned, a concept is known by its intension and extension. The intension "is its meaning, or its complete definition." This leads us to ask what the term "or" stands for. And is "meaning" something different from "complete definition"? Or is "complete definition" a detailed explanation of "meaning"? It is one thing to introduce a concept, especially one acting as a metaconcept; it's another to positively define it. This realistic attitude toward metaconcepts was explained in § 1.5.

The last interpretation of "meaning" seems reasonable, and shows the fundamental difference between the authors' object orientation and the metapattern's context orientation. We cannot overemphasize that the metapattern does not provide a positive, complete definition of an object. At most, a definition exists for what an object is *within a context*. Further, the number of possible contexts is infinite. By implication, an overall object may appear in any number of identities. Indeed, for the information set a complete, overall (information) object is given; but this is very different from a complete definition of a concept (for a set of objects) in the real world outside the information set. That complete object may well be considered an approximation of the concept definition. As the complete object changes, the definition also changes. A characteristic of such a "definition" is that it is always a relative conclusion, not a firm principle.

Despite their fundamentally different principle, Odell and Ramackers offer valuable suggestions that remain valid when considering the metapattern. For a detailed account, read Odell's excellent collection. The metapattern's theoretical foundation is formally presented in Part I of this book, particularly in Chapters 1 and 2.

Chapter 8

Dynamics

In his book *Advanced Object-Oriented Analysis & Design Using UML* Odell groups four essays into a section entitled Dynamic Issues. Two other essays appear in the Business Rules section. We discuss all six essays in this chapter.

8.1 Contextual State at Specific Time

Change and state are aspects of the same phenomenon. According to Odell, what changes in an object is its state.

But what *is* object state? In the essay "What Is Object State?" Odell's remarks are equally valid for the metapattern. Strangely, he doesn't appear to reckon distinctly with time. Contrast this with the metapattern, where time is dealt with *as a principle* (see Chapter 4, *Time*). A particular state is only valid *in an explicit relationship* to a certain point in time.

The metapattern views the concept of state contextually. A particular context is always what determines the relevant part of an overall object; the particular part has a corresponding contextual identity. The state of any such object part covers the existence of its identifying node as well as its context and intext. The state of an overall object—with an overall object's skeleton consisting of all nodes pointing to the same nil identity—is the collection of all object-part states. But is there any practical relevance in considering the overall object's state? A good reason must exist to differentiate behavior. This leads to contextual states that are largely independent (precisely because contexts are supposed to be disjunct). It is thus the contextual state rather than the overall state that puts time in proper perspective.

8.2 Dynamic, Multiple Typing

Contrary to his opening sentence in "Specifying Structural Constraints" (see § 7.3), Odell begins the essay "Dynamic and Multiple Classification" as follows: "Object-oriented analysis should *not* model reality, rather it should model the way reality is understood by *people*."

The metapattern's ontological paradigm agrees with this statement about the relationship between "the" reality and information about reality. However, in the same essay, Odell advocates that "OO analysis should not be based on any implementation technology." He also mentions that "[o]ne of the reasons why the OO approach has been so successful is because the shift from concept to implementation is smaller than with conventional approaches."

Indeed, applying the metapattern instead of conventional object orientation can narrow the gap between the conceptual information model and practical information systems. But a fundamental difference between the two extremes remains (see the paragraph about conceptual modeling in the Introduction). The gap between tools for life and living for tools can never be completely closed. Rather than attempting to close it by using a single focus, we should recognize the duality of focus and use at least two metamodels. On the conceptual side, the metapattern is a powerful metamodel. Its conceptual results need to be translated into the construction/implementation models required to switch focus to tool technology.

Odell defines dynamic classification as the system's property: an object may be declared a member of a certain class at a particular time, declassified as such at another time, and so on. The fact that no components are available for object-oriented implementation of such dynamic classification is something he views as a problem. He believes that too wide a gap exists between the information model and its implementation.

The metapattern suggests that implementation components can go a long way to behaving as the conceptual information model requires for dynamic classification/typing. First, it is not "the" object that changes its type. The change is always limited to a particular context, and within any context are existence entries to (re)construct the state of such a partial identity at any point in time.

In this way the metapattern offers more than an elegant solution to dynamic typing requirements. Such information requirements have led to the metapattern's design; the need for dynamics of information objects, among contexts and in time, have been its primary sources of inspiration.

In addition to dynamic classification, "an object can have multiple object types that apply to it at any moment. When an object is an instance of more than one type, this is called multiple classification." With traditional object orientation, then, a problem emerges whenever the particular object is an instance of "multiple classes that are not implied from a superclass hierarchy." As a first implementation solution, Odell says, every combination of (conceptual) types leads to a separate (implementation) class. (He adds that this approach has several disadvantages.) The second solution is object slicing, in which the object is divided into as many parts as there are different types.

At this point Odell is close to the concepts central to the metapattern, but although he seems to favor the second solution, he remains hesitant. The idea of object division apparently runs too much against the established principles of object orientation. Coming as he does from a world of objects and the indivisibility of any object, it's understandable that he awards the second option only exception status.

In the philosophy of the metapattern, the division of an overall object is no exception but the absolute rule. This paradigm shift in conceptual information modeling provides highly compact, elegant solutions that directly follow from the principles of context and time for many awkward problems in traditional object orientation.

The metapattern aims at multiple and dynamic typing. Each context completely or partly supplies a corresponding identity—one of possibly many of an overall object—with a relevant type. Again, this greatly shortens the gap between conceptual and implementation models. It's a precondition for making an alliance between appropriate metamodels successful (see Appendix B).

Odell ends the essay "Dynamic and Multiple Classification" by declaring his support for "enhancing OO programming languages so that these notions are directly supported." He is correct, but greater advantages are achieved by entertaining a more powerful approach to conceptual information modeling—the metapattern, for example. The metapattern's context orientation is not only richer for conceptual modeling, it's also a rigorous frame of reference for better implementation tools/components for the precision of behavioral differentiation.

8.3 "Add" as a Single Basic Operation

A student of conceptual modeling may be confused by Odell's essay "Events and Their Specification." To a conceptual modeler, the title suggests a treatise on events in the real world and how they may be modeled for optimized information services. However, the essay sums up operations that should be available for digital (not conceptual) information objects and/or relationships among those objects. He calls such operations "events," indicating that his primary perspective (at least when he wrote this essay) concerns implementation of object orientation, not conceptual information modeling. This explains why the solutions he offers remain within the scope of traditional (technologically focused) object orientation, notwithstanding how close he comes in other essays to metapattern principles (see § 8.2 on multiple typing).

According to Odell, all operations may be reduced to add and delete. The only *basic operation* required by the metapattern is add, following from the existence entry included in any registration. In principle, all information remains in the information set (see Chapter 4, *Time*).

Of course, the claim of reduction to a single basic operation is made here only from a conceptual perspective. It would be too hasty to conclude that a single conceptual operation could eventually be supported by a corresponding single tool operation. What the metapattern does is to suggest a construction metamodel. What follows should be read in this predominantly conceptual light.

The equivalent of delete is also an existence entry (an add operation). It specifies the value nonexistence together with a time value that indicates the starting time of that existence mode. (This is another example of maintaining a more abstract structure of the conceptual information model by choosing an appropriate boundary value. See § 7.2 for some guidelines on balancing modeling abstraction with boundary values.)

The radical application of the add operation for all information changes makes the information model more realistic; thus, the actual information system will perform more realistically: along an active time dimension, phenomena do not permanently disappear. Because they *existed* at some time, a reconstruction at that same time must make them appear to *exist* again. For this reason, the metapattern views time as a fundamental category; a specific time value is present for every information object and relationship.

Merely adding information could lead to an unmanageable volume, so it should be possible to remove information from the operational set before that happens. A specialized housekeeping activity is defined for that purpose, amounting to applying the "traditional" delete operation. From the perspective of the metapattern, such a delete is *not* a basic operation. The information set is not changed based on the equivalent of a real event—a change outside and independent of the set. In other words, a delete operation in the information set does not correspond to specification of a real event. This correspondence, at the heart of conceptual information modeling, does exist for the add operation.

When a cleaning operation would leave an overall object with just its nil identity, such an object has evidently lost its right to continue to exist in the information set. That particular nil identity, too, will be removed. In practice, this seems rare. All information, including past and future, is considered relevant, so it may never happen that an overall object is completely "cleaned up."

8.4 Characteristic Modeling Paradigm

Every state change—in a machine, for example—can be modeled to occur instantaneously. It follows directly that such a machine always exists unambiguously in a specific state.

The transition from one state to another (or, more accurately, the commencement of a different state) may have external effects, such as an effect on another "machine" and a resultant change to its particular state.

The smallest volume of information content, when applying digital information and communication technology, is a zero or a one. Abstracting from this smallest unit to any information object, and assuming instantaneous transitions, information systems (especially digital) exist in a specific state at any point in time. Between digits and the complete set, any subset has this finite quality. This characteristic makes digital information sets eminently suitable for simulation and/or control of other "machines" with variable states that should be as unambiguous as possible at any time.

In "Approaches to Finite-State Machine Modeling," Odell takes the inverse approach, showing the advantages and disadvantages of describing object behavior *as* a finite-state machine. When such conceptualization is achieved, subsequent implementation is straightforward because each machine corresponds to an object class.

Odell does not further explore the idea that a conceptual model assumes that "something" in reality works according to a system of finite-state machines. The behavior of those "original" machines is modeled *onto* or translated *into* object behavior, with objects acting as derived machines. Odell doesn't distinguish—as required for viable, life-focused conceptual models—between a machine-in-reality and an information-object-as-machine-in-the-information-set. He starts with the implementation and then seeks a model to accommodate it. He is right to take that conceptual model as the relevant part of reality for implementation, but he implicitly places "the" reality underlying the conceptual model in the same perspective as that model. For purposes of implementation there is no cause for confusion. However, when the modeler's activity is conceptualization rather than implementation, the absence of properly distinguished perspectives is confusing and can obstruct quality. Odell does apply his single perspective consistently; for example, he sees events primarily from the implementation point of view (see § 8.3).

Odell's approach confirms how strong the influence of technological professionals is to extend their focus, something that generally happens with the best of intentions. As the term paradigm suggests, it's nearly impossible to see beyond a particular paradigm; it is only too natural to see the rest of the world from the same perspective, too. Though understandable, it's not necessarily right. An independent, professional conceptual information modeler should ensure that such implementation bias is removed as much as possible when modeling information from the point of view of its *original requirement*. By the same token, a conceptual modeler should refrain from construction of complex information systems. The underlying paradigms are just too different to be reconciled by a single professional.

It will always be difficult to distinguish between reality and a conceptual information model when the ultimate perspective is governed by implementation. Seen from an implementation viewpoint, it's impossible to discern the conceptual information object and the assumed object in the real world. At that stage, only a single kind of object is visible—the information or (perhaps) digital object.

Again, this inevitable bias of implementation suggests the need for a fundamental change. Conceptual modelers must consider the possibilities and limitations of implementation. Above all, to succeed in conceptualization, the modeler must apply a characteristic paradigm for conceptualization. The right modeling paradigm keeps the modeler concentrating on the relationship between reality and his or her (conceptual) representative information model. The implementation paradigm has a different theme, reflecting the essential properties of the tools actually used to construct the information set structure.

The contents of Odell's essay on finite-state machines give little cause for discussion. What might be explained is that the metapattern allows reality to be modeled as finite-state machines to an even larger extent. Odell gives several conditions for abstaining from that approach, one being "[w]hen an object is viewed as being in many states at any given moment." This can be defined in more detail with the metapattern, since it is not the overall object but its contextual parts that must meet the criterion of practical "finite-stateness."

Inversely, it should be possible to define a specific context—and at the same time the type for the object part—so that the condition of finite states holds.

With "many states," Odell does not refer to the complete state of a particular object at a specific time, because this would immediately disqualify the object as a finite-state machine. He is no doubt speaking about the set of properties, each property having its own state.

An information model of a particular finite-state machine must describe each state transition. In terms of the metapattern, a transition boils down to a composition consisting of a begin state and an end state. A transition's intext will include, among other properties, the relevant conditions. A particular condition may rule that one or more states should or should not have existed previously. Such a memory is exactly what the metapattern offers as a matter of principle.

For the proper conceptual model, an important consideration is whether the finite-state machine is involved in a single, continuous process or in discrete transactions. With different transactions, details must be accommodated and the model must consider the possibility of several machines.

Odell presents specific examples in some detail. Figure 8-1, while simply an overview, adds the distinction between machine types. The metapattern invites the modeler to generate more flexible models.

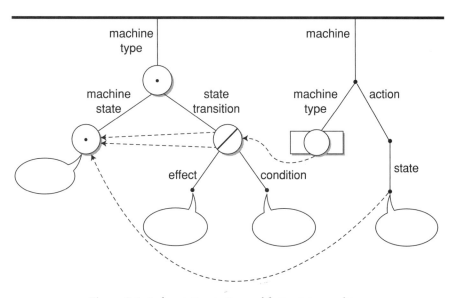

Figure 8-1 *Information pattern of finite-state machines*

8.5 Intext with Static and Dynamic Properties

Every state transition of a finite-state machine may be described with rules, but Odell doesn't refer to such machines in "Business Rules" and "Using Rules with Diagrams." The first essay contains a general categorization; in the second he offers several suggestions for integrating rule presentations in formal schemata. He emphasizes that "rules can also be executable specifications for an automated system."

To bring rules into the domain of finite-state machines, a boundary case must be defined as an assurance. This concerns preservation of state. Preservation is a special case of transition—the absence of any other state. Preservation may also be governed by explicit rules.

The metapattern is first concerned with conceptual information modeling. From that perspective, rules should be considered a property. Every rule thus appears as part of an intext, attached to a particular node. For example, in Figure 8-1, the relationship effect leads to a node that "contains," among other parts of its intext, specifications of the required rules; those specifications consist of intermediary, pointer, and/or primitive information objects.

Odell considers that conditions belong to rules. But conditions, and possibly processing rules, may be modeled separately, with everything connected by a node (see Figure 8-1).

As with all information, rule duplication must be avoided as much as possible. Rule specifications are thus modeled at the type level. A rule is always executed, however, for an object instance. Every type is present in the information set as an instance in its own right; to accomplish state transitions of a type, its metatype supplies the rules, and so forth. When a particular state transition should also affect another machine (information object as node), the rule-based action is limited to a trigger; then the rule as specified for that other machine's type takes over to establish the actual effect.

Part I of this book defines the intext as the description of the behavior of an object's partial identity in its corresponding context. So far, only static properties have been discussed, but behavior also implies dynamics. Through pointers to rules, type-based or not, each object's part with its contextual identity has the capacity to change. That changes are almost always externally triggered does not detract from this capacity. After such an impulse has been literally taken in, the partial identity itself controls its dynamics. That is to say, with access to the rules in its intext, that same intext does indeed describe behavior.

Static properties (state) may provide information for the dynamic properties (rules) to determine the next state, including possible triggers to effect state transitions elsewhere.

When the actual rule is supplied for the type rather than the instance, it is for a static property of the type. The type's dynamic properties, when specified, refer to metarules implemented as static properties of the metatype involved. In this way, an elaborate hierarchy for abstraction may be modeled and subsequently constructed.

Chapter 9

Emphasis

Part II contains a description of the encounter between the metapattern and various problems originating from traditional object-oriented modeling. A collection of essays by J. J. Odell, *Advanced Object-Oriented Analysis & Design Using UML*, provides a rich sampling of such problems. They provide excellent cases for highlighting fundamental differences between the metapattern and traditional object orientation. As has already been demonstrated in the previous three chapters, his problem cases also provide an ideal background for explaining several aspects of the metapattern in detail and for sketching some alternative models based on the metapattern.

Most of Odell's conceptual problems and solutions are presented in his book's first 11 essays. This remaining chapter of Part II reviews all of the second half of Odell's important book, which contains another 11 essays. We use them to place additional emphasis on previously explained, philosophical aspects of the metapattern. Conceptual information modeling is, after all, applied philosophy.

9.1 Degree of Freedom and Purity

Classification establishes a relationship between an instance and a type. For example, if we call Smith a man he is classified or typed *as an instance of* the male type. If we call a man a human being, we must deal with generalization: The relationship is concerned with two types, where man is supposed to be seen *as a subtype of* human being.

In "Managing Object Complexity," Odell uses a similar approach to explain the fundamental difference between classification and generalization/specialization. The difference is indeed fundamental, but Odell seems to view it as absolute.

As an alternative, the metapattern allows the concepts to be interpreted in a relative and more flexible manner. Every information object is an instance of its own complete context (§ 1.6 explains that a context *classifies* the [information] objects it contains). The particular node determines two things: what counts as instance (being the particular node itself); and which relationships and other nodes constitute its type. Of course, results differ among all nodes. Different nodes may share their complete context or—as their type—identical context subsets (see Figure 2-5 for a schematic summary).

Subtypes, as indicated by Odell, are often more productively modeled as disjunct contexts for a corresponding variety of partial identities of the overall object. In these instances, a more general type does not necessarily serve to act *only* as a node connecting more general information; it can also be the node supplying each instance with specific information as intext (but with that intext's structure being generally valid). All this can be modeled as a single hierarchy—hence the reappearance, in different locations, of the same relationship type.

However, when a single hierarchy may be replaced by a series of hierarchies without loss of options for classification, a question arises: Is the original generalization/specialization pure enough? Figure 9-1 shows the range of such alternatives.

Traditional object orientation is biased in the sense that it is ideally based on a single typological hierarchy. The relationship between information objects may thus be interpreted wrongly as a case of generalization/specialization.

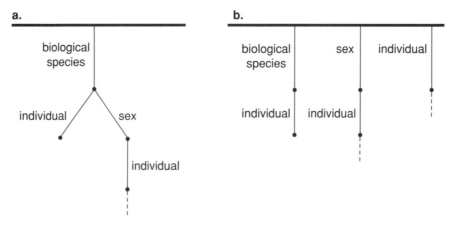

Figure 9-1 *Sorting out generalizations*

The metapattern avoids this problem altogether because context orientation does not presuppose a single hierarchy. In fact, there is no preference for one or more hierarchies. And the principle of multiple contexts seems to allow a special freedom for conceptual modeling. It turns out that, through abstraction, a homogeneous classification hierarchy results (see § 5.1), offering a purer model of generalization/specialization. The paradox is that greater freedom at implementation results in greater simplicity. A precondition is that implementation tools must incorporate the metapattern.

In the second part of the same essay, Odell explains the aggregate (a whole). For the metapattern, every intermediary information object is the identification of a whole, with intext for its parts. On its own terms, any part at the next level of specification may act as a whole itself (also having an intext for its parts), and so on. With the metapattern, no information object (node) is automatically at its simplest level. Decomposition into properties (next-level intext) may continue indefinitely. The modeler sets limits through interpretation of relevant information requirements.

Odell considers a composition to be a special case of an aggregate. A necessary condition reads that one or more parts must be present. The boundary case is the composition with just a single constituting part. The lower limit could be similarly defined for the Cartesian product in its capacity of a composition (see § 5.2).

9.2 Structural Set for Specification of Aggregates

Odell wants to prevent developers from wasting energy by reinventing software constructions. For this reason he devoted an essay, "Six Different Kinds of Aggregation," to the similarities and differences by which parts can relate to their whole and to each other. Each type (although Odell fails to mention type in this context) requires characteristic operations. After development, such operations are available for every corresponding aggregate instance.

What Odell does not elaborate upon is the conceptual modeling of the "functional or structural relationship to one another—as well as to the object they constitute." However, another essay, "Toward a Formalization of OO Analysis" (see § 7.4 for comments), contains an important clue in this regard: It defines the power set of a set S as the set of all subsets of S. This definition makes every element of the power set a candidate for modeling the relationship with the whole. Such an element may also be considered the basis for modeling relationships

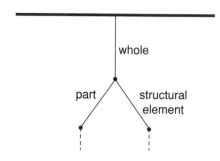

Figure 9-2 *A structural set is a subset of a whole's parts*

among the parts. It makes sense, of course, to limit attention to those particular members of the power set whose description contributes to structural under-standing, that is, how parts relate to each other and to the whole.

The (sub)set of structurally relevant elements/members of the power set of (aggregate) S is here defined as the *structural set* of S. Members of such a struc-tural set are called structural elements. The intext of every structural element, therefore, contains the model of "its" corresponding substructure of the com-plete aggregate. The concepts of whole, part, and structural set are modeled in Figure 9-2.

9.3 Rule, No Exception

"A Foundation for Aggregation" and "A User-Level Model of Aggregation" were coauthored by Odell and C. Bock. Both essays give special attention to parts that appear in various aggregates and wholes where they subsequently play different roles. An engine in a car, for example, is different in its behavior from a submarine's engine. That is why, as they suggest, engine needs to be sub-typed as car engine and submarine engine, respectively.

According to the authors, what is involved are "the parts as necessary within the context" of a car or a submarine. They further state that "current method-ologies, even though [these features] are needed in common applications," do not support that "[p]arts may be connected in certain ways unique to the com-posite . . . [that] each part has an identifiable role in the composite . . . [and that] parts may be assigned properties unique to the composite."

But now the metapattern does provide such support, even as a matter of principle. As Odell and Bock write, "[a] qua-type is a subtype created solely to support a role," a statement demonstrating their perception that such a role is exceptional. Apparently, they consider a type with *general* application as a normal case.

By contrast, the metapattern assumes multiple contexts from the start. That is, *specialized* types are the rule, not the exception. An overall object, by definition, does not lead a general existence; it only works through specialized roles within corresponding contexts. A consequence is that subtyping, as meant by Odell and Bock, is unnecessary because the various contexts (of engine, for example) constitute just as many types (Figure 9-3). Thus, every context *is* a type, not a subtype of a more general type. The metapattern does not require "context-based subtypes," as Odell and Bock actually call them. Type-on-context follows from the principle of context orientation. Figure 9-3 also shows that cardinality constraints may differ from context to context (a submarine will often have more than one engine).

An important advantage of this is that a smaller set of (basic) building blocks is sufficient to model a richer variety of information. Schemata, too, remain compact, as the contextual differentiation directly draws attention to what each *role* implies as specialization.

The authors are fully justified when stating that "[a]ggregation means that a class can describe the part structure of its instances." The metapattern limits such description to the relationships, and thereby related information objects occur at only the first level of the intext (see § 3.7). Through the principle of type-on-context, "all of the type-based services are available" for every information object.

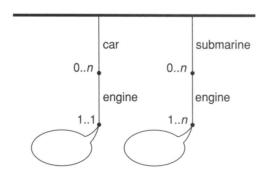

Figure 9-3 *Straightforward modeling per context*

9.4 Limitation of Patterns by Metapattern

In "From Analysis to Design Using Templates," Odell coauthored three essays with M. Fowler. The authors review a series of templates, or patterns, for basic and composite operations in information processing. Such patterns help increase standardization, which should contribute to improvements in the quality of the development process (means) and the resulting information system (end). Emphasis is placed on having specific development rules and their derived design patterns reflect both the approach to conceptual modeling and the infrastructure of information and communication technology. Whenever the modeling approach and/or the technical infrastructure changes, the design patterns must be adjusted accordingly. They also offer a general explanation as to why the metapattern, as an approach for conceptual modeling, might lead to characteristic design patterns.

Earlier in this chapter (§ 9.1), we presented a paradox: Initial distance to implementation eventually increases its simplicity. This is particularly true for the metapattern. Because context and time are dealt with structurally, uniform rules apply. Odell and Fowler see the need to list, somewhere between rule and exception, several design patterns for dynamic and/or multiple classification. They deserve full credit for already recognizing a major part of the structural nature of such patterns. The metapattern models an even more compact set of rules because the structural nature has become a matter of principle. A prominent example is the one remaining basic operation left in the metapattern: add (see § 8.3).

Because this book emphasizes conceptual information modeling, no specific patterns for processing operations are listed for the metapattern as Odell and Fowler did for traditional object orientation in "From Analysis to Design Using Templates." The manner in which they position the conceptual information model in the overall development process is relevant. The "model performs two roles: as a conceptual picture . . . and as a specification of the software components." That is, the conceptual model occupies the critical position for successful translation: It is a model, both to(ward) and before reality. The first reality lies outside the information set. For it is *as if* information will be shaped as representation of that reality (and in an operational information system the proposition is that information is indeed registered *as if* it represents reality). The second reality *becomes* and, through implementation, *is* the information set.

9.5 Context: Background at Foreground

In "Method Engineering," Odell writes about context, but in a different "context." What he refers to appears to lie outside the information set. For the metapattern, however, context also exists within the information set. It has become the critical concept for modeling the fundamental multiple nature of object behavior.

The essay entitled "User Workshop Techniques" is interesting but does not specifically deal with object orientation. There is thus no reason to discuss it here.

In "Object-Oriented Methodologies," Odell recommends object orientation for "systems in general." That is, indeed, a valuable suggestion. But is OO actually any different from the already well-known general systems approach? By the way, Odell traces the development of object orientation to its origin as "a particular kind of programming language." From that, there grew "a broader interpretation [that] means that OO is a way of organizing our thoughts about our world." This interpretation requires elaboration. In the human perspective (that is, in reality) objects never appear fully self-contained but always as a foreground against a background. The metapattern starts with the recognition of this double movement in the single act of human understanding.

The complexity of conceptual information models might be expected to increase by differentiating between foreground and background, but rather, the reverse occurs. Models become simpler and more compact. Contemplation reveals that foreground (information object) and background (context) are not absolutes. Instead, they determine each other. Their dynamics further explain that every context may also be expressed meaningfully by one or more related (other) information objects. This preserves (information) objects and their relationships as the basic building blocks of information models. However, the general approach to modeling has changed fundamentally from object- to context-oriented. Because time is included as a fundamental dimension of information, the set of basic concepts is still very limited. Applying those concepts can yield compact models featuring great variety. The actual information system is correspondingly flexible and adaptable.

9.6 Conclusion on Alternative Solutions

The metapattern does, indeed, lead to an adequate solution for all the conceptual problems reported by Odell. Metapattern solutions are especially superior where dynamic and/or multiple classifications are required. With such problems, it's *as if* the model is more realistic, that is, a closer model of reality, because context and time are fundamental categories.

From this we can reasonably conclude that this book's second hypothesis is valid: The metapattern constitutes a richer approach for conceptual information modeling than purely object-oriented approaches do.

9.7 Afterword on Context

After the manuscript of this book was largely completed, H. Kilov published *Business Specifications*, a book that deserves close study by modeling professionals, too. Particularly impressive and credible is Kilov's claim for the durability of many conceptual models.

Business Specifications is especially interesting reading for students of the metapattern because Kilov grapples with the concept of context. However, he does not yet define, nor does he subsequently apply, the fundamental equivalence among context, classification, and (conceptual) type. This paradigm shift underlying the metapattern is really necessary to establish context as a fully operational concept for information modeling.

The subtitle of Kilov's book is *The Key to Successful Software Engineering*—his stated objective is to extend the rigor of software construction to conceptual information modeling. Of course, conceptual modeling should also be rigorous and precise. Where Kilov means that this quality should be achieved by applying a construction metamodel to conceptual information modeling, the metapattern holds precisely the opposite view: It does not start from requirements about software quality. The metapattern first seeks to reflect the variety of life in the real world and to show how information supports life. The focus on knowledge for life-in-the-world requires a characteristic metamodel, different from a metamodel optimally suited for software engineering to construct the tools. This is the fundamental point throughout the text of this book.

In *Framing Software Reuse,* P. G. Bassett concentrates on software engineering itself. His ideas on reuse as a construction-time concept can be easily modeled with the metapattern. A particular frame, he argues, may be child to several parent frames, and "each parent in effect gets a separate copy to adapt." This is the principle of applied multiple contexts. Accommodating for differences, or delta, from frame defaults, adaptation resulting in an executable module may be varied with so-called ancestor frames to determine context. This construction-time frame architecture is summarized in Figure 9-4, with some "adapted" terminology. A particular frame tree, for example, is a hierarchy of construction frames.

Bassett's ideas can only be fully understood by consulting his excellent book. At the same time, a metapattern perspective might help conceptual modelers understand the important issues he raises. Bassett himself does not formalize, and thereby operationalize, context in the metapattern sense of the function of pairs of information objects and relationships. In general, he correlates context with groupings of similar "sources of change," leaving indeterminate what such seemingly varied sources are. (Essentially defining context as situation, that is, an equivalent, does not provide any practical guidelines.) A layered frame architecture should reflect such sources, with contextual similarities to be grouped by layer. Indeed, context for software consists to a large extent of information technology, that is, of other software and hardware.

An executable module is generated by a frame processor, operating at construction time on a specific frame tree. What Bassett calls context-sensitive adaptation thus yields the run-time module in which all the contributing frames' contexts are recognized. He remarks: "If an algebra of context-sensitivity lurks here, I speculate it would greatly increase our understanding of complex systems." The metapattern has prepared the ground for just such an algebra (see Part I). Actually, it succeeds because information is modeled, not only sensitive to context as Bassett proposes, but even *radically determined by* context.

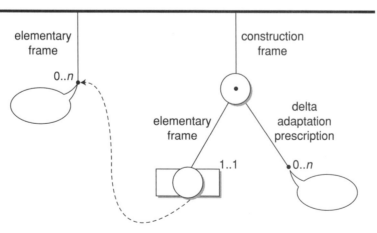

Figure 9-4 *An overview model of Basset's frame technology*

The metapattern and Bassett's frame technology could augment each other well. (The subject of metamodel alliances is treated at more length, but less practically, in Appendix B.) They fit because their orientations match, bridging the two focuses (tool use in life and tool construction). A professional modeler, applying the life focus, will guarantee that *all* information appearing in the conceptual model is externally context-specific, that it is pre-adapted by definition to contexts in reality. Again, this multicontextual precision is limited to conceptual information models. This would leave frame technology to do what it seems ultimately designed for: resolving or adapting to all differences that reside in the variety of information technology. This is strictly a tool focus, as it should be; the corresponding task of construction is big enough.

Conceptual modeling is about doing the right things. Construction is about doing things right. Proper alignment assures that the right things are done right. As Bassett implies, it gets results beyond the "reuse maturity levels" of the tool focus alone.

Part III

Pattern Analysis and Design

Chapter 10

Principle

The growing appreciation of conceptual modeling has found expression in literature during the last few years. Although the number of publications is small, especially when compared to the flood of writings on technical subjects, their quality is often excellent. One of those rare books inspired the previous section. Part III reviews three other books devoted, in part or in full, to specific conceptual information models. We follow the sequence of their original publication, beginning with *Business Process Engineering: Reference Models for Industrial Enterprise* by A.-W. Scheer (1994). The term *reference models* in Scheer's subtitle corresponds to what we call a pattern in this book.

10.1 Monumental Scope

Scheer has written a monumental work. His ambition is to present "a holistic descriptive approach" that explains at the outset why his book is rather complex. He criticizes fragmented information systems and presents an alternative version of integration that he calls ARIS, an acronym for Architecture of Integrated Information Systems.

In ARIS, Scheer unites aspects of operational information processing, which he calls views, with aspects of developing the required information systems; that is, with "proximity to information technology" levels. He distinguishes four views, three of which are data, function, and organization. The fourth view, control, adds the necessary structure to the elements elaborated in the first three views. His three levels (requirements definition, design specification, and implementation description) reflect the stages in the process of developing an information system. Note that Scheer does not require a strict sequence of development stages. From the frame of reference described in the Introduction at the beginning of this book, such a stage might very well be termed a development focus.

With the business problem as a separate component and with its four three-level views, the whole of ARIS consists of 13 components: "The ARIS architecture's descriptive views and levels are fixed, including the business problem description." In the first part of *Business Process Engineering*, Scheer explains this information architecture and suggests description methods for each ARIS component. In the remainder of the book, he consistently applies those methods to represent the reference models.

The analysis of Scheer's reference models is, as stated earlier, aimed at a more practical explanation of the metapattern. Therefore, we do not review all of his models here. In fact, in terms of ARIS, our analysis is limited to the requirements definition of the data view. However, Scheer's book deserves close study by anyone who wants to gain a thorough understanding of enterprise resource planning (ERP). He provides useful information for anyone considering application of the SAP software package, to which ARIS is closely allied. By working through almost 800 pages of *Business Process Engineering*, the reader realizes not only how complex such packaged software really is, but also that the ARIS reference models (and, by extension, SAP and other traditional ERP packages) are mainly oriented toward industrial enterprises. Scheer himself even says so in his subtitle. His book stands as convincing evidence that ERP software should not be implemented unless an organization's information systems are industrial in nature.

By the way, Scheer's 1994 industrial enterprise prototype looks quite traditional a few years later. He considered information and communication technology (ICT) an integral part of production technology, but positioned information systems as a purely administrative tool for marketing purposes. Integrated customer relationship management played no part in his reference models. This view was reasonable, considering that Internet use exploded *after* 1994. These remarks, therefore, are not meant as criticism but serve to place *Business Process Engineering* in its proper context. At the time (the first editions of his books were published as early as 1989), Scheer correctly viewed fragmented information processing as the primary problem in management and control. The emphasis on (internal) integration, therefore, was fully justified. The title provides a clue to his orientation: engineering, not reengineering. Again, as such, the scope of his work is monumental—but it is now mostly outdated as far as integrating information processing into encompassing business processes. Technology, applications, and the manner in which they are conceptualized have developed so much further that any attempt at such a detailed, all-encompassing description must necessarily fail.

But that does not detract from Scheer's extremely valuable input for exercises with the metapattern. However, since Scheer's data models are so wide in scope and presented in such great detail, we do not attempt an exhaustive review here. The selection concentrates on what is generally applicable and is further limited to opportunities for improvement when applying the metapattern.

10.2 Company and Factory Context

Scheer favors entity-attribute-relationship (EAR) models as the description method for the requirements definition (level) of data (view). He explains EAR with the example of a hierarchical organizational structure, an example that already invites remarks and suggestions for alternatives.

Every company, Scheer indicates, belongs to a single group. Unfortunately, he fails to define group; that is, in what way is a group different from a company? It seems reasonable to interpret that a group is not akin to a holding, but, rather, that it represents a geographical, market, or product classification. Scheer's model also shows factory as an entity. The constraint given is that a company may own several factories, whereas a factory is always owned by just one company. To round out the example model, a factory produces articles.

The example's modest scope quickly reveals that the time dimension is missing.

As another characteristic, all key attributes carry explicit meaning. That is, keys are constructed from meanings projected from reality onto the information as its representation. For example, the key to (or information about) a particular company is the company name. Both the missing time dimension and the present meaningfulness of identifiers make easy information adjustment impossible.

Suppose a company changes its name. On the basis of Scheer's model, the corresponding instance of the entity should then be removed. But, regretfully, there are consequences. It is still relatively easy to break the relationship, when it exists at all, with the single instance representing the mother company. Scheer is right to not constrain the number of mother companies to zero or one.

To remove the relationships with daughter companies, if such companies are so registered, requires more complicated operations. Does a relationship exist with a group? Or any relationship with one or more factories? After removal of the *old* information instance of the relevant company (and all its relationships), a *new* instance must be created (and then related to all instances of the other entity types whose relationships with the old instance were severed). However, given that the only change was in name, there is little correspondence among the single original event in reality and a cascade of events in the information system. From inside the information system it looks as if a new company was formed. But, again, the company remained the same; only the name changed.

Using Scheer's reference model, whenever a change occurs in a part of reality represented by a key attribute, disproportional efforts must be spent to keep the information set adjusted. Even worse, information may become lost. The necessary removal of old (and subsequent registration of new) information instances acts to interrupt continuity falsely.

By the way, what happens when a new company name is already being used by another company? With Scheer, this would amount to noncompliance, with the constraint of all keys must be unique. But in the real world it frequently happens that several instances carry the same name.

The metapattern accepts changing information as the rule, not as an exception that can rarely, if ever, be accommodated. This proposition supplies an important argument for *not* using meaningful or changeable information to establish structure *within* the information set. To be specific, keys should not carry external meaning. Instead, the structure is formed by unique nodes whose identifications are meaningless *outside* the information set. This guarantees a close correspondence between a change in the information set and the originating change in the real world. As shown in Figure 10-1, when a company name changes with the metapattern, the administrative change is just as specific and limited.

Some might argue that the choice of keys to support direct navigation in the information set is a matter for construction, not conceptual, models. A bal-

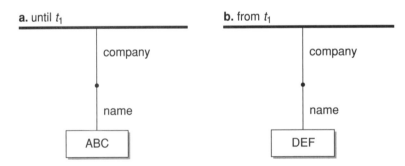

Figure 10-1 *Keeping externally meaningful information at the margins of structure*

anced view is that optimizing navigation is, indeed, a matter of construction. The principles of navigation, however, need to be included in conceptual models, because such principles largely determine how the prospective tool will be used. And tool *use* should be integrally modeled with the life focus, too. The position of a node in the overall structure is in no way based on the company name.

What Scheer presents as a hierarchical company structure is an instance of a homogeneous classification hierarchy (see Chapter 5, *Compositions*). Implementation of such a composition offers greater functionality, since the nodes of the compositional structure require more elementary information objects. Shifting the meaning of company from the element node to the composite node, as shown in Figure 10-2, is recommended.

Without considering the missing time dimension, Scheer's example provides essentially the same possibilities as the metapattern to adjust for change in company structure. What the metapattern regards as a unique node in the homogeneous classification hierarchy, he refers to as (applying EAR) the relationship of company structure. The key to this relationship consists of (1) the name of the mother company and (2) the name of the daughter company involved. What this means is that, apart from the content of key attributes, EAR and the metapattern are to a large extent logically equivalent with respect to such information structure. From the perspective of an entity, it is the relationship connecting it with other entities that provides a particular entity with the opportunity for "relationship-oriented" properties.

The correspondence with the concept of context, as the metapattern supports it, is clear. Still, entities own a privileged status in EAR, as objects do in traditional

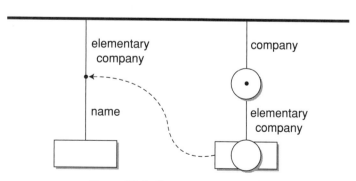

Figure 10-2 *Company as tree node*

object orientation. This is obvious from the general term for relationships that have (also) been declared an entity (in EAR); they are called weak entities. By contrast, the metapattern presupposes that such weak entities are absolutely necessary to establish requisite variety in the information set. This conviction has made context a principle, not a derivative, in the metapattern.

Since the metapattern accommodates existence and validity entries at the smallest scale of information (see Chapter 4, *Time*), Figure 10-2 goes beyond a model of just an actual state. In addition to present information, the past and future may also be, and remain, recorded. What actually counts as past, present, or future is determined by the time of relevance, that is, by the point in time at which the requested information must be valid, as well as by the current time.

When not only context but also its multiple occurrence for a particular object is recognized as a principle, Scheer's example may be taken as a starting point to develop a more general information model. Both company and factory can be redefined as organizations. It also does not seem a reasonable constraint to limit production of a particular article to a single factory/organization. A more general model avoids duplication while still opening the possibility of specialization under the heading of factory (and company). In this latter context, as Figure 10-3 indicates, article is named product.

In order to make the structure immediately visible, all relationships to other parts of the same overall object are made explicit with pointer information objects. Given an extra step, such information objects are also related through their mutual nil identity (see Chapter 1, *Contexts*). Organizational nodes x, y, and z, for example, share nil identity i. Through i, there is always a connection between, say, x and z.

As compared to Figure 10-2, the concept of company has lost its compositional nature, shifting to the more general concept of organization. But with organization now a composition, elementary organizations or organizational units are required. In the model, information on the groups to which a company belongs has been moved to the company's intext (not shown in Figure 10-3).

An alternative (not illustrated) is to disconnect both company and factory from the nil identity connecting them to organization. Instead, they could be made partial identities of the overall object, positioned as one of its other parts. Here, *position* means the composition, as introduced in Chapter 5, *Compositions*. Such a position covers all the possibilities of organization, one of its constituent elements (the other two are person and job).

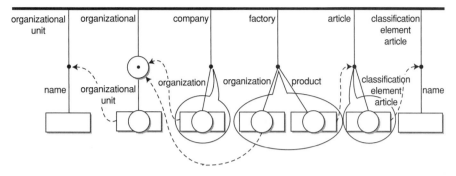

Figure 10-3 *Modeling with more abstract concepts*

Can companies and factories be imagined when not specified as an organization instance? Is it useful to add identification of a person and/or job? Upon reflection, the answer is yes. The next question, then, is whether those companies and factories are relevant for the information set. Only when the answer is yes again should the information model be broadened accordingly.

10.3 Primary Requirement

Scheer starts his main reference models from production targets. Based on what he calls a primary requirement, it's apparent which "end products, independently salable intermediate products, and spare parts derived from sales plans and customer orders" should be available at which times and in which numbers. Another way of defining a primary requirement is as the volume of "constructs" that must be ready; that is, on which, in principle, *no* further processing is required. Scheer's general name for such constructs is article. Earlier in this chapter, partial identities of the same overall object were differentiated by context and given names accordingly: article (general) and product (factory).

Contrary to the example he used in introducing EAR, Scheer does give time a central place in the reference model of the primary requirement. Time appears as an entity type. He proposes it, first of all, to distinguish between specific primary requirements, since the planning date helps identify a primary requirement. Next, the complete primary requirement for every article contains additional information such as the required number of articles and, once again, time (although now it is the time at which the required number must be available).

As a general improvement, all externally meaningful information should be removed from instruments (keys) to navigate within the information set. In this case, an instance of a primary requirement should not be internally identified by a particular planning date. Of course, the planning date may remain a property of requirement planning.

The fundamental provisions the metapattern offers for time and validity allow the information model of the primary requirement to be more radically simplified, since there is no longer a need to show a difference between a complete plan and specifications per article. Why only a plan for every article? The complete plan can always be compiled from the article plans. Such a report need not be modeled separately; what matters conceptually is that the complete plan is "reportable." And for each article-based plan, only the information that is registered as valid for the time of relevance or period of relevance will be selected from the intext. All these considerations result in a compact information model, as Figure 10-4 shows.

In Figure 10-4, many details have been left out, such as the underlying classification elements of the article composition (see Figure 10-3). This overview helps illuminate its radical nature, as compared to Scheer's model. The (ultimate) time of availability of an article batch is included as a pointer information object. In this case, we assume that the (performance) cost of the extra reference is out-

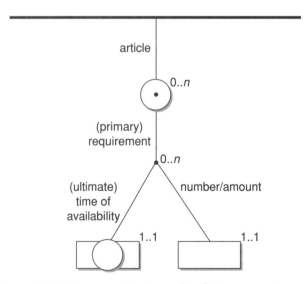

Figure 10-4 *Primary registration only, of primary requirement*

weighed by increased control along the time dimension. (See § 6.1; as an aspect of tool use, performance may be relevant for conceptual modeling.) Of course, Scheer establishes similar control through his entity type for time.

10.4 Bill of Materials, Source, and Destination

The primary requirement is an important ingredient for purchase and production planning, and serves as the basis for the capacity requirement—the bill of materials for the corresponding article. A bill of materials is defined as the list of parts and materials required before and during production.

The modularity of a bill of materials is always strictly layered. An article's first-level part may also consist of parts and materials, and so on. Enumeration of these relationships is called explosion. Taking a particular article as a starting point, repeated consultation, differentiated by explosion level, may be required to accomplish the overview of all parts and materials.

The layered modularity implies that the relevant context is kept limited, since the bill of materials as a concept does not differentiate between the several purposes a particular module may serve. Thus, explosion only carries a quantitative meaning. When the module itself appears tenfold in the next-higher module, which in its turn is required fivefold in *its* superior, the overall requirement per article is 50 module instances. If the immediate superior is only needed once, the requirement for each article is limited to ten module instances.

Scheer builds his reference model on the concept of part. In EAR, a particular structure relationship always connects two parts; one is the upper part, and the other the lower part in the hierarchical structure. Seen from the relationship point of view, one (the upper part) is a module and the other (the lower part) is a part. Inversely, but with an equivalent result, a module may be taken as a starting point for modeling. An even more compact model originates when parts or modules are considered articles. Scheer indicates that intermediate products may also be salable; that is, articles in their own right.

When applicable, a particular article's intext should contain the first level of explosion of its bill of materials. To maintain a generic model, the relationship is called part. Of course, the one or more nodes it leads to are *also* articles, but with a difference. They are actually parts *in the context* of a higher-level article. Implicitly, such a relationship always exists through a mutual nil identity, as modeled in Figure 10-5.

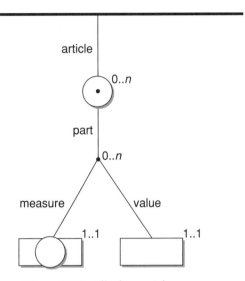

Figure 10-5 *Bill of materials*

Another possibility is through explicit relationships, in which a particular part must itself point to another article. In any case, the relevant node is supplied with relationships for measure and value that lead to primitive or pointer information objects. A pointer object for measure is recommended because it strengthens the structure of the information set.

The bill of materials only contains those "articles" for which such explosion information is useful; that is, articles that an organization produces itself in its capacity as a factory. This avoids unnecessary explosion of the bill of materials. The lowest level of detail involves the articles purchased and produced as such, regardless of how they continue to be processed.

Concrete planning requires knowledge about whether a particular "article" must be purchased or produced by the organization. Therefore, information must be supplied on the source. Scheer's reference model does not seem to recognize multiple sources for the same article.

The possibility of various sources complicates matters considerably. Suppose purchasing is an alternative to (in-house) production. What should the planning be based on? This calls for a preference, or, to use another word, default. But is such a preference dependent on, for example, the number of articles as determined by the primary requirement? And how is under- or overutilization of

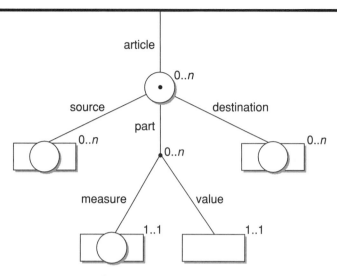

Figure 10-6 *A basic pattern for all article processing*

production capacity to be weighed? These important questions are not pursued in this introduction to the metapattern. We establish sensibility for them, however, by attributing source with the requisite cardinality in the information model.

With the meaning of article changed to a central concept of the bill of materials, more than a multitude of sources must be modeled. Similar information applies to an article's destination; in particular, whether an article is a candidate for primary requirements. There are also "constructs" that do not undergo processing for some time; those produced, for example, for the intermediary purpose of stocking. Figure 10-6 depicts how the concepts of article source and article destination may be integrated.

10.5 Transformations

Articles are often the same except for one or more attribute values; the color or the engine type may be different. But how great may differences be before the notion of the same basic article is compromised? Inversely, how far does similarity go?

These questions do not have a valid general answer. Thus, Scheer writes about transformations, which he calls variants, without a positive definition. He suggests a series of reference models to avoid what he sees as redundancy.

Similarity, however, should be distinguished from redundancy. The first is a predominantly conceptual "concept," the second a technological one. The argument that "creating independent bills of materials for similar products [leads] to an unmanageable volume of data" reflects Scheer's concern about redundancy and the devaluation of tool performance, which he attributes to a large volume of information. Such arguments were never valid for *conceptual* information modeling. Conceptually, the only worry should be whether products are, to coin a term, isomodular. When dissimilar, their differences must, as a matter of conceptual principle, be shown to exist. Of course, with ever more powerful information and communications technology available, it is becoming increasingly practical to acknowledge the full priority of ideal conceptualization. More powerful processing capacity lessens the need to compromise original information requirements.

Metapattern or not, every information model must reflect necessary and sufficient details. When a preference for compactness results in the wrong abstract concepts, the eventual information system will not perform as required. Conceptual correctness must prevail over technical arguments. Scheer's alternative models lead away from understanding the variety of bills of materials. Instead, users should be provided with the proper tools to control that real variety. They could be allowed, for example, to change identical subsets of several bills of materials through a single user interaction. However, those bills of materials are, and remain, separate.

It is doubtless Scheer's intention to create an overall simpler information system. But, as always happens without a radically conceptual foundation, he ends up with a more complex result. At any rate, the quantity of information, following from the layered modularity, is not problematic. Each transformation does not require a complete bill of materials. Additional information will always be limited to the first level of detail (see § 10.4).

It is nevertheless possible to offer a transparent provision for transformation. Again, a boundary must be given a value that at first will seem counterintuitive. That is, a transformation may be normal. This allows the information to include *everything* as a transformation, resulting in maximum generality. The result, yet again, is a compact information model, as Figure 10-7 confirms.

The possibilities for allowing transformations can be increased considerably by interpreting transformation as a homogeneous classification hierarchy.

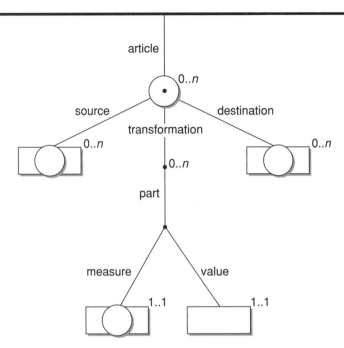

Figure 10-7 *Including article transformations*

However, this only shows that differentiating transformations is an extension of the general application of the article concept. The optimal information model is therefore already given by Figure 10-6. It proposes a single homogeneous classification hierarchy for articles that must be supplied, including all the relevant transformations (as specific articles). This abstraction in modeling should draw attention to the power of recursiveness. When information on transformations (*all* transformations, whether article-based or not) fits a more general classification scheme, the information model does not require any structural alterations. In other words, no growth keeps the model complexity stable. The requisite variety is accomplished through (variable) values for information objects while the (fixed) structure of the model remains (relatively) simple.

The interplay between the abstraction of model structure and value domains requires fundamental, creative efforts by the modeler. At most, a heuristic may be sketched. We present such guidelines throughout this book.

10.6 Types and Instances Revisited

Confronting the primary requirement with the corresponding bills of materials establishes the requirement for *all* articles—from basic materials and parts, through modules and the like, up to completed artifacts. Still, that information is insufficient for concrete production planning. Relevant stock levels, combined with times of availability, must be taken into consideration.

From this point on, the emphasis moves further away from analysis of Scheer's reference models toward the design of alternative metapattern-based patterns. His work continues to be inspiring, though, as he builds reference models in a clear, didactically convincing sequence.

Detailed analysis is complicated by Scheer's mixed use of his central concepts. Without taking the metapattern into account, it would be difficult to keep a full review compact. The source of confusion may be illuminated by pointing to the discussion in Part II (§ 7.1), where Odell presents a problem description discussing the different levels at which a concept may be relevant. The salesperson "sees" audio equipment primarily at (product) type level, whereas the inventory clerk needs additional differentiation; that is, between (product) instances.

This recapitulation highlights that Scheer writes about a part (as one example). But what he actually means is *a type of* part, and the information he models for such a part type he presupposes for all part instances.

That Scheer's implicit assumption lies with types is apparent from how he treats stock information. He writes that stock is concerned with the number of units. His perspective, therefore, is determined by part *type* (article type), not part instance (article instance).

It is interesting to change perspective, particularly at the stage of conceptual modeling. It is difficult, if not impossible, to add details about instances when starting from types. The other way around, however, presents no problem.

The only obstacle to instance-specific models could be habit. Of course, a radical instance orientation may lead to a voluminous information set. So what? If that is the level of specification needed, the conceptual information model should reflect it as a matter of principle. It is always easier to aggregate than it is to differentiate afterward, and when particular instances are removed from the conceptual model, their types remain to be specified explicitly. They serve as an entry point to reorient attention to the (variable) difference between type and instance.

It is not a simple matter to distinguish between types and instances consistently in an information model. Confusion sets in easily, for conceptual information models sometimes reflect—often implicitly—the point of view of types. Additional discipline is needed to discern as dimensions that 1) identical instances may be grouped in reality; 2) similar, but nonidentical instances may be grouped in reality; and 3) information objects must be defined. When the grouping ad 1 should also be represented by an information object in the information set, a definition ad 3 is also required; the same holds for typing ad 2. The types ad 1 and ad 2, respectively, are real, whereas the type ad 3 is more generally known as metainformation. The groupings or sets in reality, therefore, should not be considered metainformation. There are separate dimensions working.

10.7 Positional Instances

Figure 10-8 appears only slightly different from Figure 10-6. Its conceptual content, however, has changed significantly. It is now explicit that the model applies to article types ad 1. That instances of such primary types are not really identical but, instead, are similar in one way or another, may be partly expressed by the homogeneous classification hierarchy for article type; that is, by the information

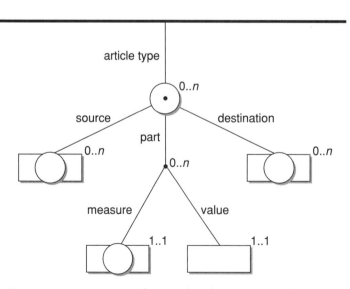

Figure 10-8 *Recognition of type rather than instance relevance*

values that have been registered to represent them. And the nodes where the relationship "part" ends also correspond, in Figure 10-8, to a set of article types, not instances. This creates the opportunity to include instances just as explicitly in the conceptual model. Only when a radical approach is taken will the information model remain simple. To emphasize this strong correlation, Figure 10-9 leaves out still more aspects.

Against the background of traditional information systems for industrial enterprises that are organized for batch production, an elaboration at the instance level is remarkable. Such a model, however, has many points in its favor. And, again, the possibility remains to exchange this perspective for type-level modeling. To look for further advantages in the next models, however, the explicit distinction between types and instances is maintained.

Figure 10-9 states the cardinality of location as being exactly one (1). This is meant as the constraint on simultaneous existence (and validity). Consecutively, an instance may appear at several different locations. Such plurality along the time dimension does not have to be indicated in a particular information model. Besides, with the metapattern, time is modeled before the fact. By the way, in the context shown in Figure 10-9, location stands for something like a warehouse; that is, a place where an inventory is held. The possibilities of an information set, however, may be easily enhanced. First, location should be limited to a purely geographical concept. Address would then be another term for the same concept.

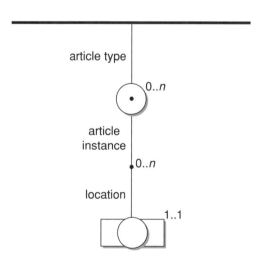

Figure 10-9 *Explicitly modeling instances, too*

The location (or address) gains importance by being placed in an adequately extended context such as *position* (see Chapter 5). Because a particular position may occupy several addresses (locations) at the same time, the very address (location) where the particular instance actually resides must be additionally specified, as shown in Figure 10-10.

Position is the Cartesian product of person, organization, and job. Indeed, the position concept also includes warehouses. But position offers far more variety, which means that warehouses will only be a limited subset of the complete set of position instances. With the position concept having much wider applicability, the "positioning" of article instances need not be limited to inventory status. Instances may be tracked at any position. If this meets a real need, one must identify all positions, including relevant locations for concrete planning. By stretching the concept of inventory somewhat, all are inventory positions. When an instance is present at the appointed time or period at such an inventory position, it follows that no additional instance need be produced. The distinction between type and instance ensures the information model's consistency. The inventory positions remain valid for all similar instances; that is, for all instances of the same type.

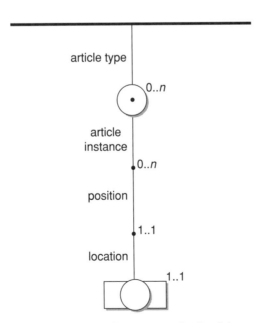

Figure 10-10 *Adding position for flexibility*

In Figure 10-11, Scheer's reference models are shown to imply considerable aggregation. When it is not necessary for every article instance to be located individually, keeping track of the total number of instances per article type is sufficient. A more generic approach would then abstract from the number, limiting the model to article types with grouped instances whose instances can be enumerated. The combined attributes of measure and value allow for more variety. Figure 10-12 presents such a model.

In practice, inventory information about article instances or aggregated information for article types will not be required indiscriminately. In order to accommodate both perspectives, we need to elaborate the context. This also provides another opportunity to illuminate a possible cause of confusion, since the article types ad 1 are grouped ad 2, based on the criterion of whether they need to be traceable by location per instance or on the aggregate. It is common to denote such grouping with the same term, type. However, here type is, and will remain, reserved as the concept for grouping similar objects. All real groupings other than ad 1 must be "typed" in a different manner; that is, by *not* referring to type. Figure 10-13 uses localization method to indicate whether an instance will be administered in the information set uniquely (on an individual basis) or on aggregate (with similar instances grouped together). This, by the way, illustrates a nodal information object determining how an intext is structured. Based on two localization methods, therefore, two types exist (in the sense of

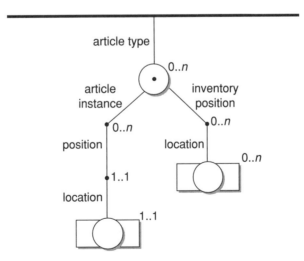

Figure 10-11 *Possible and actual positions for instances*

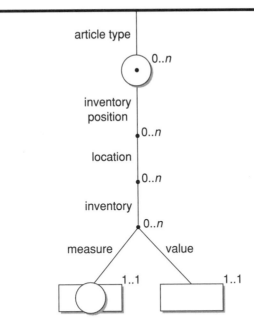

Figure 10-12 *Modeling aggregates of instances*

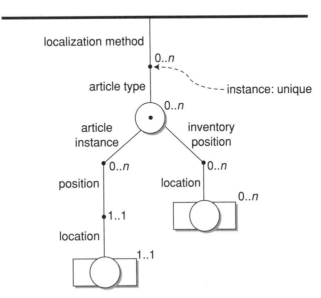

Figure 10-13 *Localization mode of unique instances*

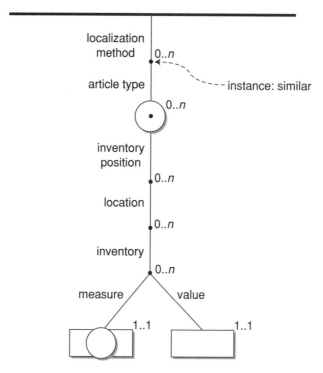

Figure 10-14 *Localization mode of instance aggregates*

metainformation) for article types. Figures 10-13 and 10-14 present elaborations for both cases.

These figures also show that the metapattern's basic notation is kept as limited and simple as possible. Sometimes, however, conceptual precision requires that additional information be included in the model. This may always be done through appropriate notes. How notes are composed and where they are placed in the model is at the discretion of the modeler.

10.8 Fundamental Variety

We hope that this review of Scheer's reference models as well as the presentation of additional models and patterns have demonstrated wider opportunities afforded by the metapattern. Every time, it seems, it pays to search for a more fundamental model, rather than to try and solve a particular problem. When we use abstraction in modeling and simultaneously allow for a growing set of specific information values, the resulting information set will entertain greater variety. The problem as originally stated will then turn out to have been a single phenomenon in a wider field of opportunities.

A correspondingly wider orientation in modeling invests the information set with the potential to act as a solution for all related problems. Fundamental attention to variety, applied at the earliest possible stage, always makes subsequent modeling efforts easier, yielding simpler additional conceptual information needs. Whenever possibilities can be shifted to the infrastructure, problems require less specific energy to be solved properly. For example, the position in its capacity of the Cartesian product of person, organization, and job appears in many contexts. It is advisable to remove it from any particular application. Instead, position belongs at a more fundamental level; that is, in the infrastructure where correspondingly leaner applications may be based. This reduces the overall complexity of an information system. These benefits, however, require close attention and a broad view during conceptual information modeling.

Chapter 11

Alternatives

This chapter continues the presentation of exercises with the metapattern based on Scheer's monumental book, *Business Process Engineering*. Once again we stress that the patterns shown here are not meant as completely operational alternatives to Scheer's reference models, in which he strives to include almost every detail of the industrial mode of production. The analysis of his work is limited to fundamental patterns. The alternatives remain fundamental (if anything, their fundamental nature is shown more explicitly) and, therefore, address only major points. Scheer's book is recommended to any reader interested in a thorough and specialist treatment of an integrated information system for industrial enterprises.

11.1 Serial Size

Starting from the primary requirement, says Scheer, the explosion using bills of materials results in gross purchasing and/or production requirements. The net or real secondary requirement is determined after confrontation with the available inventory. For relevant reference models, Scheer applies the same reasoning as for the primary requirement. That is, he models an overall requirement, which is subdivided into one or more items for every part (article type). This secondary requirement leads to orders.

It seems, later on, that Scheer only applies general microeconomic criteria to establish the order volumes. For example, the available production capacity is not taken into account. He defines overall orders, with items for every article type. More items for the same article type reflect the difference between purchasing and production. In his reference models, Scheer includes many details that are left out here.

One of the alternative patterns (see § 10.3) does not even show the overall primary requirement. It can always be produced as a report from the requirements captured for every article type.

The analogous alternative for orders is to leave out modeling of the overall grouping. The order concept thus applies directly to article types and even article instances. In fact, the whole secondary requirement does not need to be administered separately, since it can always be constructed from orders. Where § 10.7 suggests differentiating between the localization methods of unique and similar, respectively, an equal distinction may be useful for something called serial size. When the value of the serial size is instance, apparently every article instance is ordered individually. With the serial size set instead at group, instances of one and the same article type will be bundled in a particular order. The conditions governing order volume should then be specified elsewhere in the information set. Again, Scheer consistently supplies all such details in his models. They are left out here to maintain a clearer perspective on the fundamental characteristics of the alternative patterns.

Figure 11-1 sketches a pattern for the instance mode of serial size. It must be emphasized that the order appears *in the context of* an instance. This might seem illogical, since the instance only comes into existence through execution of the order. The meaning of such an unorthodox model, however, is more understandable when an order is taken as an aspect of an instance. The presupposition of instance makes it possible to arrive at a more compact model of *all* aspects. Also, Figure 11-1 tries to communicate how little information is

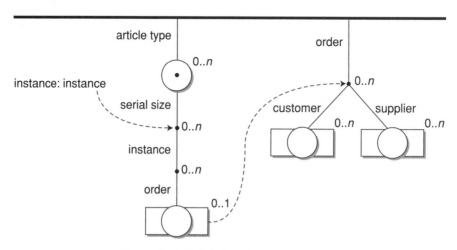

Figure 11-1 *Serial size of unique instances*

required for an instance-sized order. An intext may even be omitted completely when a pointer information object is modeled. Client and supplier (as one example) may then be included as properties of the same overall (production) order, but are further specified with intexts through a partial identity in a different context.

In this book, customers and suppliers are perceived as instances of position almost as a matter of principle. This helps us arrive at an identical model for all order types, as is also Scheer's intention. Indeed, he already uses a single classification for customer orders, purchase orders, and production orders. The differentiation according to serial size is another example of an investment in a more complex foundation, used to establish a more complete and ultimately more compact information model. Figure 11-2 shows the model for a serial size of instance aggregates.

Now that instance and group have been defined as "instances" of serial size, the next question is whether, for any article type, only one of those instances is valid at some time. By showing a particular cardinality, Figures 11-1 and 11-2 already favor multiplicity. This choice makes control more complex but the opportunities with the information set increase accordingly.

Pay special attention to the coexistence of localization methods for article instances (§ 10.7) and serial size. On the basis of the instances supplied in the previous examples, four combinations result. The matrix is shown in Figure 11-3.

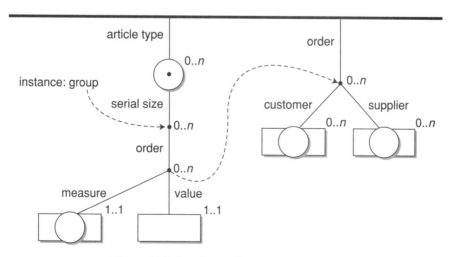

Figure 11-2 *Serial size of instance aggregates*

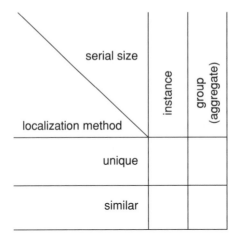

Figure 11-3 *Combinations of localization method and serial size*

A three-dimensional matrix originates when such a sizing method also exists for the primary requirement. Such a (primary) requirement size could, at a minimum, take on the values of instance or group.

11.2 Timing and Scheduling

Time is an important aspect that we have dealt with only in the abstract thus far. Several (types of) points in time may be defined. First, for a particular order, the earliest time at which it should be available might be specified. Then a final time might be given. Thus, if it appears that the order will be delivered late, creating a problem, an action may be triggered.

For points in time to be specified properly, much information is needed. Scheer goes into this at length. Because the emphasis here is on exercises using the metapattern, not on fully developed models, we make only a limited selection from his multifaceted approach.

To keep the information model compact and generic, even a unique article instance is modeled to have an article type (of course, what is given for such a type only applies to that single instance). Thus the bill of materials for an article type contains a list of ingredients, but it is not a recipe. A procedural prescription is required to optimize timing.

Suppose that production of a certain article instance starts at t_1 and that an instance of a different article type must be available for assembly at t_2. Starting at production of their encompassing article instance, for the latter part instance an extra period with the duration of $(t_2 - t_1)$ is available for purchasing or (in-house) production. A more complex situation occurs when several instances of the same article type are to be processed, and where their temporal requirements for availability differ per instance or subassembly of which they are a part. When n subassemblies are involved, a series of points in time from t_2 up to t_{n+1} should be considered, or, as an equivalent, a series of intervals from $(t_2 - t_1)$ up to $(t_{n+1} - t_1)$.

In Figure 11-4, the model of the bill of materials has been extended to include information to support (improved) timing of orders.

The quantitative measure of (instances of) the article type to be processed continues to be a property of part. The idea is that the measure will never change. Only the value will change for different procedural steps.

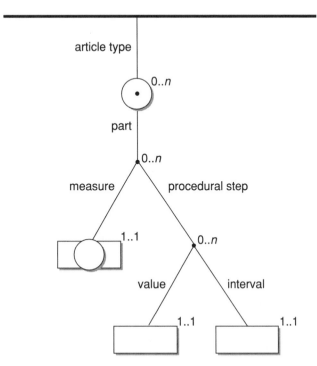

Figure 11-4 *Information for order planning*

In addition, differentiation on the basis of serial size is an interesting option to consider. In this case, the procedural step is the obvious anchoring point in the information model. It would then be possible to specify a particular article instance for assembly, although this only makes sense when the encompassing article instance is produced with the identical serial size (that is, as a *uniquely* administered instance).

Figure 11-5 shows both intext structures, as determined by the respective values for serial size, side by side. The diamond-shaped symbol indicates that the model contains a juxtapositioning of (information) types, based on an equal elaboration of types-on-context.

The information needed to schedule orders may also be modeled using an inverse approach. Then, instead of the bill of materials, the processing proce-

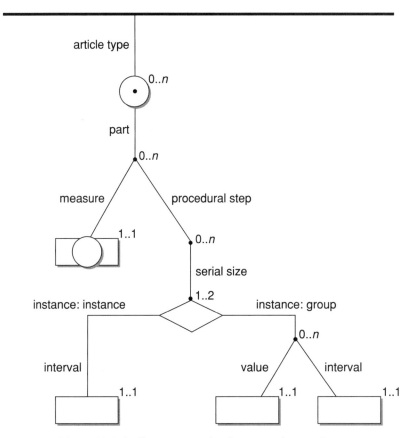

Figure 11-5 *Differentiation of order timing by serial size*

dure is taken as the reference point. Figure 11-6 shows such a model and includes some minor alterations applied to minimize duplication of information in the operational set.

With this model, the information for scheduling and timing is more directly available. A disadvantage is that an extra action is needed for the explosion of the primary requirement; that is, through the procedural steps for every article type. Of course, when both information requirements deserve equal priority, the metapattern allows differentiation into corresponding contexts, each optimized for the requirement that founded it.

Using this example, we can model a more or less universally valid article type. Added would be both its appearance (or context) as an aggregate, serving to place the bill of materials; and its appearance/context as a product, where the processing procedure could be "intext-ed." Such partial objects, belonging to a single overall object, are, at a minimum, always connected through their mutual nil identity. See Figure 11-7 for an overview.

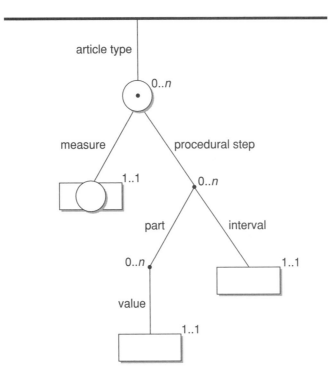

Figure 11-6 *Scheduling from a procedural perspective*

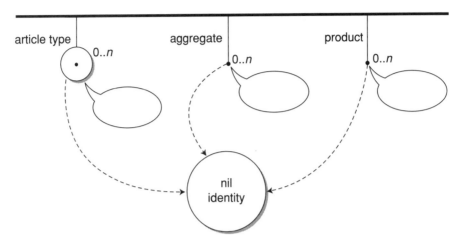

Figure 11-7 *Different contexts for optimization of different information requirements*

11.3 Production Series

As long as the focus remains on product requirements, Scheer is correct in not taking production capacity and the like into account (even for the secondary requirement). However, it's reasonable to question whether he introduces the order concept too early in his reference models. He pays attention to requirements tracking, for "[t]he information flow between requirements and orders is . . . essential for controlling the flow of materials." We later understand that he refers primarily to conditions for order tracking.

The resulting complexity may be avoided by eliminating the idea of purchase and production orders when occupied with requirements. A consequence is that the patterns in § 11.1 turn out to be premature. What is called an order is better considered a secondary requirement, differentiated as needed to fit (secondary) requirement sizes. Seen in this light, the secondary requirement must be given its own separate space in the information set because the subsequent establishment of orders is no longer strictly determined.

Upon more reflection, it's preferable to provide an extra differentiation of customer, purchase, and production orders, respectively. Scheer goes into detail developing those reference models, which is understandable in the context of his book on industrial enterprise and the engineering of their business processes. But here, inspired by the differentiation, a more fundamental question arises: What purpose is actually served by a production order? The answer is that such an order is a means, nothing more and nothing less, to improved control of production. This, in turn, leads to a desired end: fulfilling the primary requirement. Such control is easier to achieve when production orders are already specified, taking the availability of production capacity into account. A particular production order already reflects its feasibility, based on available information. That is, the order-as-plan is understood to be perfectly executable. However, when the plan does not hold up to reality, it should be possible to substitute the earlier production orders for more realistic ones.

A particular production order is concerned with similar article instances to be produced as a group. Therefore, it is more precise to talk about a production series rather than a production order. It is then possible to distinguish clearly between type and instance. A type of production series provides information valid for the production processes of all article instances to be produced within the framework stipulated by the series type. An instance of a production series is then identical to a group of concrete article instances that (1) will be produced, (2) are in the course of being produced, or (3) have been produced.

This is another distinction not made by Scheer. In his reference models, the term "part" appears extensively. Its meaning, however, is always that of part type. As a consequence, he lacks an elegant mechanism for capturing and providing information about part instances.

As we've said, on many points Scheer goes into much more detail than do the metapattern exercises provided here. Thus, the pattern in Figure 11-8 only contains the outline of an alternative.

An important benefit of the standardized mechanism for validity entries is that different plan versions pertaining to a product series need not be modeled explicitly. When a new plan is declared valid, the old plan is automatically allocated an nonvalid status. This metapattern principle is explained in § 4.7.

Also remarkable about the alternative pattern is the repeated appearance of position. This composition covers many "classical" entity types treated separately by Scheer (such as organization, factory group, factory, factory department, employee, workstation group, and workstation). The variety that the Cartesian product of person, organization, and job provides is large enough. Because one or more of the constituting elements may be left undetermined as a boundary value (see § 5.2), a distinction is always possible between a manned and an unmanned workstation, for example. The manned option is realistic when considering a specialist contribution, requiring a particular expert in person. By the way, it is indicative of Scheer's thoroughness that he supplies a

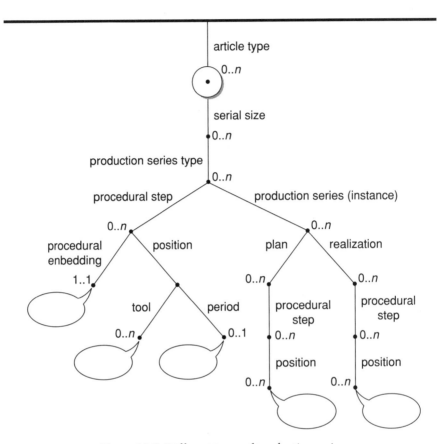

Figure 11-8 *Different types of production series*

detailed reference model for human resources management. For an alternative, more flexible approach using the metapattern, we earlier mentioned the position as the basic building block. As we'll see, the position continues to appear in many contexts, enhancing the compactness and robustness of a great variety of conceptual information models.

11.4 The End of Reviewing

Following further along in Scheer's book, *Business Process Engineering,* would now only result in diminishing returns for our purposes. For one thing, his objectives are different (see § 9.1). Recognizing them makes his great attention to detail understandable—even admirable. But an equally detailed exposition would surely obstruct insight into what the metapattern has to offer. Also, the main points of the viable alternative information models, as presented here, would likely suffer from too many details. An appropriate citation from Hay, whose book is reviewed in the next two chapters, reads: "In order to maintain perspective, it is important to begin by capturing general concepts."

A second reason not to continue our review of Scheer's book is that the alternatives presented here now diverge considerably from his reference models. The distance between them, as the elaboration proceeds, becomes increasingly difficult to bridge. The choice in Part III is for a broad presentation of pattern analysis and design, not an in-depth treatment of a single application domain such as industrial enterprise. In the spirit of a general tour, we now turn to two other books as guides to inspire the metapattern's practical applications.

Chapter 12

Positions

In 1996, D. C. Hay published *Data Model Patterns: Conventions of Thought.* In the foreword, R. Barker classifies traditional entity modeling as passive. But, he continues, "[t]here is a more active form of modeling . . . which has a model predict something that was not previously known or provide for some circumstance that does not yet exist. Such models are invariably much simpler, easier to understand, and yet deal with more situations than mirror-image models. . . . If we can model in this sense, using simpler and more generic models, we will find they stand the test of time better, are cheaper to implement and maintain, and often cater to changes . . . not known initially."

As Barker so eloquently indicates, the metapattern is designed to support such an active modeling approach. Real success is achieved only when a professional modeler is involved; perhaps she or he will be inspired by Hay's work to design specific, useful patterns. To gain maximum benefit, modelers are advised to consult the original source, *Data Model Patterns*. Out of respect for the book's composition, as well as for easier reference, our review follows the sequence of the contents.

12.1 Introduction

Hay starts his introduction with a definition: "A data model is a representation of the things of significance to an enterprise and the relationships among those things." He adds a helpful footnote to explain why he favors such a compact, popular definition, for "[i]t is easier to suggest to a business manager that you would like to discuss the company's data." For such reasons, Hay writes about a "data model" (instead of, for example, an "entity/relationship model"). Here, the same concept is called a conceptual information model—information model, for short. From the perspective of the metapattern, Hay's definition makes it immediately clear that he accords primary ontological status to *things* and not to something like context.

Hay emphasizes, as does Barker, a fundamental orientation toward information modeling. In his view, a model should first and foremost express what is *invariant*. Those properties are often difficult to distill from conversations with people directly involved in business processes, like employees. They will often report and stress incidental problems; that is, derivations from structure. The paradoxical nature of the modeler's contribution is now to emphasize what is essential on the one hand; that is, the model should preferably stress what is invariant, fundamental. It is precisely such an emphasis on structural invariance that will instill trust in stakeholders and thereby, on the other hand, promote actual change. Hay thus attempts to solve the paradox between renewal and continuity. He then makes a claim for standardization, going beyond a notation for information models.

More important is what he calls, and uses as his book's subtitle, "conventions of thought." Only through conceptual agreement, combined with a shared notation, will communication be simpler and more successful. Communication can be improved further by consciously discussing patterns. Hay, too, sees patterns as "starting points, showing ways of looking at a business situation that should allow an analyst to quickly come to terms with the most important aspects of it." (In this book, the analyst is called a modeler or designer.) Benefiting from such a start, the modeler should find it simpler "to apply creativity and imagination."

Everything Hay puts forward is equally valid for the metapattern. In fact, the metapattern adds to the power of patterns, since it encompasses generic mechanisms for multiple contexts, time, existence entries, validity entries, and audit trail (accountability). As Hay claims, a benefit of conventions is that "entire categories of decisions do not have to be made." Conventions equal infrastructure. They have already been adequately cared for through those generic mechanisms.

What Hay calls semantic conventions are equivalent to our patterns, which are based on conventions for syntax and representation. The latter refer to positional conventions, including rules for the configuration of (graphical) symbols in schematic figures. Following his introduction, Hay discusses those three convention types in a separate chapter.

For syntax and representation, the metapattern also has its so-called conventions. However, as we discussed in Chapter 1, these are developed informally due to their simplicity. The differences among Hay, Odell/UML, and Scheer do not matter here, since all patterns in this book are sketched using the metapattern's notational "conventions."

The remainder of this chapter and the next take on Hay's invitation to consider his patterns as providing specific starting points.

12.2 A Play of Positions

According to Hay, almost every information set contains information about persons and organizations. For that reason, he starts his parade of patterns by applying those concepts. Because a person and an organization not only have different (types of) properties, but also share (types of) properties, an encompassing concept serves a useful purpose. Hay calls it party. Person and organization are thus considered subtypes of party.

A similar effect is reached by the metapattern through contexts. One overall object will have partial identities in the contexts of party and person, respectively. Another overall object will appear in the contexts of party and organization. Figure 12-1 shows the case of two overall object instances. It is, actually, almost identical to Figure 3-11, the only difference being that party substitutes for customer.

In Chapter 5, *Compositions*, the position is outlined as the Cartesian product of person, organization, and job (including the shifted meaning of organization and job—both as nodes in a homogeneous classification hierarchy). This makes the pattern in Figure 12-1 obsolete. The position concept also goes beyond what Hay subsequently presents as relationships between person and organization. He starts with employment, defining it as the general composition of person and organization. Next, each employment can cover one or more assignments; that is, instances of the composition, a relationship of employment and job.

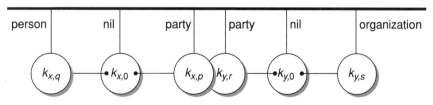

Figure 12-1 *Multiple contexts, rather than multiple subtypes*

The alternatives given here are somewhat difficult to compare with Hay's patterns, since he uses the word position in place of the more limited concept of job (or even job classification element). Here, position is used in the broad meaning established in Chapter 5.

Hay's pattern is surely elegant. It supports a person entering an employment assignment with one organization from which he or she may be given another employment assignment, even with another organization. A more or less equivalent extension of the concept of position is described in § 5.3.

When metapattern notation is applied, Hay's information model appears as shown in Figure 12-2. As a departure from Figure 12-1, pointer information objects in Figure 12-2 make cohesion inside the model more clearly visible (instead of the "invisible" cohesion through the mutual nil identity).

Combining the ideas behind Figures 5.8 and 5.9, the position concept leads to an enriched pattern. It is more flexible because the distinction between employment and assignment is no longer needed, thereby keeping the extension to the minimum. The assignment from employment elsewhere may now go beyond a single (other) employment, as explained in § 5.3. It works because a position is an "open" hierarchy of position elements. In addition, all information objects (and relationships) include their own existence entries. This automatically provides assignment with the required time-based information, as shown in Figure 12-3.

Condensing variety in the position concept requires intelligent application of corresponding information values. By issuing the value [undetermined] to one or more constituting elements of position to form instances, a powerful subset is achieved. Using position, it is logical to include job descriptions (no doubt

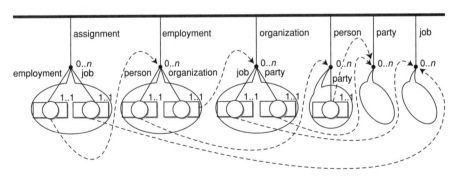

Figure 12-2 *An intermediate level of flexibility*

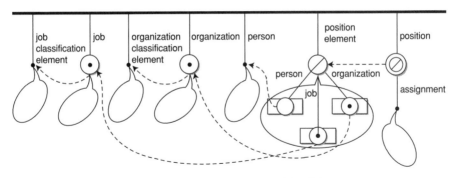

Figure 12-3 *Position-generated flexibility*

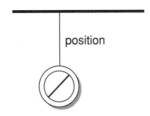

Figure 12-4 *Shorthand notation for a homogeneous tree of Cartesian products*

dependent on a particular organization) in the intext instances of position instances having a person value of [undetermined]. Then, a performance evaluation based on a job description will belong to the intext instance of the position instance holding identical values for organization and job, but with the relevant person indicated by the corresponding element of the position.

Because the position regularly appears in patterns, the building block shown in Figure 12-4 represents the complete subpattern given by Figure 12-3 (excluding the assignment). From now on, the constituent elements are only shown when modeling their respective intexts is relevant.

12.3 An Extended Space for Relationship Management

Hay consistently strives to gain understanding about a limitation. Then, in a later step, he tries to avoid or work around such limitations.

It is an excellent approach to modeling. As an example, Hay counsels against "defining employee as an entity" (Scheer still does so). But including only employee as a type in the conceptual model reflects too limited a perspective. Instead, Hay starts by introducing the entity type of employment. An instance of employment combines instances of a single person and a single organization. Next, he introduces the entity type of job[1] and replaces employment with job assignment. Such an assignment combines a single person and a single job, with job dependent on a single organization.

A position, as explained in Chapter 5, directly joins person, organization, and job. Position is at least equivalent to job assignment, but it is also equivalent to Hay's employment. Or, in a reverse formulation, the set of instances of employment consists of the subset of position instances where the instance of the job component is valued [undetermined].

This interplay is not bounded by just persons, organizations, or jobs: All three constitute parts of position instances. The boundary of the play of positions is widened ever more by establishing position as a homogeneous classification hierarchy (see § 5.3). What Hay remarks on in his introductory chapter is especially applicable to the position pattern we have presented here: "[. . . V]ariations can be made to reside in the *contents* of data, rather than in the *structure* of those data and the programs built to manage them." Similar conclusions are drawn in this book (at the end of § 10.5, for example). Determining an optimal conceptual information model is all about balancing model structure abstraction with value domains. Applied again to the example of the position, it should be clear that such a single pattern can provide an enormous variety. Through the abstraction, necessary differentiation disappears that would elsewhere be implicitly provided by separate entity types and their relationships.

The metapattern opens several ways to model the required differentiation. The simplest model results when there are no differences required in the structure of the intexts. This is something like a reference to a positional classification, of which one or more instances may be contained in the intext of a particular position instance, as shown in Figure 12-5. Whether a specific combination of person, organization, and job instances entails a job assignment (as one example) will "only" be clear from the value of the positional classification.

---

1. As explained in the previous paragraph, the term Hay uses is *position*. This term, however, is already used here in a different, much wider meaning. Thus, Hay's concept is renamed *job*.

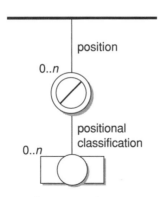

Figure 12-5 *From specific to general structure with specific content*

Often, however, differentiation is needed to support diverse behaviors. As a consequence, the intext's structure must be correspondingly characteristic. As a basis for such differentiation, as many different contexts must be modeled as there are behavioral types. There could be, for example, positions *as* employee, or *as* customer, or *as* debtor and/or creditor, or *as* supplier, or *as* delivery point, and so on (see Figure 12-6). The "original" position remains available to provide a context for an intext that is (more) generally valid.

Note that Figure 12-6 does not show any pointer information objects; for example, no reference is made to a position in the intext of a customer. The assumption is that the cohesion supported by the joint nil identity is adequate to meet information requirements.

As a Cartesian product, the position concept/pattern unites the traditionally divided sets with information about so-called internal and external organizations. The overriding idea is relationship management. As far as the pattern is concerned, all differences between internal and external positions are removed.

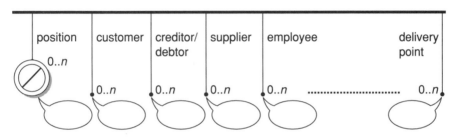

Figure 12-6 *Contexts for behavioral differentiation of positions*

A thoughtful approach determines that labels such as internal and external are always relative. Suppose two organizations share a single information set. What is internal? And what is external? For such reasons, it is advisable *not* to model such relative distinctions. That Hay does not show this additional flexibility in his patterns is surprising, considering his otherwise open and sophisticated modeling approach. In general, the responsible modeler should be extremely conscious of his or her own perspective. The metapattern allows all contexts to be explicitly treated as variables. A boundary-less space of contexts is an impossibility; but now, at least, the space of potentialities is enlarged.

To exploit modeling opportunities, the metapattern suggests questions such as: Cannot one and the same person be both employee and customer; that is, could partial identities be juxtaposed? The prefix "juxta" should alert the modeler that additional flexibility is needed for the information set. From the point of view of one organization, a particular employee has supplementary jobs (positions) elsewhere. A general perspective will show the person to play a constituting part in several positions, none supplementary to any other. The concept of position supports universal juxtaposition. When a specific perspective is relevant, a corresponding selection can always be obtained.

12.4 Connectivity

One of the practical reasons that Hay models person and organization as subtypes of party is that the structure of address information is likely to be identical. As we have shown, a richer alternative to party is position—a broader base that proves useful for many varieties of so-called connectivity. Hay restricts his patterns to physical locations such as addresses. But why are addresses important? They are a means for communication. A wider perspective on communication includes geographical locations where people meet, where deliveries can be made, and so on. Increasingly, however, communication travels in ways other than direct physical contact. Thus, a more general concept would be what is called connectivity here.

A conceptual model of connectivity could start out with communication types. A particular communication type encompasses one or more characteristic communication channels and/or address types. Let's take money transfer as an example of a communication type instance. A certain amount of money could change ownership through the channels of cash, check, pin code transaction, or electronic transfer.

Today, when organizations usually transfer money to their creditors electronically, the bank account number must be known to the paying organization *as an address*.

At the moment, such an address is used exclusively for purposes of money transfer. But let's consider whether that same address might be valid for any other instance of communication type. Is an account number specific enough to also serve as an e-mail address? In this case, it is a bad idea to merge the means for different communication channels, because it would mean that, when the account number changes, the position involved needs to be "connected" differently with e-mail. In addition, the term multimedia speaks for itself. An e-mail address serves several kinds or instances of communication type.

The pattern for connectivity is only crudely and incompletely sketched in Figure 12-7. The details of different address types vary greatly. An international standard now exists for "account number" at financial institutions. Physical addresses have so far been standardized only in certain countries. Thus, presenting a detailed pattern is beyond the scope of any book. The pattern wants to convey (as much as possible) a foundation model for future, often unknown, instances of communication types with their characteristic channels, address types, and, ultimately, specific addresses. The concept of address type is particularly useful to bridge differences in the structures of actual address information.

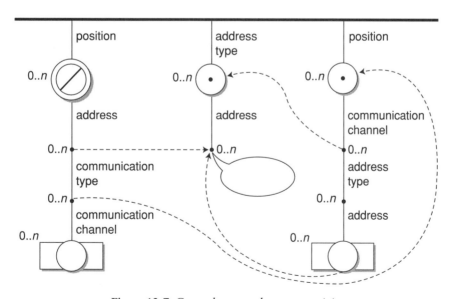

Figure 12-7 *General approach to connectivity*

The sequence in the address intext is quite arbitrary. It really does not matter whether the references for each particular address (reference), as well as references to communication types and channels, come before or after. The reverse order would require just as many references by starting with communication types and channels, and closing the model with specific addresses. The potential multiplicity requires explicit rules for information selection and retrieval. Suppose a particular position has several account numbers at its disposal. To which of those is the actual payment to be made? Or at which delivery address are the goods to be handed over? When the choice cannot be made by default, the information for decision making must be supplied in the context of the transaction(s) implying payment, delivery, and so forth. As illustrated, the pattern does not show such elaborations, though they are often vital.

Hay has added to his address pattern a separate entity type, called placement, to indicate the period during which a particular party may be reached at a particular physical address. With its standardized mechanism for time-factoring information, the metapattern does not need such additional concepts in its specific information models. Conceptually, the existence and validity entries for the pointer information object in a position's intext (that pointer referring to a specific address) take care of time and accountability management in a generic manner.

In his pattern, Hay also raises the issue of relating physical addresses to geographic locations. He wants to avoid problems that might occur when a certain geographic area does not fit the already-existing classification hierarchy of geographic locations (as when a lake has "parts" in different countries). Such knotty problems are easily untangled and subsequently handled by modeling corresponding contexts. As expected, Hay looks for a solution using subtypes. He is right when he points out that the hierarchical segmentation of geographic locations can be extended to the level of what he calls sites. The practical suggestion here is to apply the concept of (geographic) location to everything identified in a comprehensive atlas. Thus, a town or a village is considered an instance of location. A physical address for traditional mail delivery would require additional information, such as street and house number, with details dependent on a "local" standard.

12.5 Explicit Relationships

The concept of position was described in § 12.3 in the context of relationship management. As a matter of principle, the metapattern presupposes a context for that concept of relationship management. (This context is different from that governing the concept of relationship meant to connect objects in the information model.) What follows here is an explanation of what a relationship is in relationship management; that is, for relationships among positions.

Theoretically, creating nodes in a homogeneous classification hierarchy may continue indefinitely. Organization and job are examples of (nodes in) such hierarchies. Position is also patterned hierarchically, as Chapter 5 suggests. In their turn, positions may be used as elements in another type of hierarchy.

On the one hand, elaborate but compact patterns offer interesting possibilities; on the other, the price of abstraction may get too high. Who can still sufficiently understand the underlying model? Who can adequately use the tools based on it?

Although we take such concerns seriously, a composition with explicit positions as its constituting elements seems required. Hay makes a similar suggestion, but stays with his earlier construct of party for membership.

Because position is a richer concept than party, a relationship consisting of positions offers more variety than Hay's relationship of parties. Still more flexibility is added by going beyond characterizing the relationship as a whole. Instead, the role of every constituent position could be explicitly stated. Otherwise, a single perspective often threatens to dominate what is available as information. With roles for every position, such danger is absent (that is, when the modeler acts responsibly). For example, take the relationship between John Smith and Jane Williams. Despite different last names, he is the father, she is the daughter. With their respective roles specified separately, the ambiguity that might reside in whole-relationship labels such as family or parent/child, is ruled out. With role at the level of the participant, rather than the relationship as a whole, it is also possible to change the cardinality of role from just one to at least one. It depends on the requirements.

As another point of departure, Hay limits relationships to two participants. But because the alternative pattern registers each participant with a characteristic role, a relationship can involve any number. The next question is: In what way is a relationship with many participants still different from an organization? The answer, following metapattern logic, is that is does not really matter. An extended concept of relationship—a structure between positions—offers additional possibilities to meet information requirements. Which conceptual information model is actually chosen depends on the particular problems and/or opportunities with information. With more variety available, as shown by multiple relationships between positions, an information set is more likely to satisfy real needs.

As stated earlier, a positional relationship is what the metapattern defines as a composition (see Chapter 5, *Compositions*). The role a position instance plays in a relationship instance may be indicated with information already elaborated as jobs. And roles not yet instantiated should first be added as jobs.

It might seem strange to consider being a father or daughter a "job," but again there is a trade-off to make. In the context of a positional role it *is* different information. So, there might be something in favor of integrating jobs and other roles. If not, a separate pattern for roles is in order.

Each position participating in a positional relationship will itself already contain a job component. The extra role for every participating position is necessary to adequately describe it *in the context of* its relationship with the other positions. Figure 12-8 gives an overview.

An equivalent model, shown in Figure 12-9, makes the concept of participant explicit. It is now represented by a more intermediary information object.

With finely grained existence and validity entries everywhere, a metapattern-based model of positional relationship does not require the time aspect to be specified explicitly. Hay must make time explicit; indeed, he does so where he identifies a requirement for it. But it remains a special requirement, as time-factoring at all levels of information modeling is not fundamental to his approach. As such, it is not universally "present."

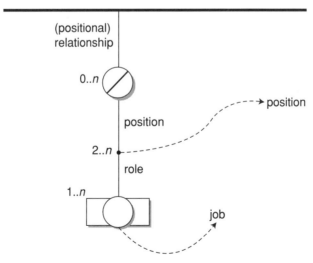

Figure 12-8 *Every position plays an explicit role in a relationship*

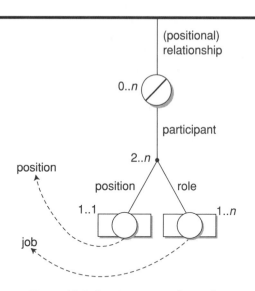

Figure 12-9 *Participant as relational position*

12.6 Analysis and Synthesis

Hay concludes the third chapter of *Data Model Patterns* with some general remarks. He asserts "a bias toward creating the purest models possible, with an emphasis on describing things in terms abstract enough to encompass a wide range of circumstances."

Though every modeler should share this bias, what can be considered "purest"? Can purity be objectively measured? This chapter provides a number of alternative patterns, all selected because they offer an even larger functional variety. It is possible to obtain considerable improvements with corresponding opportunities. But these alternatives are not final, that is, "purest." They, too, must be thoroughly analyzed, inviting ongoing synthesis that leads to even more powerful patterns.

Such dialectics of modeling are undoubtedly what Hay meant to express. Indeed, a modeler achieves his or her best results if he or she generally strives for *pure* models. But directed attention should simultaneously be paid to the particular (organizational) strategy the information set is built to support. Thus, Hay correctly offers the sobering advice that "[y]our client or user will have a particular problem to be addressed quickly and in terms that he or she understands." Therefore, it will always be convincing to give a demonstration of something that really works. In this way, a responsible modeler may hide the more general structure (solution space) from view of the client/user whose primary interest remains a specific solution. A surplus in the solution space will make many later adjustments relatively straightforward (sometimes no structural change will even be necessary). When flexibility is available, all that might be needed is additional instructions for use.

Chapter 13

Publications

The books by Scheer and Hay present data reference models (for requirements definition) or, in what amounts to the same *concept*, conceptual information models. When such models are reusable, they are also called patterns.

Although both books deal with conceptual models, their contents differ greatly. Scheer addresses a specific set of enterprises (that is, industrial enterprises) while attempting to integrate all aspects of information systems. Long before UML, his aim was unification. Hay, taking the inverse approach, limits his attention to "conventions of thought," that is, to the aspect of conceptual information modeling. He addresses all organizations in attempting to present patterns and subpatterns that are as generally applicable as possible.

13.1 Short Comments

As an expert in modeling, Hay produces patterns of a better quality (especially with respect to their essential flexibility) than Sheer, who seems more of an expert in the management and control of industrial enterprises. Whatever differences we assume to exist between them are exemplified by the contents of Hay's chapter on assets (on which we make no extensive comment here). What is relevant from the perspective of the metapattern has been discussed in previous chapters dedicated to Scheer's book. However, a few short remarks are in order.

Hay makes a distinction between single-element-oriented and lot-oriented asset management. The alternatives, presented earlier in response to Scheer's reference models, stressed the same fundamental requirement that was modeled multidimensionally. What we earlier called an article type, however, is a more limited concept than Hay's asset type.

His broader idea is even easier to model with the metapattern. Among other contexts, article type may determine a particular, separate context, whereas another partial identity of the same overall object can have the more widely applicable asset type as part of its context. The patterns in Chapters 10 and 11, sketched as alternatives to Scheer's work, have this in common with Hay's patterns: The same model applies, as much as possible, to both discrete and bulk assets. A relevant measurement must be specified for bulk assets, making unambiguous interpretation of the known quantity possible. But at some point, distinction between what is discreet and what is bulk is unavoidable. Again, Hay reverts to subtyping. As a contrast, the metapattern suggests a more logical model; logical, that is, once the idea of multiple contexts (differentiation through contexts) is grasped.

Hay clarifies the frequent necessity of establishing several perspectives on the structure of assets and also mentions the bill of materials. He advises that insight into the relationships among assets may also be required with respect to electronic connections, safety considerations, or even their incompatibility. The metapattern suggests a corresponding set of contexts.

To meet the requirement of differentiated asset behavior, Hay models behavior as a property of asset type. Indeed, that counts as a pattern for meta-information.

Hay is also interested in the dynamics of organizations. It is commendable how far he succeeds in maintaining a general model. The real variety, however, is enormous. Therefore, just like Scheer, Hay makes some early assumptions in order to protect his patterns from unwanted divergence later. Unlike Scheer, he is fully aware of such modeling decisions, pointing them out as a professional, responsible modeler should. For example, he explains that (work) orders are usually directed at individual persons. It also happens, he says, that organizations are involved in order processing. For this reason he chooses what he calls "the conservative approach," and denotes the more general concept of party as order participant.

Interpreted differently, this is not conservative at all. But it is always safer to apply the broader concept. A model even more certain to match variety would let positions, instead of just parties, participate in (work) orders (see § 11.3).

In another model, Hay's choice is to restrict time sheets for submission by persons only. Again, position is the safer option. With time sheets modeled implicitly on the basis of the universally present existence and validity entries, Figure 11-8 matches Hay's order-related pattern to a large extent. Note, however, that Figure 11-8 speaks of a plan rather than an order.

Scheer presents far-ranging, detailed reference models oriented toward determining total production costs. Hay does not provide as many details, which helps us maintain an overview while studying his patterns. We suggest that allocating positions, rather than just persons, to orders entails much more flexibility. It follows that in order production, the use of machine assets can also be brought under the heading of positions. Through organization and/or job, such asset instances may be known as "properties" of a particular position instance. Given the position instance involved, relevant components of the costs of order processing are immediately available. Note: Several position instances should be permitted to contribute to the "work" required at a particular procedural step. (Procedural step carries the meaning proposed in § 11.3, not the meaning Hay presupposes for his patterns.)

Hay summarizes real events as an activity; he calls a prescription for similar activities a procedure. Chapter 11 shifts the meaning of procedure. The general prescription is a procedure type, with the actual instances of work contributions being procedures.

Actually, the general attitude of interest in *intended meanings* is more important than the actual use of language for properly understanding models and patterns. Such understanding is essential for translating from one frame of reference to another (when such translating is still necessary after fundamental understanding). In this book, the term position reflects an elaborate conceptual information model in its own right. Thus, important parts of this book can only be understood when the intended meaning of position is perceived.

Hay proceeds to differentiate order (sub)types for production, maintenance, and projects, among others. The metapattern's answer, as usual, is to define a corresponding set of contexts, each allowing differentiated behavior. How behavior actually departs from one context to the next remains without comment here. Such details do not provide additional insight into the metapattern and its opportunities. Also, such industrially oriented patterns are reserved for our review of Scheer's work. However, anyone who wants to gain a general understanding of conceptual information models and patterns for industrial organizations is well advised to start with Hay's book and then move on to Scheer's. The patterns presented here should stimulate a "bias" (see § 12.6) to create even more generic alternatives.

13.2 Contractual Positions

When he models around (formal) contracts, Hay articulates yet another modeling guideline: "[A]s modelers, it is important to step outside the immediate perspective of our clients, in order to identify what is truly going on." Though a modeler cannot always claim absolute truth, Hay is conveying sound advice: It usually pays to look for a wide horizon; if you do, many advantages follow. For example, a sales contract and a purchase contract are supported by one and the same pattern. The only requirement is that participants be explicitly stated.

In a further abstraction, an identical pattern can hold for all contracts. Hay does not mention that the application of such a pattern need not be limited to contracts to which the administrator of the information set is a party. If participants are explicit, third-party contracts may also be included. Hay does not mention this opportunity, probably because he models *from the point of view of* a particular organization. An indication is his sentence that he "continues this filling-in [of information models] by discussing the organization's relationships and transactions with the outside world." A flexible information set, however, often needs a modeling point of view that lies *above*, whether inside or outside a particular organization (or any other unit instance). A more robust model will always result. No structural changes are necessary when something that was inside at one particular moment is moved outside the next.

Again, substituting position for party results in a more general pattern. Still more general is a pattern including positional relationship, as defined in § 12.5. An additional advantage of this wider perspective is that the limit of having (only) two positions participating in a contract is removed. As usual, such abstraction leads to a more compact model, as shown in Figure 13-1.

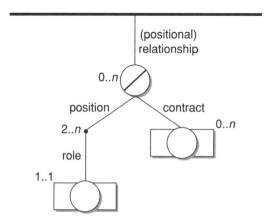

Figure 13-1 *Abstraction: questioning assumptions behind constraints*

The pointer information objects in the intext of a particular relationship refer to contracts in possibly varied contexts (with intexts structured with corresponding variety in their own right). Note that a (positional) relationship is a composition of positions (and their respective roles in the relationship). From the inverse angle, a single position, itself a node in a homogeneous classification hierarchy built from position elements, may also be considered a (boundary case of) relationship. Then, apart from any other position instances missing, even its own role in the "relationship" will not be specified. At any rate, the position concept is useful for relating contracts—for example, employment contracts between people and organizations.

13.3 Radical Simplicity Through Inherent Mechanisms

A significant difference between the models of Scheer and Hay is that Scheer ascribes only indirect influence to customers on product development. His intermediary concept is marketing. To Hay, a customer is a subtype of party, which is here a partial identity in the customer context (another partial context is almost certainly position). He believes that a customer may have a direct influence on product specifications.

In the structural sense, the "originating" organization is considered one of many potential participants in product specification. Conceptually, it does not matter whether this organization's influence is major or not. What might be important for a conceptual model is that "outside" contributions to product specifications are often subject to additional conditions; for example, to meet security concerns. When differences in tool use have conceptual implications, they need to be fully recognized. To arrive at an appropriate model, the essential question to be answered is whether different participants exist for the activity under consideration. Any differences will lead to corresponding contexts in order to provide the basis for diverse behaviors.

Building upon the more basic pattern around contracts, Hay continues "filling-in," this time in the direction of project management. For that purpose, he presupposes the involvement of other parties or positions. He also discusses the very real occasions when one or more participants to a contract change. Seen here against the background of the metapattern, his suggested solutions are particularly interesting: "[I]t is advisable under these circumstances to include a CONTRACT ROLE for 'former buyer,' 'former seller,' and so forth. A more disciplined way to accomplish the same thing would be to always draw up a new CONTRACT any time the PARTIES change, and to record the fact that the second contract is *derived from* the first."

The metapattern offers a solution of radical simplicity. The "old" contract participant is provided in his intext with an existence entry consisting of the relevant point in time and the value nonexistence. Referring to exactly the same point in time, the new participant is added to the intext of the contract instance. With Hay understandably concerned about accountability, it's hard to imagine a more immediate audit trail than that inherently secured by the metapattern.

Given the composition of Hay's work, it is not surprising that the patterns presented here as alternatives repeatedly include the concept of position. Because Hay rightfully views party as a fundamental, prominent concept, it makes a frequent appearance in most of his patterns.

Position is an even more complex, richer concept than party, as amply demonstrated throughout this book; thus, many patterns may be simplified through its application. As Scheer's reference models often build on different fundamental concepts, they do not lend themselves to "positional simplification" as much as Hay's.

There is really no paradox to this simplification process. What is always relevant is the total variety, which can never be neglected. The simplest model results when real complexity is addressed as early as possible. The inherent mechanisms for time-factoring, existence, and accountability do just that. Powerful basic patterns, as for position, help keep the final information models extremely compact yet powerfully flexible.

13.4 Content and Form

Hay devotes considerable space to bookkeeping and financial accounting patterns. From our vantage point in Part IV, these patterns seem to lack important abstraction; it looks as if Hay is entangled in traditional layouts for relevant reports. Elsewhere he indicates that a modeler should abstract from all-too-specific reports: "Indeed, a major challenge to systems analysts is to refuse the client's request simply to mimic a current report. The objective [must be] to see how to get underneath a body of data's current representation in order to understand its inherent structure."

From the perspective of the metapattern, an essential aspect must be stressed: There does not exist a single, absolutely valid structure for information. What can be realistically imagined is knowledge of structure, with structure always in a particular context. From this starting point, it is radically simpler to model the structure of information and to qualify reusable models as patterns. As Hay does not model beyond traditional concepts for financial accounting, ample room for improvements exists. However, such alternatives are not presented here as a reflection of Hay's work. Instead, Part IV presents a separate case, extending the author's earlier work on conceptual models for financial accounting.

At the end of *Data Model Patterns,* Hay again seems to critically investigate conceptual traditions. This is how a professional modeler contributes most—by finding models beyond tradition. With new concepts, more abstract models can be increasingly flexible, robust, and compact. The particular subject Hay treats near the end of his book is the last one we comment on here. Again, alternative patterns are presented.

Hay starts by attempting to clarify what a document *is*. He states that two meanings are common: documents "as representations of other data, and as things of significance in their own right."

His entity (type) of document refers to contents only. He no doubt means, in this case, document-as-representation. He introduces the concept of copy to signify a document-as-thing. Thus, a copy is the form in which the contents are published. Indeed, such a distinction needs to be made. But then it seems curious for Hay to classify the publication date as a property of document, rather than copy. It's even more remarkable when considering that he shows an awareness of electronic publishing, in which thinking in terms of a series of simultaneously produced copies is outdated.

The fact that Hay mixes two structure types in his discussion is a bit confusing. First, he views a document as elementary, and all sorts of documents may be combined into a hierarchical structure. A document can be a part of zero, one, or many other documents. In order to reflect such variety, Hay conceives of a separate structure element, equivalent to a relationship-as-entity in EAR. The essence is that a structure element is a means to supply an information model with necessary differentiation. As such, it shares many aspects with the concept of context. (On this equivalence, see several remarks made in § 10.2.)

Second, Hay assigns meaning to what he calls structure within a document. Initially, a contradiction seems to occur with his principle of a document pertaining to contents only, but he means the structure of those contents (that is, the mostly conceptual composition).

This conceptual structure is seen as a property of document type. Hay next considers his first structure type for document types. When necessary, document types may also be hierarchically related. For this purpose, he introduces corresponding structure elements into his pattern.

Again, the metapattern allows all such structure elements to be eliminated, as their intended purpose is better served with explicit contexts. Figure 13-2 reproduces Hay's general pattern in terms of the metapattern.

In his well-established manner, Hay elaborates from what he modeled as fundamental at an earlier stage. He hypothesizes that people and/or organizations may be involved in several ways with documents and/or their copies.

By limiting the concept of document to contents, it is easy to model a relationship between author and document. In Hay's view, an author is a person or an organization. This makes it a party in his more general frame of reference. Since a particular party-as-author may be involved with several documents, and as a particular document may originate from several authors, Hay needs a separate entity type in order to secure precision in his model. Such an extra type can be omitted with the metapattern, since a particular context provides all the required precision by definition.

Distribution is modeled by Hay in a similar way. On the basis of his definitions, distribution concerns copies rather than documents. Something called a distribution plan (Hay speaks of subscription) may pertain to a document type. Access permission may be specified for individual documents, and/or, more generally, for document types. Similar rules govern clearance permission. However, Hay does not make clear the difference between prescription and actual occur-

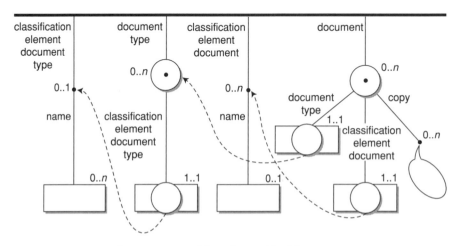

Figure 13-2 *Modeling the world of documents*

rences. Perhaps the *prescription* reads that every document of a particular type should be cleared by a particular job holder (position) before any copies are distributed. But what about the *execution* of the prescription for a specific document and its copies? Actually, this distinction between prescription for a role, execution by a role, and their subsequent abstraction simply leads to more general alternatives to Hay's patterns. The distinct, explicit roles disappear from the information models; roles are now parameters of a more general variable.

Given the relationships in Figure 13-2, the concept of information scope encompasses everything from document type to copy. For example, when permission must be obtained to distribute a particular copy, such clearance could first be considered as a property of that copy itself. When no such permission is specified, a first aggregation of scope is document. An even wider scope is provided by document type.

Even more abstract is the concept of role scope. Remaining with the case of permissions, (at least) two values of role scope exist: prescription and execution (and more as required). Substituting position for party results in a highly compact pattern for involvement.

Note that in this model, an instance of the intermediary information object itself is attached to an instance of information scope, which refers (through mutual nil identity) to an instance of either a copy, or a document, or a document type. The abstraction, illustrated in Figure 13-3, is of a radical nature. The concepts introduced are no doubt far removed from the (current) frame of reference of the real people involved. However, it always pays to at least try to

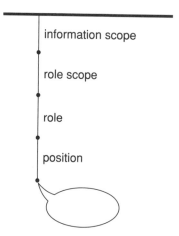

Figure 13-3 *Inventing concepts for flexibility*

push the limits of abstraction. Even when the ultimate information model is less abstract, we gain a more general understanding through such attempts.

13.5 Subject Classification

The emphasis on contents, which Hay attributes to his concept of document, makes document the logical choice to contain its subject classification. Note that subject classification is used here with its traditional yet powerful meaning from the theory and practice of libraries.

Another worthwhile idea of Hay's is that he does not confine himself to single terms. He makes sense by stating that it is especially the other entities in which users will be interested but "[t]hings get more complicated as we realize that DOCUMENTS may have as TOPICS *anything else* of interest on the data model." Retrieval of specific documents—and subsequently, by definition, access to particular copies of them—should be accommodated through those objects-as-subject. Again, the metapattern affords a simple, even trivial solution, since a document is just another context (see Figure 13-4). The subject entry may refer to parts of any overall object in the information set. A thesaurus may be integrated into the set but its terms will now be supplementary for subject classification, rather than its primary tool (as in separate library information systems). Of course, even if of a supplementary nature, a powerful thesaurus should build upon a characteristic pattern. Such a pattern is presented in § 14.6.

A more general model results when information scope (as defined in the previous paragraph), rather than document, is fitted with subject classification, as that wider concept also includes document.

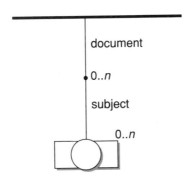

Figure 13-4 *Documents are about subjects, too*

The most radical subject classification of information in a particular set occurs when *any* information object can be attributed with (other) objects-as-subject.

The patterns Hay presents for indexing confirm that he does not treat time as a matter of principle. Whatever is registered apparently counts as permanently valid. The price for such inflexibility may be high. Subject classification, in particular, requires vigilance, as both terms, and the meaning(s) of terms, may and will change. This calls for "maintenance" of subjects and their attribution to (other) information objects. As repeated throughout this book, the metapattern supports such maintenance with its primary mechanisms for existence and validity values.

13.6 A Single Idea About Contents

We mentioned earlier (§ 13.4) that Hay creates some confusion with two structure types, one internally oriented and the other externally oriented. From such a double perspective, his subsequent problems in arriving at an unambiguous model of contents versions are perfectly understandable. In addition, a lack of basic attention to the dimension of time keeps a simple, compact model from being "invented."

An alternative is to remove document, as interpreted by Hay, from its central place in the information model; that is, remove the requirement for the primary existence of a document (until and unless copies of it appear). The pattern is made simpler by hypothesizing that the original document is a version (by definition, the first). Suppose a second version is created. One of its properties could be its source—in this case, the first version. In all fairness, it must be said that Hay points out a similar mechanism of chaining versions, though it is less fundamental. Note that a more abstract model structure is attained by definition of the appropriate boundary value. In this case, it is the choice of version to be a universal property that needs a version value set for the original.

Another improvement in the direction of compactness lies in eliminating the distinction between external and internal structure. As a consequence, the conceptual composition of a document is described on the basis of other documents and the like. Radically applying a single idea to the modeling of the internal structure means even an individual character sign could ultimately be treated as a document in its most detailed contents. In most situations, this is not a practical level of decomposition. However, important exceptions are easy to imagine. A notary public's information system, for example, should optimally reflect all modifications to an official act.

Hay also deals at length with differentiation of conceptual composition. A general structure is attributed to document type, with possible differences as properties of a particular document. A relevant comment from the metapattern's perspective is that what actually needs modeling is, as always, fundamentally a set of necessary and sufficient contexts. Another comment in favor of an alternative is that patterns in which a single structure type governs conceptual composition are more compact.

13.7 From Creation to Publication

The patterns developed by Hay around the concept of document are, at closer inspection, somewhat biased. His models seem oriented toward information systems for business settings; that is, for the for-profit sector. By claiming that his models are patterns, he correctly omits too-detailed characteristics of specific business sectors. However, an industry exists that is predominantly occupied with information as its core product type: publishing.

Developing patterns for a publishing house provides a perfect opportunity for insight into the variety of information's form and contents. Almost from the start, Hay's basic orientation is impossible to maintain. A publisher's product is information content, but it is evident that the information's form must also count as a product. As a consequence, the meaning of form must *not be derived* from contents. Rather, contents and form should be juxtaposed as equally valued aspects.

To gain a more neutral perspective, it is helpful to view the configuration of publishing activities as a process. At the early stages, emphasis should be placed on activities of creation—that is, contents. At later stages, however, the emphasis shifts to publication—the marketplace of readers. A reader buys a publication on the basis of what he or she perceives its contents to be. But from the publisher's point of view, the product at those stages is better characterized as an embodiment, with the contents as a necessary condition of the form. By the way, Hay puts forward most of the nuances required to arrive at an adequate model. He states that particular contents may be constituted by other contents, and indicates that the same set of contents may act as an element of a diversity of encompassing sets of contents. He also stipulates that what is distributed is not contents but, rather, form. Lacking is the notion that form may be structured. With Hay, a copy is directly derived from a document.

A publisher's perspective, however, highlights the idea that several copies may constitute an encompassing copy. Such an aggregate, called a set in the publishing world, does not need to have its origin in a document specifying the copies' structure. It pays for a publisher to abstract from copy-as-instance, leading to the concept of copy type and a homogeneous classification hierarchy made up of its instances. Hay's frame of reference and corresponding terminology do not easily support this pattern development; Figure 13-5 sketches a first alternative with different concepts. Cardinalities are not specified; again, they seem obvious.

Focusing on a publishing company, it soon becomes clear that what is called a contents element is still insufficient for requisite differentiation. A much greater variety, just looking at contents, exists. This is captured in Figure 13-6. Apart from its title, a contents element may have version, language, and art form as its characteristic properties. This amounts to the contents element being a composition with the four concepts mentioned earlier as its constituting elements. For increased flexibility, we advise modeling all four constituting concepts as homogeneous classification hierarchies in their own right. Art form is particularly difficult to conceive from the perspective of an average company and its information systems. But for a publishing house, the ability to distinguish between the art forms of text/prose, music/arrangement, or film/documentary is a primary requirement. Such differentiation is especially important when contents are based on other contents: a movie script derived from the text of a novel, for example. By the way, the contents element as a composition is still

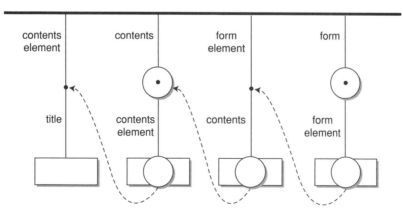

Figure 13-5 *A foundation for relating forms to contents*

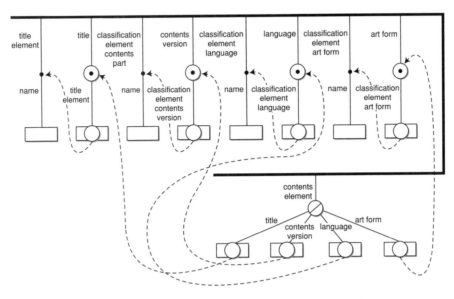

Figure 13-6 *Fundamental variety of contents for publishing business*

quite similar to Hay's pattern. Contents version, language, and art form taken together determine what he calls document type.

The contents element, which itself has now become quite a complex composition, is positioned to take part in several other encompassing contents, as Figure 13-5 suggests. In publishing processes, however, the transition from contents to form element requires differentiation comparable to the way in which the contents elements are constituted as a composition. The essential question is: Are the elements determining the variations of form? Contents are most relevant, followed by what can be termed imprint, design, and production group. Similar to contents element, form element is a composition constituted by four (other) elements. This makes the model, as illustrated for form element (Figure 13-7), structurally similar to the presentation in Figure 13-6 as the model of contents element. How contents elements are modeled is not repeated in Figure 13-7.

Finally, how form element and form are related remains identical, as Figure 13-5 shows.

Continuing from the perspective of a publishing company and its processes, insight is supported even more by imagining a line drawn between contents-oriented (information) objects and form-oriented (information) objects. On the

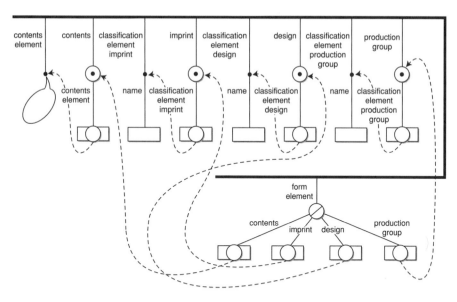

Figure 13-7 *Variety of publishing forms, linked to contents variety*

contents side, the emphasis is on creation, editorial changes, and the like. With form, relevant activities are concerned with production, marketing and sales, inventory management, etc.

The perspective can be subsequently broadened to allow for information requirements of (production) companies. Intriguing opportunities become visible when an article instance is considered as a particular instance of a publication. The flexibility, well known to publishers with respect to reprints, redesign, and so on, appears to a large extent closely comparable to varieties of article types. Through the introduction of an extra differentiation—between what is produced (products) and sold (articles)—the processes outlined for publishers are equally relevant. For example, the patterns for design element and product type may be extended, as shown in Figure 13-8, when a corresponding requirement exists along the lines of contents element and form element as detailed earlier.

Instances are missing from the patterns sketched so far. The basic idea is that instances are only relevant to form elements (products). For example, no instances are administered separately of complete encyclopedia sets (to mention a rapidly disappearing "product" in book form) but instances of the individual volumes. Of course, the number of complete sets can always be derived from available volume instances. With the focus on volumes, a publisher may

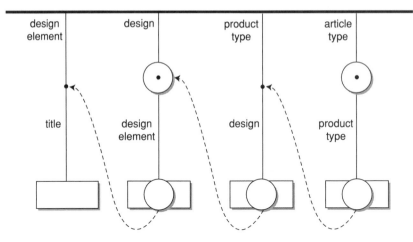

Figure 13-8 *Looking for parallels between publishing and production*

develop different forms (form types, actually) while delivering corresponding instances on the basis of actual demand. That is, as long as the inventory of required instances of form elements goes.

13.8 Dynamic Publications

The inspirational nature of patterns originally developed for information systems in publication processes should not come as a surprise. They show a powerful combination of both singularization and abstraction. Consequently, a broad variety of information requirements is supported. The same variety is a precondition to adequately modeling information required to manage rewards.

Authors are important to the success of a publishing company. The conditions negotiated between author and publisher can vary widely. Often, an author will receive a money amount (royalty) for every "article" instance sold. Usually, the amount is computed as a percentage of the article's net price. Different percentages may be agreed upon for combinations of language area, distribution channel, contents version, production group, design, and so forth. And to the extent that (other) consumer articles (article types) acquire cult status, their creators, too, will demand similar conditions from producers. For those reasons, it is sensible to gain insight into publishing processes and their traditional complexity.

An additional reason to use a publishing perspective is introduced through the phenomenon of dynamic publications. Suppose a page on the World Wide Web constitutes a publication. To retrieve it, the consuming surfer makes a certain payment. The whole of the Web page is then best considered an overall form consisting of one or more form elements. This makes it possible to characterize form element x as constituting part of the whole page up to time point t_1, but as from t_1 no longer. The elegant result is that whoever retrieves the Web page before t_1 also pays royalties, through the publisher, to the author of the content which formed the basis of form x. But for all hits after t_1 the author will not receive payment, at least not for his x in the context of that particular Web page.

The metapattern easily supports such dynamics. For example, how a Web page is constituted may be changed without altering the (partial) identity of the page as a whole. Of course, the inherent mechanism for time control makes such simplicity a reality (see Chapter 4, *Time*).

The flexibility will be severely injured when copyright agreements are only possible between a publisher and persons in the capacity of author. Had Hay modeled around financial reward for publications, such models would undoubtedly have shown his concept of party. Here the even richer concept of position appears. Hay would probably model copyright agreements as contracts. As a consequence, not only the author-as-position but also the publisher-as-position are explicitly present in the model. By placing a particular contract in the context of a particular (positional) relationship (see § 13.2), several authors and/or publishers may be combined, at a single stroke, to participate—nicely reflecting what happens in the real world.

Therefore, a pattern supporting a wide variety of multiple participation is not a luxury at all. For every individual contract participant (position) involved, particular rights and duties as agreed upon must be specified at the required level of detail. A publisher will attempt to acquire rights as broad as possible with the least number of conditions. In fact, conditions at the level of contents element give maximum flexibility. Then, for every form in which the contents element in question appears (is published), the general conditions hold. A more limited scope exists when separate conditions are agreed upon for a particular contents element in the context of particular (encompassing) contents. Such conditions hold for all forms in which those contents appear through the medium of a form element. However, this is a limitation in scope from the perspective of the publisher. Even more limited is a copyright agreement based on a particular form element.

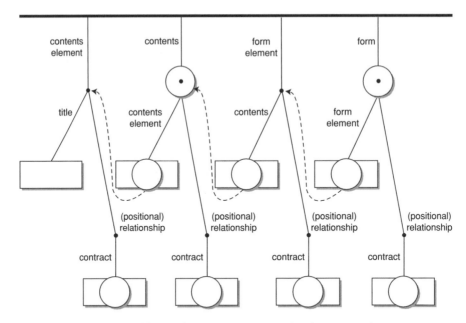

Figure 13-9 *Publishing business as an example of contractual variety*

Finally, some popular authors can negotiate separate conditions for different instances of form types. This is not as odd as it might seem at first. A concert in its capacity as an individual performance is a good example of a separate form instance. So is a particular tennis match. Star performers demand and receive payment as agreed for such stand alone events. All such contractual variety is included in the pattern of Figure 13-9.

The repetitive nature of the pattern illustrated here is evident. It is therefore advisable to compound the four information objects in a different, encompassing context. This is similar to what Figure 13-3 presents as the concept of information scope. Actually, all kinds of positions play different roles in publishing processes. Often, no explicit contract exists for their participation. In those cases, direct relationships with positions occur (relationship as given here means connecting information objects in general). Thus, contexts are created for positions in which their relevant activities, differentiating between planning and realization whenever necessary, are specified as intext. The general idea is much like what is fundamental to patterns for other production processes.

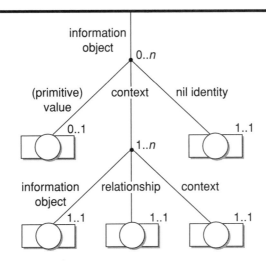

Figure 13-10 *A model of the metamodel*

13.9 Summary

Ending *Data Model Patterns*, Hay claims to present "the ultimate example of a metamodel." How strong is his claim? Starting from a different principle—context rather than Hay's "thing"—a different and even more compact "fundamental" metamodel results. Such a model of the metapattern itself, as explained in Part I of this book, is presented in Figure 13-10. As an exercise, every reader is invited to falsify this metapattern's model; that is, to find out what might *not* be right about it. The metapattern was originally designed as an improvement. Perhaps it, too, can be improved upon.

Chapter 14

Trails

In the series of pattern books we reviewed in Part III, *Analysis Patterns* (1997) is the third and last. Its subtitle, *Reusable Object Models,* succinctly describes the subject. In his foreword, M. Fowler states that "[i]t is valuable to base a computer system's design on [how people perceive the world] and, indeed, to change that perception." This is exactly how tools may change life. Different and new ways of organizing information, including processing in its widest sense, can inspire new organizations. And that is "where business process reengineering comes in."

It is thus surprising to read in R. Johnson's foreword to Fowler's book that "[p]atterns are supposed to describe reality, not invent a new one." It does not seem to fit *Analysis Patterns,* where Fowler tries hard, and with justification, to present patterns as ingredients for innovation in other organizational aspects and in their overall configuration.

14.1 From Related Pairs to Context

The Hay and Fowler books are similar in many ways. This is be expected, since both authors orient their patterns on business practices at the most general level. Fowler takes a cue from address information structured identically for persons and organizations. Like Hay, he arrives at the concept of party, with person and organization as subtypes.

Fowler continues with the assumption that organizations may be related in several ways; that is, a number of relationship types exist for organizations. Organization x, for example, is accountable to organization y for production, and to organization z for marketing. Two related pairs of organizations result, in this case (x, y) and (x, z).

A name often encountered for such related pairs is structure element. Those pairs usually appear to model hierarchical relationships. Starting from types, instances of structure elements are classified by them. The pattern that Fowler presents for structured organizations can simply be translated with the meta-pattern shown in Figure 14-1.

Again, the structure elements as defined and applied by Odell, Scheer, Hay, and Fowler always refer to the relationship between *two* entities, objects, or whatever. A more general outlook recognizes such a paired relationship (type) as one occurrence among many others. Remarks to this effect appear in §10.4, where they specifically relate to the bill of materials.

Like a list of ingredients, a traditional bill of materials is characterized by strictly layered modularity: a module essentially protecting the inside of one module instance from the other module instance of which it is a constituting element. This also blocks modeling of any boundary crossing effects. Suppose that a module x exists, with module a as one of its constituting elements. (A more exact account is to state that such a relationship between module types x and a controls whether an instance of type a is an element constituting an

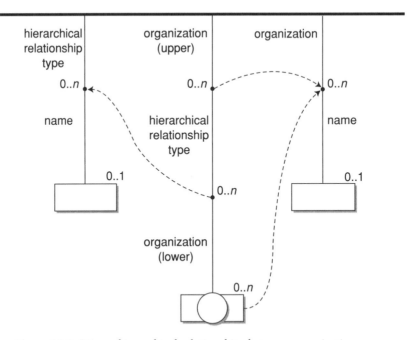

Figure 14-1 *Binary, hierarchical relationships between organizations*

instance of type x.) Suppose, too, that module x is an element of both module y and z. The point is that the behavior of a in y/x may be different from a's behavior in z/x.

Scheer tries to counter the difficulties remaining with strictly paired relationships. He elaborates types of structure elements for different purposes: requirements explosion, production, marketing and sales, and so on.

Diversity in behavior is extremely easy to model with the metapattern, which was developed to deal with such static and dynamic variety. For each behavioral type identified, a corresponding context is established.

Take test results, for example. Complete information would still be lacking when only the behavior of a as an element of x is administered. The differentiation between behaviors of a in y/x, and z/x, respectively, is easy to recognize as essential.

The sufficient specification of contexts is always governed by what is required to reflect relevant behavioral differentiation. Returning to Fowler's patterns for organizational structure, any alternative modeled around organization as a homogeneous hierarchical classification already offers plentiful variety. What is still missing, however, is Fowler's typing of hierarchical relationships. It turns out that a choice exists among options.

One option is to use the potential of the relationship between two information objects more fully. So far, those relationships have only been indicated by simple names, but each relationship is also an information object in its own right. Therefore, its values may originate from a homogeneous classification hierarchy, for example. At the highest level of such a hierarchy, the most general type of relationship would appear. Figure 14-2 presents this option. To accommodate this kind of specification of relationships between information objects, the symbolic language of the metapattern has been extended accordingly; the relationship of organization is a node in its own right, too.

A second option to register a hierarchical relationship type is to do so in the intext of one of the participating organizations. It seems logical to make it a property of the hierarchically lower organization.

A third option is to limit flexibility. Even with the metapattern, why not model traditional structure elements in their capacity of paired relationships? The hierarchical relationship type would then be one of its properties. Fowler and the other authors whose work is reviewed in this book do this. In § 9.2, the concept of structure element is changed, exhibiting an element from a set's so-called power set.

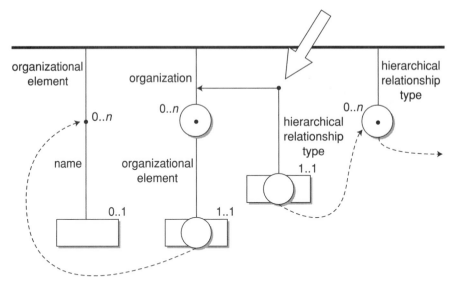

Figure 14-2 *Using a metapattern relationship as a collection of information objects*

14.2 Operational Knowledge

Fowler elaborates extensively on modeling the mandatory nature of the organizational level. Assume that a particular organization is a company type. In Fowler's example, as a lower organization it can only be related to a higher-level organization typed as a division.

Most often, such control details are not worth the effort. When authorization is properly managed, it guarantees that only responsible, expert users will register information about organizational structure. Practically seen, rules governing structure may remain outside the information set, recorded and applied by knowledgeable users while illustrating the inclusion of tool use in the conceptual information model (in this case by *not* including formal structural rules).

This practical solution for a specific problem should not distract from the fact that Fowler brings up a very interesting *type* of problem. His own abstraction is to distinguish in conceptual information models between a knowledge level and an operational level. "At the operational level, the model records the day-to-day events of the domain. At the knowledge level, the model records the general rules that govern this structure. Instances in the knowledge level govern the configuration of instances in the operational level." This is similar to the problems discussed by Odell with reference to product types and instances (see § 7.1). It always depends on the perspective of what must be counted as a type or as an instance (and when). A distinction cannot be assumed with absolute validity.

Several general remarks address this fundamental issue at the conclusion of § 10.6. The *operational* serial size provides an orientation for additional understanding. When we mean a size of individual instances, a single knowledge level may be useful. Serial sizes that amount to groups of instances require two knowledge levels. The first of these, though from a different perspective, is to a large extent also assigned operational meaning. Clear examples abound in information sets for industrial processes, since a product design refers to a product *type*. This also holds for the production prescription. Governed by the same type, the process should result in similar product or article instances.

To conclude, Fowler offers an interesting, necessary distinction. However, beyond a certain complexity, a further distinction than the one he proposes is required.

14.3 Almost Positions

Fowler elegantly broadens his modeling scope by imitating relationships between parties from hierarchical relationships between organizations. He places party relationships within the wider frame of (hierarchical) accountability. Person and organization being subtypes of party, a pattern results for all accountability relationships between persons and/or organizations. He extends the scope further by defining job (Fowler: post, Hay: position) as a subtype of party. His idea of a party is *either* a person, *or* an organization, *or* a job.

In this book position is defined as a Cartesian product; that is, the intersection of *and* a person, *and* an organization, *and* a job. Simply put, any composition does not require separate structure elements, for, by definition, the position *is* their composition.

In their capacity as compositions, positions are individual information objects, too. As such, they may participate in relationships. Theoretically, creating compositions from elements that are themselves already compositions may be continued indefinitely. In general, step-by-step elaboration equips information models. What ultimately matters is this: Operational information sets are equipped with greatly increased variety. This approach was explained earlier (see § 13.7).

By the way, adding the concept of job establishes a fourth alternative to modeling hierarchical relationship types for organizations. A job does not have to be limited to something-that-a-person-does. It is an equally convenient concept to indicate the role of an organization—perhaps a role pertaining to the particular organization itself. In any relevant context, something like a role might be included to specify how an organization fits in the relationship with another organization.

14.4 Authorization

Both Hay (reporting relationship) and Fowler (accountability) give ample attention to formal relationships between what both call parties. Starting from positions, many of those relationships are already implied. As with any powerful composition, it is simpler to enhance the variety of conceptual information models. With the concept of position, a strong foundation for authorization is also available.

Authorization is understood here as the collection of rights a particular user has to the use of an information set. If a majority of employees are subject to explicit authorization for use of information processing tools, it seems superfluous to create separate information objects about employees merely for authorization purposes. Logic dictates an integration with the information set(s) for personnel management. Strangely enough, such integration is rare. Modelers, too, are set in their habits; many fail to see the opportunities for integration provided by the almost complete coverage of information tools among people in organizations.

Against current tradition, as with several alternatives this book presents, it is logical to view positions as users, too. As we noted in § 12.3, by referring to an extended space for relationship management, users need no longer be limited to (internal) employees. Indeed, any position may be declared a user of the information sets under control. From a general, positional perspective there is really nothing fundamental separating internal from external users. They can all be awarded use rights, as appropriate. This broad foundation for authorization greatly assists process integration beyond the boundaries of individual (traditional) organizations.

Use rights for information may be specified along two dimensions. The first places emphasis on processing. What needs to be determined for the system-as-tool is the set of information transactions for which the user is authorized. The particular information involved is secondary. In a manner of speaking, it *automatically* comes with the transactions.

The second authorization dimension concerns values of information. The main question here is to what information does the user have access?

Of course, information systems that support and incorporate organizational processes always provide access to information through a choice of transactions. The two authorization dimensions are not exclusive but must be applied in harmony. The practical question is what weights must be attributed to them. The transactional nature of information processing is emphasized here. As a consequence, value-oriented authorization will be specified *in the context of* transaction-oriented authorization.

Transaction, by the way, is yet another example of sloppy terminology. What is actually meant is transaction *type*. As we just suggested, an authorization is meant to cover all instances of similar transactions on the information set.

It should also be possible to specify an authorization for a unique transaction instance. Such an ultimate level of detail has been mentioned previously, as for example with a unique article. To keep the model generic and compact, when authorization is oriented at transaction instances, a transaction type is also considered its own instance. This ultimate case of authorization is not pursued in the following discussion.

The simplest way to organize a wide variety of transaction types is, again, to create a homogeneous classification hierarchy, as shown in Figure 14-3. The general idea is explained in Chapter 5, *Compositions*.

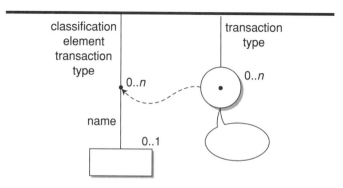

Figure 14-3 *Transaction as a node from a homogeneous tree*

The next modeling step is to relate positions to transaction types, either by placing such types in the intexts of authorized positions, or vice versa. Both alternatives are illustrated in Figure 14-4. Further development of the pattern elaborates the second alternative. The reason, by the way, is not that it is intrinsically better; whatever is favored must always be decided by the actual requirements addressed by the conceptual information.

Each transaction type concerns certain types of information objects. With the metapattern, such a transaction scope can be redefined as a subset of contexts as relevant to differentiating the behavior of information object instances. In short, the pattern under development here merely mentions information object types. In the context of a transaction type, information processing may be specified at an even more detailed level; that is, limited to particular information object instances of the type under consideration. There are many methods, partly dependent on type, to identify relevant instances. For example, an exhaustive list of instances may be given, or boundary values may be specified; then, all instances obeying the value range qualify. Any set of criteria may be used; such methods have in common that an instance's eligibility is determined dynamically. Those often detailed rules are not elaborated upon here, as they are beyond the scope of the main structure of the authorization patterns.

What has been determined in general about authorization for a transaction type only provides a basis. It is now possible to shift emphasis from transac-

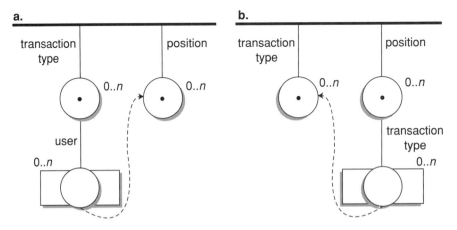

Figure 14-4 *Positions authorized for transaction types*

tion to information. Again, there should be room for specifications for separate users.

A distinction between default values and "real" authorization is convenient. A default value can make using an information system much easier. Users greatly appreciate such provisions.

The possibilities for specifying information types and values in the context of a particular position/user must conform to what has been determined for a transaction type in general. This rule is not represented in Figure 14-5, because such rules must account for different information object types. The patterns here are meant to convey overall insight into issues of authorization and how they might be modeled.

In § 4.7, the outline indicates that the metapattern offers fundamental provisions for audit trails and accountability. Any change to any information object includes a reference to the user involved, and to the transaction applied. By integrating authorization with the play of positions (see § 12.2), users appear in validity entries *as positions*.

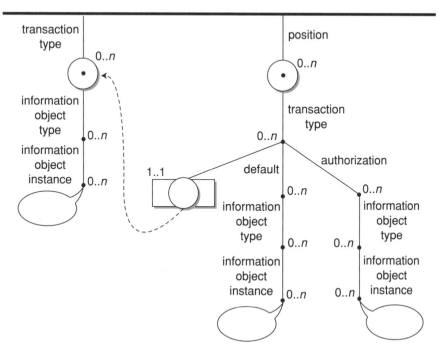

Figure 14-5 *Overview of transaction-oriented authorization and defaulting*

14.5 Phenomena in Observation Objects

Another correspondence between Hay and Fowler is that both give extensive treatment to observations and measurements. Whereas Hay takes his cue from test laboratories, Fowler's basic orientation is on developing patterns to support medical diagnosis, proceeding in the direction of more general patterns. For example, he consistently defines every quantity as a composition with (as named here) a measure and a value as its constituting elements. This allows every quantitative observation (or measurement) to be registered in its original measure and corresponding value, and whatever conversion may be relevant is always possible at a later stage. For this purpose, Fowler has integrated conversion ratios into his patterns. The disadvantage of his approach is that the number of ratios increases in exponential proportion to the number of measures, since a ratio is needed between each pair of (relevant) measures.

With a large number of measures (for example, with monetary currencies) it pays to introduce an additional measure to serve as a general unit or to define one of the existing measures as such. This reduces the burden of ratio maintenance to an arithmetic proportion. No longer are ratios required between each measure pair. Instead, for each measure, a ratio that specifies conversion to the unit measure is sufficient. As a consequence, conversion between two ratios will take two steps. The second step is based on an inverse ratio; this is implicitly defined by the original ratio. In this way, a quantity known in a particular measure can always be converted into a quantity in any other measure, provided that those measures are basically compatible.

From observations of quantities, Fowler moves on to observations of qualities. For the latter, no explicit measure is used. In fact, a more general notion than Fowler's is this: Defining the outcome of a qualitative observation is a classification process. From this broader perspective, one sees how to create even more elegant patterns. Fowler takes the concept of person as the observation object for medical diagnosis. For him, a person—that is, the corresponding information object—is not decomposable. Thus, covering his subject properly, Fowler introduces separate phenomena. In his view, a particular observation establishes a relationship between a person instance and a phenomenon instance.

However, the inverse approach eventually results in a more transparent model. A medical person can be represented as being different from a so-called natural, indivisible person. Only such a medical person provides the context for a choice of phenomena. This general set of phenomena should, first of all, be given its own structure; that is, how can subsets of phenomena be possibly related? When necessary, such a structure could even be differentiated for organism species. An example of such a species is the human being. An interesting coincidence—if it is a coincidence—is that traditional classification schemata already exist for organisms. A foundation for an alternative pattern, therefore, resembles Figure 14-6.

It is also possible, on the basis of this pattern, to exploit the hierarchical classification of (types of) organisms to allocate a broader horizon to phenomena. Suppose cow, chicken, and human are all defined as subtypes of a single, more general type. If so, their shared phenomena actually "belong" to such an encompassing type. The implied inheritance makes a purposeful grouping of organism types all the more manifest.

Fowler does not wrestle with this problem, but his pattern is less generic. The alternative is not presented as being inherently superior. What it should illuminate is that there always *is* an alternative. For example, the main ideas behind the current alternative could be developed further. Figure 14-7 only shows a pointer information object referring to a particular person; that is, to the information object that represents that individual. However, an even more general model is possible (if not, the generalization leading up to organism type would have been unnecessary). Note that in Figure 14-7 observation now provides a denominator for both qualitative and quantitative "measurements." This denominator has obtained a more general scope as compared to Fowler's patterns and allows for simple extension. Any rules for observation instances may

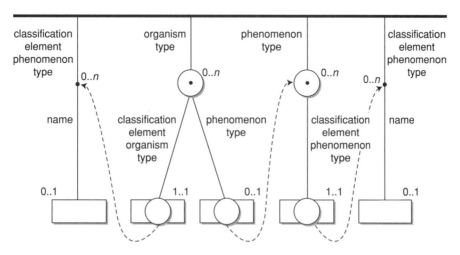

Figure 14-6 *A foundation for diagnosis, medical or not*

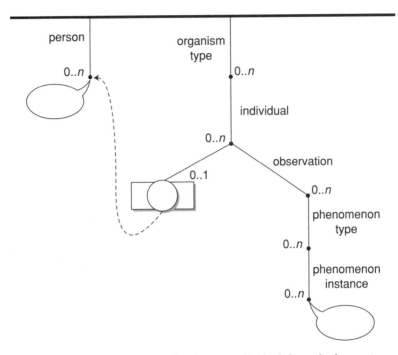

Figure 14-7 *Phenomena are related to an individual through observations*

be summarized for observation types. An applied protocol (that is, a particular protocol instance) should be considered part of the relevant observation instance.

The pattern illustrated in Figure 14-7 remedies a shortcoming of Hay's modeling approach to samples and other materials undergoing laboratory tests. Like Fowler, he views the observation object as something indivisible, notwithstanding the greater variety of such real-life objects appearing in his patterns. By replacing organism type by article type and individual by article (instance) in Figure 14-7, even richer patterns result.

14.6 Thesaurus

For practical purposes (and for the information sets supporting them), an important question is how detailed the typing of information should optimally be. Abstracting from the way in which Fowler applies the concept of quantity, any subject may be described as a composition.

There is nothing novel about this idea. In fact, such generalizations have long been used. A rich tradition of libraries with uniform classification systems exists, supporting a wide variety of subjects. With the volume of information sets growing exceedingly fast, subject classification becomes increasingly vital. The idea here is that controlled subject descriptions provide structure for information not yet otherwise structured.

A richly structured classification scheme is commonly called a thesaurus. The importance of a thesaurus goes far beyond information retrieval. What should be considered is general access to information—in other words, access to information in general. As requirements of this general nature will appear again and again, a subpattern of a thesaurus must be available (it also serves to model observations separately modeled by Fowler).

The thesaurus, as modeled here, has been inspired by the work of the Indian mathematician S. R. Ranganathan (1892–1972), who designed what is known as facet analysis. His main idea was that every subject should be parsed to yield a maximum of five facets, with each facet given a separate description. This parsing rule may, whenever required, be applied to any facet thus obtained. Thus, a higher-level facet could, in its turn, be described by facets, too. To arrive at a sufficiently complete description of the original subject, he applied as many repetitions of faceting as necessary.

Ranganathan prescribed facet types and the order in which chosen instances must be specified. His choice of fixed facet types and their citation order was personality, matter, energy, space, and time (PMEST). See Figure 14-8.

The point of subject classification is that, generally speaking, an observation object or instance is accessible through the particular subject instances attributed to it. This requires the object instance to be catalogued accordingly; it amounts to access to the object instance through one or more subject indices.

Since Ranganathan fixed the sequence of facets, that is, he determined a citation order, this keeps the (library) catalogue limited to a subset of all facet permutations. The catalogue is only open to those subject descriptions that satisfy the predetermined citation order. The reason that Ranganathan spent so much attention on a very limited subset, but one that would still adequately support access and retrieval, was because his mechanism of facet analysis was intended for manual use in often voluminous libraries.

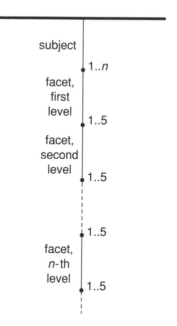

Figure 14-8 *Abstract model of Ranganathan's facet analysis*

Of course, the practical limitations he had to allow for are no longer relevant for applications of digital information and communication technology. For conceptual models, such considerations should be set aside. It is therefore *conceptually realistic* to broaden the orientation beyond Ranganathan's already general scheme. His principles, however, remain valid and clearly visible.

First of all, the precondition of the five particular facet types may be removed. Instead, variable facet types are introduced. As such, a facet type is nothing but a radical application of the concept of measure. This explains why the thesaurus pattern presented here follows the discussion of Fowler's patterns for observations and measurements.

This comparison supports the notion that a complete facet instance may include one or more values. A series of words may serve the purpose of acting as values. A minimal number of words in a series is zero. Besides words, a facet instance may contain a single constant as a value; of course, a constant value may be symbolized by one or more words. This helps create an even more compact conceptual information model. To keep the presentation as accessible as possible, (qualitative) words and (quantitative) constants are modeled separately here. As with Ranganathan, a series of one or more facet instances describes a particular part at a particular level of a particular subject.

In Figure 14-9, the word "series" appears below at the right as an aspect of cardinality. The facet instances—in the context of subject part—are given a particular sequence, too, which must be maintained.

Just adding "series" is sufficient for a conceptual specification. Implementation can be achieved through various mechanisms but are not relevant at this stage of modeling.

The pattern as shown can be made even more compact by using words for the classification elements of facet types. Then the intext of those classification elements does not consist of a name given by a primitive information object. Rather, a pointer information object is required, referring to a word node elsewhere. The same logical cohesion exists on the basis of a mutual nil identity. Without a separate pointer information object, however, practical navigation to establish the relationship of shared nil identity takes an extra step.

Fowler raises the question of whether the values to be attributed to observation instances should be predefined separately as a domain for each phenomenon type. By reframing the problem in terms of a thesaurus, several solutions appear feasible, since a facet type may be considered synonymous with a phenomenon type.

A compact mechanism to help translate Ranganathan's conceptual approach to an even more general foundation focuses on the recursive application of subject part. Every facet that describes a part of a subject part at the first level, may, in its turn, be expanded as a subject part. Structurally, this is comparable to a traditional bill of materials where the extrapolation of modularity is consistently limited to (just) the next level of specialization. Thus, a full overview of a particular

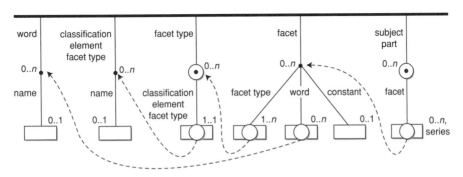

Figure 14-9 *Removing some of the constraints in subject classification*

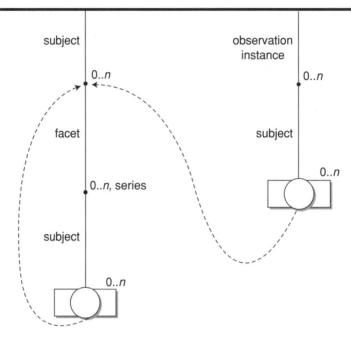

Figure 14-10 *Joining general concepts into a compact model*

subject part also requires an explosion. Subsequently, and still following the same comparison between subject classification and bill of materials, doubt could be raised as to whether it is sensible to continue speaking of subject *part*. Indeed, the whole and its parts again appear to constitute relative concepts, with their relationship at the very center of the modeler's attention. Thus, subject part may be replaced by subject. Whenever multiple subjects are required, this is adequately controlled through the observation object (observation instance). Various subjects may be attributed to a particular observation instance for the purpose of improved access and retrieval (see Figure 14-10). What this figure does not show in detail, however, is a provision to avoid circular regression in subject classification. But it must be ruled out for a subject-oriented description of a particular facet to rest on a subject already described by that same facet instance.

14.7 Indexing

The thesaurus pattern presented in the previous section has deliberately been given a wide scope. Due to its variable facet types, it also serves as a metalanguage supporting the principle of semantic modeling. However, the primary goal when applying a thesaurus is to improve access and retrieval of information (objects). To achieve this goal, indexes are eminently suitable. The current section does not introduce the concept of index as a technical mechanism into an otherwise conceptual discussion. It appears, perhaps surprisingly, that the highly recursive nature of the thesaurus pattern also requires a conceptual notion of index.

We have seen how any subject may be described on the basis of a thesaurus. A structure has been outlined in which the smallest scale elements constitute intermediary level descriptions, and so on.

In the inverse direction, a correspondingly meaningful indexing structure should cover a subject's breakdown. One index, then, gives access to (other) information objects when is the whole subject is considered. A second index, already with a greatly diminished horizon, could be built from separate facets, but include their own specialization with subjects at all lower levels. This would make information objects accessible by index through any facet-based subject classification. Yet another index—or, rather, index type—could encompass all the facet series pertaining to subjects' first-level descriptions. Or every facet by itself, without any further specialization, may be indexed to provide conceptually controlled access to information objects. As modeled in the previous section, a particular facet at a particular level is also constituted by (other) elements. It is possible, therefore, to extend the model to include indices on facet type, word series per facet type, separate words, and even constant values. Of course, as the depth of classification covered decreases for an index, more information objects answer to a query in which it is addressed as a type of criterion. Dependent on real information requirements plus the relevant information's characteristics, indices must be chosen as useful or even necessary in this overall spectrum.

14.8 Standardized Time Management and Control

The pattern designs in the last few paragraphs seem, when seen from a specific perspective, quite different from what Fowler presents. But it is precisely the word *pattern* that suggests applications in areas that often seem widely remote from a pattern's origins. Both Hay and Fowler emphasize that patterns they designed for one purpose may be useful elsewhere. There is much wisdom in their words, and it is for such reasons that this book offers many seemingly unrelated patterns. We hope that further study will show that they correspond meaningfully in many, often unexpected, ways.

In general, Fowler in his patterns shows more appreciation than Hay of how information depends on time. But where time is allowed for, it is always with incidental provisions. A universally valid mechanism, as the metapattern provides, is nowhere suggested.

Fowler, for example, rightly states that a particular observation needs to contain a double temporal indication. There is first the point in time, or the time period, at which the observed phenomenon is considered valid. Second, the point in time when information about the observation was registered should also be known (and included in the registration). He notes that an observation instance may be cancelled at a later point in time. Because Fowler does not specify whether a cancellation is also fitted with time indications in its own right, it is impossible to judge how complete his pattern is. With the metapattern, management and control of temporal information is highly standardized. At the basis of this mechanism are existence and validity entries (see Chapter 4, *Time*, for a fundamental explanation).

Fowler's patterns are mainly taken as cues to follow alternative trails, rather than being directly reviewed. Thus, we have covered only three chapters from his book *Analysis Patterns*. Many patterns developed here do not build extensively on the metapattern capabilities to support multiple contexts within information sets. Still, they are of interest because they confirm that the metapattern supports a more generally applicable approach to information modeling. What greatly helps is that universal details to represent existence and validity of information are standardized at the smallest relevant level. This is a liberating force, as the modeler is now free to direct his or her attention to other aspects. And it is always on that variety of the real world that the modeler should concentrate. What is "really" different (and relevant) must be reflected in the conceptual information model. Many examples are presented in this book to support the view that a playful modeling approach—at once unrespectful of traditional conceptual boundaries and productively building on tradition—will often lead to interesting, widely applicable modeling results.

Chapter 15

Nails

"To a person holding a hammer, everything looks like a nail." Sayings like this point out that bias is inescapable. Behind every idea is *a* paradigm.

Professional designers of conceptual information models can never completely escape their own preconceptions, either. In fact, it is just *because* designers possess knowledge and experience that their services are appreciated and contracted. But modelers should always be aware of their own bias, understanding their own personal orientation as completely as possible. Only then will they be able to alter that orientation as different modeling problems require.

Fowler, a recognized professional modeler, openly states that his observation and measurement patterns originated for purposes of medical diagnostics. This account of origins makes it easier to understand his subsequent explanation of how those patterns might be used for corporate finance. Knowing their origin makes it simpler to develop alternatives. It should come as no surprise that alternatives in this book reflect one of the author's own important preconceptions—generally applicable access to, and retrieval of, information as inspired by a rich tradition of theory and practice in libraries.

15.1 Pattern Transfer

Fowler begins by broadening the observation object from person/patient to object of care, so that, for example, population and enterprise segment qualify as its subtypes. He goes into some detail as far as modeling types of enterprise segments is concerned. This corresponds to the recommendation made earlier to factor an observation object into a system of relevant phenomena. An observation instance is then considered a particular phenomenon-in-context. But it appears that an enterprise segment, as defined and elaborated by Fowler, is not based on the object differentiation mentioned here. In terms of the metapattern, a few remarks will explain how he constitutes a segment.

Several dimensions are given, each modeled as a homogeneous classification hierarchy. A particular enterprise segment is the composition of values for all relevant dimensions. However, a complex mechanism is required to achieve what has been normal practice under the label of data mining.

The usual approach to filling a data warehouse is to gather information about operational transactions. Those transactions, rather than enterprise segments, must be described using dimensions defined by Fowler. In general, he chooses to call enterprise segments transactions rather than observation objects. By focusing on enterprise segments, Fowler reifies a concept. The model supports a wider variety when dimensions are kept as abstract as possible. From a source of adequately described transactions, reports of any enterprise segment may be dynamically produced as long as the required intersection has been made available through registered properties of transactions.

But why should dimensions be limited to descriptions of enterprise segments? Actually, they can accommodate any subject, which brings the approach back to the discussion of a thesaurus. Any thesaurus capable of supporting homogeneous classification hierarchies provides the necessary and sufficient mechanisms for selection and retrieval. The analyses Fowler seeks to support by his enterprise patterns essentially reflect the more general requirements of selective access to relevant information. As relevance changes, the reach of the mechanism of selectivity should also be variable. Indeed, this is where a hierarchical classification scheme proves especially useful.

Through his attempt to transfer a pattern from one application area to another, Fowler has made an important and interesting contribution. He should not be criticized because his pattern will perform less than optimally in the new environment (it will more than likely not be a perfect fit). But there is the question of overall elegance and efficiency. Fowler's goal can be reached more simply with different, more general patterns.

15.2 Basic Operations of the Metapattern

From the perspective of the metapattern, Fowler's remarks on identification and existence of (information) objects are also interesting. His observations may be reduced to the metapattern's basic operations as elaborated in Part I.

Fowler states that an explicit identification scheme is a guarantee of unique information objects. That is correct, but he limits his view and, therefore, his patterns to external identifications—distinctions made by users of the information set. The metapattern makes some important discriminations beyond this traditional idea of identification.

The uniqueness of the (external or conceptual) identification may be restrained to periods during which such identifying information is valid. In this view, it is possible that two different information objects might share their external/conceptual identification, but never simultaneously. For this reason, the metapattern does not penalize erroneous registration of (externally/conceptually) identifying information in the sense that it may not be corrected. It always can, provided a user is authorized to do so.

Suppose that a user has selected a wrong element from an externally determined list in order to identify an information object. The effect (not the information itself) can be undone through a validity entry, after which the correct registration may follow. Of course, the error (or fraud) must first be detected.

Sometimes, as Fowler suggests, what originally appeared as separate (information) objects should be a single object. The metapattern allows the intext of one object-in-context to be transferred to another object-in-context. The basic mechanisms involved are, on the one side, validity entries supplying the value nonexistence from the relevant point in time; and, on the other, establishing new relationships. The superfluous information object continues to exist in the information set. However, its intext now contains the relevant existence entry. Besides providing an audit trail, this makes it easy to undo the joining of objects when and if, at a later stage, they are separate information objects, after all.

Fowler also signals requirements to copy and replace information. Because of the metapattern's active management and control of time, Fowler's actions of replace and supersede are identical, amounting to adding information.

Fowler writes about appearances of a particular information object: "but sitting behind it is another object—the object essence." Apart from its focus on life requirements, rather than the tool focus that Fowler seems to keep for his ideas on (information) object existence, the metapattern offers still far more variability. It is explicit variety at the conceptual level that the metapattern seeks to model. Some confusion may arise as Fowler applies conceptual notions, but he does so implicitly from the perspective of digital objects inside the tool. According to the metapattern, an overall (real) object appears in many contexts, with just as many partial identities. For its essential identity, the nil

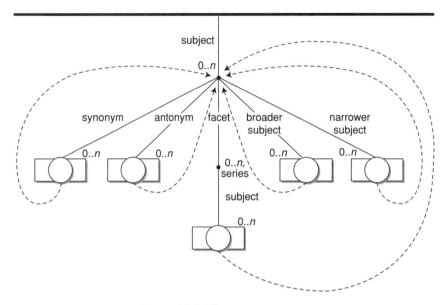

Figure 15-1 *Thesaurus structure*

identity is defined, its only purpose being to guarantee cohesion among all partial identities (to Fowler: appearances) of the overall object.

Finally, Fowler remarks about object identity that information objects may to a large extent be equivalent. As a matter of principle, the metapattern suggests just as many contexts as there are behavioral differences. When considering subjects, (all kinds of) relatedness between concepts may be expressed *within* the thesaurus. Through such relationships, therefore, a thesaurus offers additional opportunities for selection and retrieval, opportunities surpassing the limited set of subject allocations to particular information objects. A thesaurus may lead from one subject to others as they relate to the original subjects as, for example, synonyms, antonyms, broader subjects, and narrower subjects. Figure 15-1 provides a structural overview of such a thesaurus.

15.3 General Ledger for Accountability

Fowler also occupies himself with patterns for financial accounting. However, he does not draw any connections between his chapter "Observations for Corporate Finance" (see § 15.1) and the chapters "Inventory and Accounting" and

"Using the Accounting Models." An explanation for the lack of conceptual integration might be that he, like Hay (see § 13.4), follows the tradition of financial accounting in its capacity as an *independent* control mechanism. According to this tradition, a financial information system should reflect *all* changes. Of course, money is what determines the guiding perspective. The changes in monetary values are registered using unambiguous categories; that is, financial transactions are consolidated in the general ledger accounts (accounts, for short).

An obvious problem is that ambiguity is always present in information requirements of complex organizational processes. But Fowler does not yet conclude that his paradigm for financial accounting is causing the problem. He continues to see (general ledger) accounts as a focal point. Additional measurements are needed to arrive at the requisite variety of the information set.

Since Part IV of this book presents alternative patterns for financial accounting, what follows here is a limited commentary on Fowler's patterns.

Elsewhere, Fowler stresses the wide applicability of his patterns for observations and measurements. In § 15.1 we have already stated that financial analysis may benefit from a more general modeling approach. But such benefits are even larger, and more easily achieved, when transaction rather than enterprise segment is taken as the primary observation object. If the concept of transaction is to properly serve this purpose, any transaction instance must be registered, including all relevant references to subjects (called dimensions by Fowler).

Reports are then generated through selection and retrieval on the basis of subject-directed criteria. As an intermediary step, information may be processed from a temporary set derived from the total information set. A conceptual model need not bother with actual reporting steps: They are issues for construction.

Remarkably, Fowler does base journalizing groups on transactions (and he is right to do so). He does not make it clear, however, that any journalizing entry may contain (references to) instances of observation objects. Because he fails to make this connection, his patterns remain oriented toward accounting practices that were meaningful and even optimal for manual execution. This bias shows where he models separate summary accounts, even hierarchically organized. Such accounts are useful for strictly manual production of reports because they already contain large parts of the answers to probable questions. But summary accounts also significantly contribute to complexity, and there always will be questions to which those accounts do not provide direct answers. Therefore, as long as reports are compiled with sufficient speed, they should all be based on the single set of information about basic transactions.

Combining subjects as nodes in a homogeneous classification hierarchy greatly enhances the possibilities, and a pattern with no summary accounts is simpler and more compact.

A (still) extreme view of monetary values is that they, too, may be represented as a subject to be included in a journalizing entry. This "quantity" is modeled separately in Figure 15-2, where the whole of the value is thought to consist of instances of currency, direction, and amount. The concept of direction is an abstraction that fits double entry accounting. The two values of direction are plus (+) and minus (–), respectively (or debit and credit).

Note that a logical condition for a complete journalizing group is that all entries share the same currency. This condition is not shown explicitly in Figure 15-2. Also, with double entry accounting, the balance of a complete group should always be zero. Separate monetary changes, as described by individual entries, cancel each other out. This overall balance is created because some items reflect a source of monetary value and others reflect their destination. Thus, the direction of a monetary flow, as defined by a transaction, is from a source to a destination.

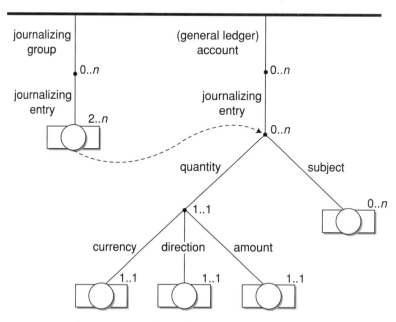

Figure 15-2 *Traditional pattern for general ledger*

In Figure 15-2, the details of journalizing entries are modeled as properties of general ledger accounts. As its intext, a journalizing group contains only references to journalizing entries. This is sufficient to establish an audit trail. The points in time of the transaction itself and of its registration need not be modeled explicitly when applying the metapattern.

A journalizing group is not identical to a transaction. It may be useful to express this difference as part of a pattern. This extension is illustrated in Figure 15-3. The intext of a transaction (instance) may contain other information than that traditionally defined as necessary and sufficient for financial accounting.

A classification, or chart of accounts, soon shows its limitations when a multi-perspective information set is required. Fowler's proposal for memo accounts serves to underline this conclusion. One of his examples concerns making reservations for tax liabilities. To him, such a reservation does not pertain to *real* money. In Part IV, the idea of what types of money may be considered real is stretched significantly by introducing different appearances (which, in their turn, correspond to stages, or phases, during organizational processes). A budget and contract, for example, are both real, but their mode of reality differs from money as it *appears* as the actual means of payment.

To support special perspectives, Fowler models derived accounts. But those are completely superfluous when transactions have been classified through relevant subjects (which may or may not have been included in journal entries). Fowler's patterns are also unnecessarily complicated as a result of his modeling posting rules. Countless derived postings are no longer beneficial because modern information and communication technology guarantee that *timely* reports are supplied when based on original entries.

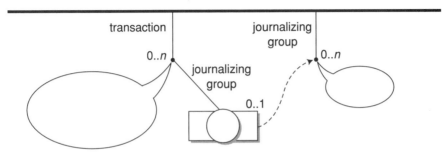

Figure 15-3 *Usually, more than financial information is needed about transactions*

Actually, Fowler is not far removed from a more fundamental approach. He writes that "all entries are predictable from the initial entries and the posting rules." The same result, based on a considerably simpler and more compact pattern, is achieved with the original entries rather than relying on summary accounts and/or derived entries. However, original entries are always needed. They serve information requirements best when directly related to transaction type (instead of account type, as Fowler suggests). This is shown in Figure 15-4. When relevant, events within the financial information system may be interpreted as transactions, thereby maintaining the possibilities of posting rules for (internal) derived journalizing groups and their entries.

Fowler has maneuvered himself into a dilemma by aiming, starting from necessarily unambiguous (general ledger) accounts, at a multiperspective pattern for organizational management and its corresponding information requirements. He seems aware of this: "A common problem in dealing with accounts is when there is more than one place to book an entry." However, his remark shows that he maintains the account as the central concept in his patterns, keeping elegant and more powerful solutions out of reach. Through applying various balancing entries, it is possible to maintain a journalizing group's monetary equilibrium while the same amount (or rather, quantity) is posted at several accounts. Those "multiple accounts" represent the different points of view supporting corresponding reports.

However, an equal or even larger variety in reporting may be obtained by including multiple subject references in journalizing entries to a single account. It is correct that from Fowler's perspective "[t]here is a certain amount of arbitrariness in choosing which accounts hold the main stream of money." As the patterns in Part IV illustrate, a primary organizing criterion is still required for

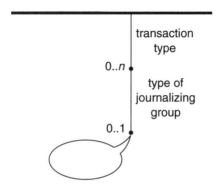

Figure 15-4 *Journalizing entries are transaction (type) specific*

the chart of accounts. The most general case builds around the concept of responsibility (or accountability) as just that criterion. Like Fowler says, "[a]ccounts work best within relatively static structures." To support more dynamic information requirements, the more flexible subject classification is far more suited (and so are the patterns on observation Fowler presents).

Limiting the orientation or choice of accounts strictly to the provision of information on formal accountability presents opportunities for improved information to support other perspectives. A general ledger account should only be created when it can be shown to serve a real accountability requirement. "[W]henever we are trying to represent an aspect of an entry, we have a choice between an attribute of an entry or a new account level. The decision is based on what part of the account behavior you need." Generally speaking, Fowler is right. What is lacking, however, is a specific, practical criterion on which to base the choice of accounts. Therefore, it is understandable that the patterns in a later chapter of his book, dedicated to a particular application, suffer the risk of being used arbitrarily. His example pertains to an organization that provides services, dealing with processes without clear relationships to "the mainstream of money." What he sketches seems more appropriate to label as a process-oriented information set. No explicit accounts are required as long as relevant information is properly channeled into the general ledger, establishing accountability at the necessary and sufficient level of aggregation.

The general idea behind conceptual modeling is to eliminate as many technologically oriented concepts as possible; and for those that remain, there must be awareness of their technological origin. Many accounting concepts originated during its long history of manual practice. It thus pays to question every concept now that digital information technology is available. Does such technology only exist to make manual application more efficient? A concept such as summary account should elicit strong doubts about its contribution to a fundamentally effective accounting system. In fact, a manual system could be just as effective without summary accounts, only far less efficient. The modeler should take this as a hint to eliminate the concept. Using the same rationale, memo account and derived account may also disappear. But what about the original information requirement? Indeed, it did not disappear, and probably never will. The conceptual information model should contain concepts necessary and sufficient for effectiveness (life focus). Efficiency is really not an issue at that stage of development. But an ill-performing, inefficient tool does not solve the life problem of relevant information requirements. Beginning with construction models, the issue of efficiency must be fully addressed. But that is not the metapattern's focus: effectiveness is.

Fowler continues to present other patterns beyond those discussed here. However, they are either too general or too specific to warrant their review in the light of the metapattern.

How Fowler deals with planning is interesting as a conceptual framework. When applying the metapattern, the guiding idea is that both proposed and implemented activities always require a particular context to develop the relevant intext.

The largest part of *Analysis Patterns*—the part that treats conceptual patterns—concludes with three chapters about trade in financial products. Their analysis here would not be useful, since they explain no additional metapattern characteristics. Those subjects are also too specialized for this book, which seeks to provide relevant patterns for a wider audience.

15.4 Conclusion on Analysis and Design

In Part III, we introduced and reviewed important books by Scheer, Hay, and Fowler. A major objective was to show that their reference models and information patterns may also be expressed using the language of the metapattern. It was not necessary to treat their work exhaustively, but rather selectively.

Often inspired by their models/patterns, Part III presents many alternatives and even some entirely new patterns. As this section developed, one could see a growing distance from the work under review. The increasing lack of correspondence was also due to the fact that Scheer and, to a lesser extent, Fowler, treat many subjects other than conceptual information models and resulting patterns. The focus of this book, on the other hand, is kept on conceptual modeling as much as possible.

Has the metapattern succeeded as a tool for analyzing a wide variety of information patterns? Has the third hypothesis, as formulated at the beginning in the Preface (see *The Book and Its Parts*), been made sufficiently credible?

The presupposition is that together the three books reviewed in Part III contain a sample of patterns representative of overall variety. As the language of the metapattern has nowhere shown any lack of expressive means to formally present patterns taken from those books, the metapattern may indeed be considered an appropriate tool for analysis of all kinds of information patterns.

However, Part III goes well beyond supplying credibility to this claim. At varying levels of detail, it also contains many patterns covering entirely new ground when compared to the contents of the books reviewed. But whatever the merits of these new, original patterns, they are not all directly derived from the application of the metapattern. Rather, the metapattern greatly assists us in arriving at and maintaining a high level of conceptualization in modeling. As such, the metapattern, too, is nothing more or less than a powerful tool that will only yield equally powerful results when professionally applied. What makes life much easier for the modeler is the metapattern's standardized conceptualization of existence, time, and validity aspects. Their treatment is fundamental, which means that they are adequately covered in any model. Fowler, for example, still states that "historic mapping [...] is not supported in any method that I am aware of." In fact, the metapattern does support "this [...] vital pattern for many information systems." And through differentiation of contexts, the metapattern helps solve often complex problems of information modeling. When specifying details, we can now limit attention to a single context "at a time" (provided we frequently ascertain that all contexts are and remain disjunct). Applying the metapattern shifts the fundamental choices in modeling from objects to contexts. The primary status of the concept of context makes this paradigm shift perfectly logical.

Part IV

A Case of Financial Accounting

Chapter 16

Family

Previous comments (see § 15.3) may have given the reader the impression that this author has strong modeling ideas about financial information sets. Several ideas have been extensively documented, as in my book *Aspecten en Fasen,* published in 1991 (in Dutch; the English translation title is *Aspects and Phases*).

That book treats many subjects other than conceptual information modeling and models. Its subtitle tries to capture the scope: *Notes on relational accounting, organizational information, change, etc., vice versa.* Still, conceptual modeling and models are at its core. At the time it was written, the term pattern had not yet been coined to indicate reusable conceptual information models, which is exactly what *Aspecten en Fasen* provides—reusable models or patterns. That book also originated before any explicit description of what is presented here as the metapattern. What is new in this book? Some of the earlier book's patterns are repeated, in this and the next chapter, in metapattern notation. In addition, as a recent development, the metapattern has improved them, resulting in some new patterns with increased conceptual coverage. A major contribution has been the increasingly deliberate application of some compositions (the concept of composition is defined in Chapter 5). This chapter contains an overview of the "classic" patterns and Chapter 17 outlines the major improvements.

The patterns were originally designed to overcome basic problems with the traditional method of fund accounting applied by Dutch ministries and other institutions of central government. This accounting method is called, in Dutch, Kameraalstijl. Its name is derived from the word chamber. The original meaning of room was transferred to indicate the institution governing from it, such as Chamber of Commerce. As far as the author knows, no equivalent exists in the United States, where fund accounting is also based on double entry accounting. The author's solution rested on a synthesis of Kameraalstijl and double entry accounting, making the resulting method of relational accounting suitable for both government institutions (public sector) and commercial organizations (private sector).

16.1 Prototype for Interpretation Management

Before presenting specific patterns, it is useful to emphasize an important characteristic of financial information systems in general, and of general ledgers in particular: its explicit orientation to time (even time with a double meaning).

Suppose that a transaction is registered as a journalizing group. Such a group contains both the transaction date (more specifically, a point in time) and the registration time. Because strict requirements for auditability exist, a fundamental rule holds that, once consolidated, a particular journalizing group and all of its entries must remain unchanged. If a correction is necessary, the effects of original entries are reversed by new entries and then the correct information is registered. Should this new information also prove incorrect, this process of correction is repeated.

The combination of time points for (1) the transaction proper and (2) its registration secures a complete audit trail. It suffices, for example, to reconstruct that during a certain period—that is, between successive points in time—incorrect information has been held in the information set (as formal journalizing groups) *thought to be valid*. The inverse journalizing entries have neutralized the original entries, those discovered to be nonvalid. Such neutralization is an implicit mechanism to declare (other) information nonvalid.

The combined mechanisms of the following four items have long held the status of immutable tradition in financial accounting: (1) double entry accounting, (2) double temporal orientation (both transaction time and registration time), (3) permanence of consolidated journalizing groups and their entries, and (4) correction through neutralizing entries. As a result, it has become difficult to unearth the actual objective those mechanisms supposedly serve. That objective is to guarantee an unbroken audit trail as far as interpretation of registered information related to time is concerned; that is, whether information is or was valid or nonvalid.

When this basic objective has been clearly restated, the next question is whether the mechanisms mentioned previously are required to achieve it. Does an alternative exist? Do such concepts have their origin in efficiency, that is, in the limitations of the application of a particular technology? Or are they really (more) conceptual; that is, required for a tool's effectiveness?

Rhetorical or not, the answer to such questions is that, indeed, the metapattern supplies an elegant, compact alternative. The double temporal orientation is standardized, as a matter of principle, with the metapattern. Every information object has, according to the metapattern, other information objects connected to it that reflect changes in *both* its existence *and* registration. A property of every existence entry is the time at which the existence value starts to be valid. As Chapter 4, *Time*, describes, there is a choice between two existence values: existence, and nonexistence.

In addition to one or more existence entries, every "regular" information object has one or more validity entries. Each of these also contains, among other information, the time at which a validity value (valid or nonvalid) starts to be "valid," and the corresponding time of registration.

As far as financial accounting is concerned, the mechanism of double entry accounting plus such standard mechanisms of the metapattern provide an alternative guarantee for completeness of an audit trail. With this as a reference point for further modeling, the meaning of a consolidated journalizing group can change. Even any part of a journalizing group and/or entry may be changed independently. What remains to be controlled is the appropriate authorization of the user. Double entry accounting requires that the whole of every journalizing group must retain its monetary balance. But inverse journalizing groups are no longer required; any correction may be limited to the original mistake (with, if necessary, any information exceeding the journalizing group's monetary balance registered by one or more additional journalizing groups). Such simplicity appears logical to anyone not acquainted with the tradition in financial accounting. Inverse journalizing was once convenient. It becomes an obsolete mechanism when the manual tradition of accounting is critically investigated, since properties of existence and validity may now be practically handled at a more fundamental level, as with the metapattern. In fact, conceptually, modeling should always concentrate on what the prospective tool implies for the user, rather than on the tool's internal workings.

However, traditions or paradigms are difficult to change. One reason for inertia is that awareness about the relationship between the objective (in this case a comprehensive audit trail) and mechanisms (from double entry accounting to inverse journalizing) has disappeared. With the objective out of controlled reach, the need to cling to familiar mechanisms is often established more firmly. In general, such power of tradition is also an obstacle for consistent application of the metapattern.

In order to make the exchange of ideas as rational as possible, we have started with explicit modeling of the double temporal orientation. After all, that is how patterns for financial accounting in *Aspecten en Fasen* originated, without consideration of the metapattern. Those patterns, therefore, are to a large extent well within a powerful tradition of interpretation management, of which the general ledger, supported by an elaborated combination of control mechanisms, is an important prototype.

16.2 System of Systems

The patterns for financial accounting, as sketched by the books reviewed in Part III, start from a detailed assumption. They invariably run into problems because that assumption lies *within* the modeled information system. The inability to externalize assumptions is typical of specialist approaches.

The problems are caused by using account as the fundamental concept. Even when that concept is too narrow for requisite variety, it is still maintained. But an account is not an end; it is also a means for financial reporting. Such was no doubt its original purpose many centuries ago. Considering it as a means makes it easier to reconsider as a concept. Is it really fundamental to financial accounting? Might a different meaning not be more effective?

Here in Part IV, accounts are not the primary basis for relevant patterns. What is considered first is a complete financial accounting system, which helps bring the accounting organizational entity into focus. It then becomes evident that several such entities may be relevant, and that those organizations are also related in some way. In fact, an often important constituting reason for their close relationships is that organizations exchange information obtained from their respective financial accounting systems. The independent organization and its independent financial system is, according to this view, not an exception but the simplest case of cohesion. So, as a rule, several related organizations exist. The simplest case is represented by a single organization; consequently, cohesion is reflected by a (boundary) value stating its "absence." By using abstraction and corresponding boundary values intelligently, the modeler can always arrive at more compact, flexible models.

In the original patterns in *Aspecten en Fasen,* no explicit distinction is modeled between organization and (its) financial accounting system. The basic assumption referred to the information system annex organization. The added assumption of related systems requires that, for each information system, all other information systems with which information may be exchanged are known. Figure 16-1 provides the model of networked accounting systems.

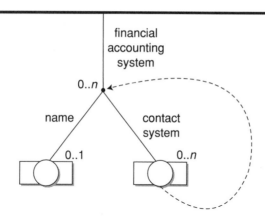

Figure 16-1 *A network of accounting systems*

Implicitly, such a model assumes equivalence between the system of organizations on the one hand, and the system of financial accounting systems on the other. This has proven too simple. But then, such *were* the assumptions of the original alternative.

At this stage of pattern development, it is still possible to connect to the accounting tradition. The obvious step, then, is to add (general ledger) accounts for every financial accounting system. However, that would bypass a vital opportunity for improved compactness and flexibility.

In order to recognize and appreciate the alternative, it is necessary to keep the model focused strictly on the administrative organization. A general question about an organization is: What does it do? An equally general answer is: It is involved in organizational processes. It appears that *process* is a very powerful concept for patterns in financial accounting.

16.3 Dimensions and Phases

What happens *within* processes? A general (but for acquisition of requisite variety, useful) answer is transactions. It is obvious that complex processes generate transactions of all types and sizes.

In view of information requirements, the next question is whether there exists a single, meaningful criterion to classify transactions. By actually zooming in on the financial aspect of transactions, we can see that every transaction requires an *explicit decision* for its realization. This criterion holds, for example, for allocation of a budget, for agreeing on a contract, for a transfer of a payment, and so on. Through abstraction, it is possible to postulate separate phases of decision making during overall processes. In the original alternative, those phases are strictly consecutive. Another early idea is to establish phase as a variable. This means that all processes need not follow a predetermined, absolute route of phases in decision making. Their possible sequence could be determined ad hoc; that is, separately for each organization annex financial accounting system. Each system thus acquires its characteristic series of (transaction) phases, as shown in Figure 16-2. To control the information flow between a particular financial accounting system and its so-called contact systems, the definition of relevant phases in different systems must be coordinated.

A purely one dimensional succession of phases, however, is untenable in more complex processes (with their correspondingly complex official rules for financial management and accounting, as in the central government ministries of the Netherlands). In hindsight, it seems extremely simple to label a straight succession of phases one dimensional. But this concerns the very concept with which the pattern was enriched greatly: dimension. To understand how, we give a short introduction to the Fourth Amendment to the Government Accounting Law (Comptabiliteitswet) of the Netherlands. That particular amendment

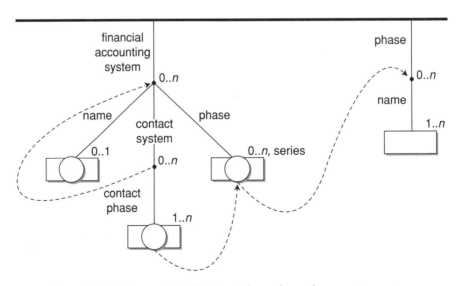

Figure 16-2 *Characteristic (decision) phases for each accounting system*

replaces the single cash-oriented budget with two goal-setting amounts. In addition to, and with priority over, the cash budget, a contract budget is specified for organizations and their processes. Then, during the relevant budget period, an executive organization should exceed neither the allocated cash budget with its payments, nor the allocated contract budget with its committed contracts. In popular terms, this is called the double lock on spending. The Fourth Amendment requires a double orientation to the financial aspect of transactions. To model these orientations, the concept of (temporal) dimensions is best. It even leads to a more general abstraction, since there is no reason to limit its values to the cash dimension and the contract dimension. For example, investment dimension is often realistic; that is, an orientation focused on the time during which the investment budget is allocated.

Adding specific dimensions does not undermine phases. One phase still follows another, but now every series of phases is limited to a particular and primary dimension. In addition, phases may be linked across dimensions. Through such relationships, phases acquire one or more secondary dimensions. This means that, at the inspection level of phases, relationships may be unambiguously modeled. The phase of the cash budget, for example, is related to the phase of the contract budget. This relationship is necessary, since the contract budget for a particular period is distributed to form parts of the cash budget for one or more periods. Because a distribution mechanism is involved, the phases of contract budget and cash budget, respectively, are linked through a distribution relationship. Inversely, it holds that all cash budget amounts that refer to the same contract period (which is a calendar year for government institutions in the Netherlands) must total the contract budget allocated for that period. In the same way, the phases of actual contracts and their cash-flow estimates are linked through a distribution relationship. With the Fourth Amendment of the Government Accounting Law of the Netherlands still under consideration, it is logical that the phases of contract budget and contract are also related; the phases of cash budget and cash-flow estimates of contracts should also be related. These are called consumption relationships—actual contracts "consume" the cash budget.

The payment phase occupies a special place in the configuration. As a rule, payment reflects the last decision phase of processes. Therefore, *all* dimensions converge in payment. As such, payment is connected with consumption relationships to all of its earlier phases.

The phased configuration of a financial accounting system, enriched by dimensions, is meant to support purposeful registration of transactions. Corresponding to phases, a separate ledger exists for every phase. Such ledgers are symbolized by cubes, making it simple to sketch an overview of dimensions and

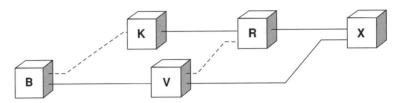

Figure 16-3 *Minimal configuration for compliance with Dutch government accounting law*

phases. Figure 16-3 presents the pattern for a single financial accounting system along the lines of the combined requirements (both contracts and cashflow).

In Figure 16-3, a consumption relationship between phase ledgers is represented by an unbroken line. A dotted line means a distribution relationship. The single (capital) letters represent phases as follows:

B—contract budget
K—cash budget
V—(actual) contracts
R—cash-flow estimates of actual contracts
X—payments (and receipts)

When **B** is replaced by **I** (investment budget), a model results that is suited for private sector enterprises. Note that this involves the contract dimension changing to an investment dimension. The contract dimension focuses attention on the period during which actual contracts are agreed upon. With an investment dimension, attention is primarily given to whatever is considered an investment, from investment budget through contracts (and possibly other intermediary phases), up to payments. All transaction instances during these phases (or of these types) should also include a reference to the period during which the initial investment budget was approved. Until now, the Netherlands' government has viewed contracts and the contract dimension, rather than the investment dimension, as sufficient to control "real" investments.

16.4 Primary Dimension

For registration of the financial aspect of a transaction, it's necessary to know to which financial accounting system the relevant journalizing group and its entries belong. Then comes the choice of the proper phase.

A rule states that a transaction/journalizing group is always limited to registration in a single phase ledger (and, by implication, in a single financial accounting system). Another rule is that every phase ledger is governed by the monetary equilibrium of double entry accounting. Balances hold on a smaller scale than the general ledger as a whole, and auditability is correspondingly simplified and improved.

A journalizing group consists of two or more entries, by the definition of double entry accounting. A single journalizing entry refers to exactly one account in a general ledger or, rather, in a phase ledger. All entries to all accounts of a particular phase ledger must have as property at least one shared dimension. This is called a phase's primary dimension. The primary dimension of entries to the contract budget phase ledger is the contract dimension. According to the Fourth Amendment, this is also the primary dimension of the contract phase. In that specific model, the phases of cash budget, cash-flow estimates of actual contracts, and payments have the cash dimension defined as their primary dimension.

Theoretically, the number of primary dimensions in a financial accounting system is unrestricted. Figure 16-4 includes the investment dimension and retains the contract dimension. Including the cash dimension, this makes for three primary dimensions. But take note that a more logical idea is to shift actual contracts from a place along the primary dimension of contracts to a place along the primary dimension of investments. However, in the Netherlands, the Fourth Amendment to the Government Accounting Law has not yet been superseded by new legislation. Based on dimensions and phases, an improved accounting model is already available. See *Aspecten en Fasen* for a more detailed analysis.

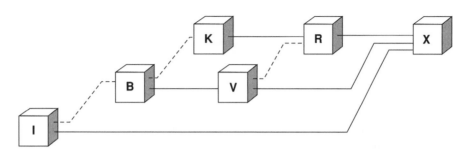

Figure 16-4 *Investment dimension added to minimal configuration of phase ledgers*

16.5 Related Accounts

It may be specified, per individual account, whether a single journalizing entry contains one or more references to other dimensions (besides the mandatory reference to the primary dimension of the phase ledger in question). Suppose that phase ledger **R** holds an account for the distributed cash-flow estimates originating from a particular account in phase ledger **V**. Every entry onto that **R**-account will then include a cash control period, because the cash dimension is primary; but that same entry must also mention a contract control period. However, the balancing entry in the journalizing group for the transaction (with the cash-flow estimate of the actual contract here as the transaction) will most likely be posted at an **R**-account with no relationship to a **V**-account. In such an inverse entry, just the relevant cash control period is required as information for dimension.

Even though the conceptual model has already been developed in some detail, what constitutes an account has still not been defined *from within*. Rather, it is the relationship *between* accounts that determines the essential information in journalizing entries.

Because each phase ledger may contain many accounts, all figures here abstract from individual accounts, showing only phase ledgers. Thus, only relationships between phase ledgers are visible, instead of the more detailed ones between accounts in different phase ledgers. It should be clear, however, that such relationships between phases only indicate the possibilities of account relationships. It may be concluded that account relationships sometimes skip phases. A payment account, for example, may be directly related to an account in the phase ledger of the cash budget, rather than through an account in the phase ledger of the cash-flow estimates of actual contracts. It all depends on the specific requirements of the accounting organization itself and of the larger system of stakeholders in which that organization participates.

16.6 Intersystem Relationships

The relationships among accounts may cross the boundaries of financial accounting systems. In fact, as account relationships secure cohesion and constitute a configuration of phase ledgers within a single financial accounting system, they also hold the overall system of such systems together. Examples of types of relationships among accounts from different financial accounting systems are delegation, reporting, and informing. The rule for such intersystem relationships is that they are allowed only between and among accounts in ledgers for identical phases. Figure 16-5 provides an example based on the models shown earlier in this chapter for separate accounting systems.

Figure 16-5 shows two financial accounting systems on two hierarchical levels. Phases **I**, **B**, and **K** are concerned with (financial) objectives; that is, they contain amounts that may be spent. Therefore, information flows through delegation relationships between accounts in phase ledgers. Direction flow of these relationships follows tradition from top to bottom. Such a hierarchy should not be confused with relative importance of levels; all are important because they all contribute essential activities.

Phases **V**, **R**, and **X** are "filled" with transactions during implementation by the operational organization, sketched at the lower level; the information, aggregated as specified, flows "up" through corresponding reporting relationships.

The internal requirements for financial consolidation should inspire a particular organization to choose a characteristic configuration for its overall financial accounting system. To keep in step with external requirements in a minimal fashion, identical dimensions and phases must be shared between constituting elementary accounting systems. Figure 16-5 shows complete correspondence. A realistic departure might be that the **R**-phase ledger is omitted at the upper level.

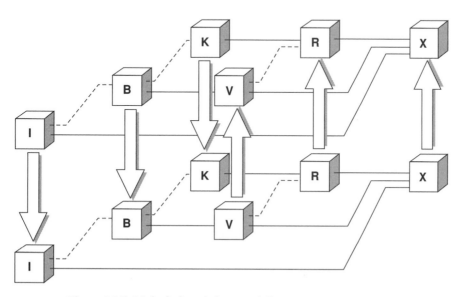

Figure 16-5 *Linked phase ledgers in different accounting systems*

Without even specifying an account, we have laid a rich foundation for a conceptual information model. It may even be considered a result of *not* specifying the concept of account in anything but a general fashion. The ideas and arguments presented so far in this chapter may be summarized with the metapattern as shown in Figure 16-6.

This pattern yields a more specific and at the same time much wider meaning to the concept of chart of accounts. Traditionally, such a chart, or classification scheme, holds the rules about which accounts may be instantiated.

The system of accounts presented thus far governs the dimensional orientation between phase ledgers in a single financial accounting system, as well as the

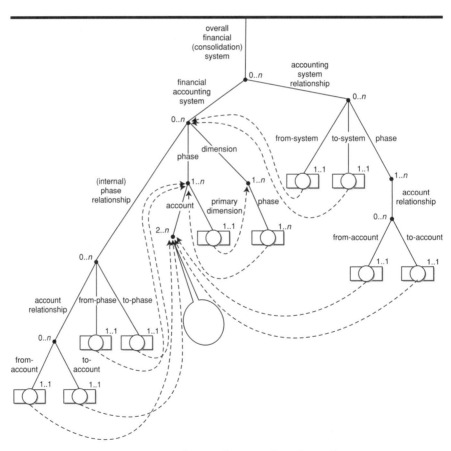

Figure 16-6 *Overview of original pattern for relational accounting*

flow of information between financial information systems in an overall financial consolidation system. To a certain extent, such configurations are often coded implicitly through account numbers. However, this does not result in generic, flexible conceptual models. Particularly where variety is large and changeable, explicit account relationships are better.

In general, a sure sign of a conceptual modeler's professionalism is in abstaining from proposing external meanings to provide internal structure for the information set. Information uniquely identifying an information object at the technological level should not be based on any of a real object's properties.

16.7 Subject Classification of Transactions

A transaction can be seen as an overall object, in which a journalizing group, one of its partial objects, represents the financial aspect of the transaction. Stated more clearly in terms of the metapattern, the journalizing group *is* the transaction in the context of financial management. As other relevant partial identities of the overall object appear in the information set with their contexts and corresponding intexts, information per context may be kept to a minimum. This raises the question of how elaborate a journalizing group and its entries should be. Overview is guaranteed, even without any duplication. Information about partial identities from different contexts can always be combined. Figure 16-7 provides examples of traditional functional contexts,

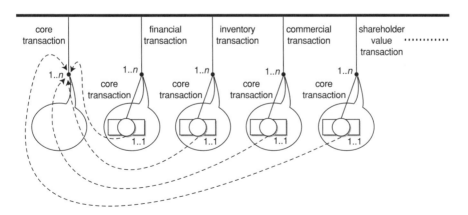

Figure 16-7 *Functional contexts for partial identities of transaction*

which can now be integrated because they all reflect *partial* identities of an overall transaction.

However, a journalizing entry must also contain references to particular subjects (see § 15.3). With the metapattern, there is no difference between a reference to a "normal" information object and a reference to an information object created for selection and retrieval. We presented the latter before as a term from a thesaurus.

The rule underlying the patterns here is that a journalizing entry may contain an indefinite number of subject references. Actually, it is often possible to structure subject classification of transactions to a very large extent. This opportunity is rooted in the existence of relationships between transactions. A possible denominator for specific transactions is, for example, a case. With respect to a particular case, an organization could commit itself through a contract; that agreement would then count as a transaction. Another transaction is probably payment of the bill, received after products or services have been delivered as contracted. Those transactions can be related when both the contract entry and the payment entry refer to the same case-as-subject.

Special subjects, deserving a separate status in journalizing entries, are quantity and all references to relevant dimensions. Only the latter—dimensional information—is missing from Figure 15-2. It has been added to the pattern shown in Figure 16-8, applying the rules for dimensions as explained earlier in this chapter.

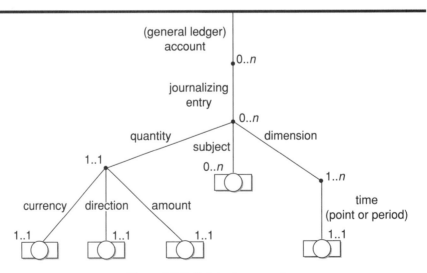

Figure 16-8 *Entries to accounts*

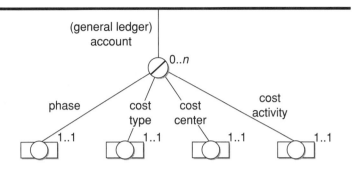

Figure 16-9 *Ledger account as Cartesian product*

16.8 Accounts

In this chapter, the patterns for financial accounting end with general ledger accounts, the basis for traditional information models. Use of the account concept must be necessary and sufficient to establish (1) dimensional differentiation *within* financial accounting systems and (2) information flow *between* financial accounting systems constituting an overall consolidation system. To serve these purposes, accounts may be given "names," which for flexibility's sake should exclude any external system references. What is then needed is for all required "systematic" relationships to be explicitly determined. Reports do not require any such meaningfully "coded" account identifiers; the unrestricted possibilities of subject classification offer all the reporting flexibility required.

However, to improve acceptance by those who cherish accounting tradition, we advise creating conceptual account identifiers with which they themselves will be able to identify. A successful tactic for change is to view an account identifier as a composition. Its constituting elements are phase, cost type, cost center, and cost activity, as shown in Figure 16-9. Of these Cartesian product elements, only phase and cost type should be considered mandatory. Therefore, when no other value for cost center and/or cost activity is registered, they retain their default value of [undetermined].

Chapter 17

Variety

The patterns for financial accounting presented in Chapter 16 are oriented toward integration with other *aspects* of organizational processes and their corresponding information requirements. Together with the emphasis on process *phases*, the ideas behind the title *Aspecten en Fasen* (*Aspects and Phases*) should be clear. Since its publication in 1991, the author has continued to develop financial accounting patterns resulting from the increasingly explicit formalization of the metapattern. The multicontextual approach optimizes information integration. Observed superficially, model changes and enhancements often seem minor. What counts is the real increase in variety made available through improved patterns.

17.1 Positional Accounting Systems

In the original patterns, no explicit relationship is modeled between the organization and the financial accounting system. When, inversely, an organization is defined to serve as a unit of financial management, a simple model results (Figure 17-1). Because the same organizational element can appear in multiple organizations—that is, in various contexts in the corresponding homogeneous classification hierarchy—it is possible to define organizations separately for financial management. For that purpose, even relationships may be used as a mechanism for differentiation (see Figure 14-2).

Although the possibility now exists, we do not recommend too many definitions of what amounts to the same organization. Even when organizations coincide with financial accounting systems, their underlying concepts or types should be modeled separately.

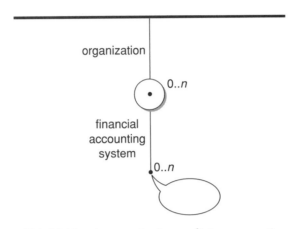

Figure 17-1 *Making the organization explicit as accounting entity*

Next, does the concept of organization (with actual organizations represented by nodes in a homogeneous classification hierarchy) provide sufficient variety? It is impossible to give a comprehensive answer. The inverse approach leads to the assumption of relating a financial accounting system to a position rather than an organization as shown in Figure 17-2. The question is what the extra variety, provided by the constituting elements of person and job, consists of. And do real information requirements exist that are served by the richer model?

It's evident that a far more finely grained system of accounting systems may be configured, and purely organization-oriented accounting systems continue to be possible. For "just" organizations may be considered a subset of all positions (where the values for person and job are both [undetermined]). However, based on the compositional nature of position, a financial accounting system can also be defined for a particular person holding a certain job, or even for a person only. All such accounting systems would still fit within their overall system of financial accounting. An individual salesperson, for example, might completely administer her or his "own" financial accounting system; it would then maintain information flows with one or more financial accounting systems of a more organizational nature. The organization employing the salesperson allocates sales budgets and must be informed about negotiated sales contracts, perhaps establishing one or more phases in between for additional management and control of sales processes.

Anyway, there are no restrictions introduced when moving from a strictly organization-based to a position-based system of (financial accounting) systems.

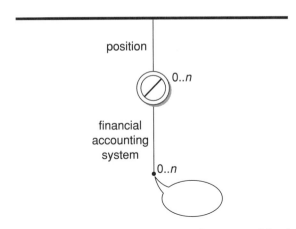

Figure 17-2 *Again introducing position for increased flexibility*

This positional perspective should also be applied to the information flows between separate financial accounting systems. The obvious rule is that two such systems may maintain a flow relationship only when a relationship has been formed between their underlying positions. Those positional relationships have already been described earlier (see § 12.5). Compared to Figure 12-8, Figure 17-3 shows some more details of the intext of the positional relationship.

The difference between Figures 12-8 and 17-3 emphasizes that large variety is characteristic for conceptual modeling, too. The modeler tries to construct a

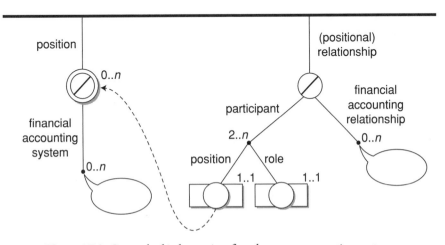

Figure 17-3 *Control of information flow between accounting systems*

general framework, then attempts to make changes necessary for the conceptual information model to fit the actual requirements of a particular case. Patterns are meaningful as starting points; a really useful model often needs at least some customization.

17.2 Configuration Management

As we described in Chapter 16, information objects belonging to several types determine the overall behavior of a particular financial accounting system. Which dimensions exist? Which phases? What are the (internal) relationships between phases? And, based upon the latter, which relationships have been defined between accounts? How are the accounts identified externally or conceptually? Which subjects may be referred to in journalizing entries?

All of this information provides structure to an accounting system. Although many different systems may exist, several of those accounting systems probably share structural characteristics in their overall configurations, and therefore they also share structural information. Those correspondences must be recognized to simplify management of a configuration of financial accounting systems.

It might appear the easiest solution when a pointer information object referring to an instance of a financial accounting system is defined as a mandatory subject for every journalizing entry. Essentially, this guarantees that reports may be generated based on that particular criterion.

However, each financial accounting system is first and foremost part of a context that determines behavior of accounts and journalizing entries posted to them. Every relevant context, therefore, must be differentiated into an ordered collection of information objects, necessary and sufficient to uniquely determine appropriate (additional) behavior.

Again, how can we simplify configuration management when those behavioral parameters are identical? It turns out that the variety of position-based financial accounting systems may require additional measures. Suppose the explosion onto position instances from its homogeneous classification hierarchy occurs as in Figure 17-4.

When one or more financial accounting systems have been defined for position 5, they may get their behavioral parameters supplied by the financial accounting system defined for position 2. However, such *inheritance* is only unambiguous when position 2 maintains a single accounting system. Without a

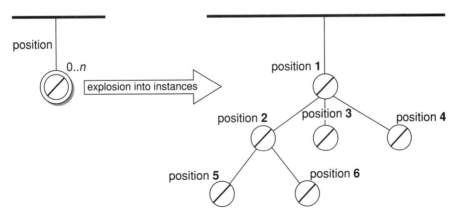

Figure 17-4 *A tree of position instances*

guarantee to this extent, the financial accounting system from which behavioral parameters must be derived should be explicitly referred to. As such, this is just an example of the possibility of multiple inheritance.

Of course, position **2** (and its financial accounting systems) may not have (all) behavioral parameters available itself. Then, at least in this example, the route in search of parameters leads to position **1**.

There is an alternative. The hierarchy in financial management, as represented by the configuration of position instances, does not presuppose correspondences in the behavior of their respective financial accounting systems. Instead, just one of the constituting elements of position may provide superior orientation for behavioral similarities. In practice, it seems logical to view inheritance of behavioral parameters from an organizational perspective. Starting from a particular position instance, the values for person and job should both be replaced by [undetermined]. This yields the position instance that might provide the required information objects as part of its intexts. Sticking to this example, organizations are nodes in a homogeneous classification hierarchy. Starting from a particular node, the intexts of superior nodes may also be inspected in search of parameters.

Combined, several mechanisms establish a wide horizon for inheritance. What all kinds of inheritance share is the implicit nature of how successive potential sources of parameters are addressed. The horizon widens following the route through an information network that has probably been defined for different purposes. It is a bonus when previously structured information *also* serves the purpose of supporting configuration management in financial accounting. However, are divergent purposes well served in the long term by merged mechanisms?

The system will always be more resilient when a separate, characteristic support structure is created for configuration management of financial accounting. Rather than inherit parameters through more or less implicit relationships, we should include explicit references. Their only objective is to support common use of behavioral parameters for financial accounting throughout an overall configuration of accounting systems.

One extreme on the spectrum of common use is when a particular financial accounting system is structurally identical to another. The other extreme consists of the case of the two accounting systems being completely different structurally.

When structures correspond completely, and the structure of one system is already known, a single reference suffices for the structure of the second, the idea behind Figure 17-5. Any accounting system may have a multitude of behavioral parameters listed. But for some systems, only a single parameter is sufficient; that is, the reference to another system whose structure is identical. In fact, it is advisable to create a separate, even semivirtual, accounting system whose only purpose is to serve as reference for structural information to other systems. The variety of such structural references is determined by the requirements for optimal configuration management of accounting systems.

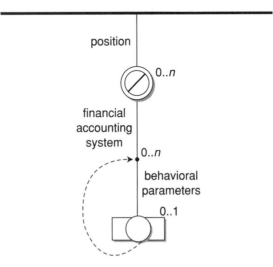

Figure 17-5 *A parameter may be a reference*

When the number of differences between behavioral/structural parameters is small, it could still be efficient to take another accounting system's structure as a starting point. If so, all differences must be stated explicitly. A cost type, for example, may *not* be used in the derived accounting system. Such exceptions help clarify the problem that shared parameter use requires mutual understanding. It does not matter where the possible prohibition on use is registered, that is, in one financial accounting system or the other. Whenever information is shared, coordination is necessary. Where such coordination information is physically located, and how coordination mechanisms are technologically implemented, are *not* conceptual issues.

Figure 17-6 includes differences in the intext of the financial accounting system that inherits behavioral parameters from another accounting system.

As the number of differences with respect to the reference accounting system grows, configuration management increases in complexity. Depending on the circumstances, a particular number of differences will prove critical in the sense that a reference for behavioral/structural parameters is no longer advantageous. Along

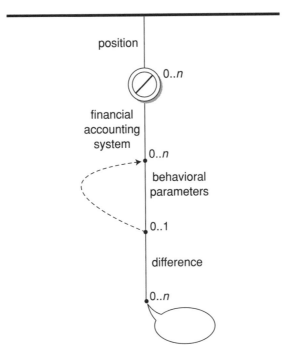

Figure 17-6 *Making differences between configurations explicit*

this stretch of the spectrum, however, not all parameters are different between the two accounting systems under consideration. It might thus be useful to group structural information by parameter type. Dimension, phase, phase relationship, account, and so on, would all be instances of such a parameter type. Again, we stress that the reference might not be completely relevant. So, even with this more limited horizon for inheritance it should be possible to include differences.

As Figure 17-7 indicates, for a particular parameter type, it is possible to refer to several sources; that is, to more than just one other financial accounting system. Of course, management of differences becomes more complicated.

Differences have a right to exist; that is, they are *really* relevant, whenever one or more other financial accounting systems serve as examples (or prototypes) for behavior, including structure. In addition to references to other systems and any differences that might be necessary to define as a result of those references, it

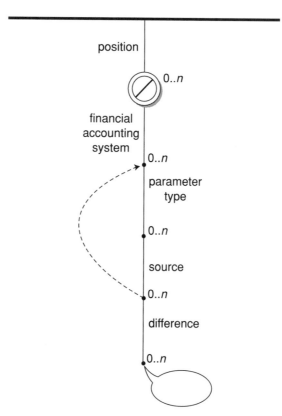

Figure 17-7 *A variety of sources for configuration parameters*

should always be possible to define behavioral parameters directly for every financial accounting system. In Chapter16, this has already been ruled for dimensions, phases, phase relationships, accounts, and account relationships.

In this chapter (and throughout the book), all the patterns for configuration management are general, since the real variety in configurations of financial accounting systems is extremely large. That variety can only be generally indicated; more details would distract from major design choices. But even such general ideas about configuration management are not available in most patterns presented elsewhere. Why they are lacking is explained by their respective perspectives. It is difficult to start modeling with individual accounts and then bring their configuration into the model. This more general level of inspection can only be properly brought into models by giving the overall configuration a conceptual status of its own. In order to arrive at an elegant result, this should be done at the start of modeling.

17.3 Constituting Elements of Account

Information processing by fast, modern technology contributes to a significant decrease in the *practical* importance of independent account identifiers in general, and of account numbers in particular. For a wide range of reports, subject references registered through journalizing entries provide a superior mechanism. Still, the possibility of more variety in account identifiers—achieved simply by modeling an account as a Cartesian product—offers advantages. The number and types of constituting elements are impossible to determine universally. But there is a way that proves adequate in most cases, in which a particular account identifier consists of references to instances of at least phase and cost type. Constituting elements may be added instances of cost center and cost activity (see Figure 16-9).

As stated, the practices of financial management are so varied that it becomes unrealistic to universally define what cost type, cost center, and cost activity mean. These concepts may be given their meanings within a separate financial accounting system as a context, since *explicit* account relationships regulate information flows between accounting systems and serve to translate between different meanings.

In the original patterns documented in *Aspecten en Fasen,* specific cost types appear as atomic information objects, as do cost centers, cost activities, and phases. The variety of the information set is greatly increased when all those

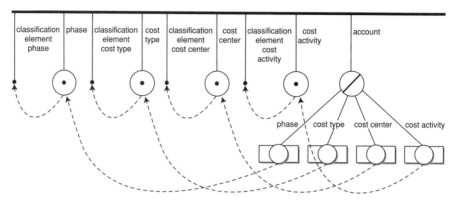

Figure 17-8 *A foundation for accounts with increased variety*

concepts are changed and modeled as nodes in as many homogeneous classification hierarchies (see Figure 17-8).

A hierarchical classification, however, introduces overlap by definition. A cost type at a particular hierarchical level, for example, encompasses all cost types reachable at lower levels from that node. When all such nodes may also act as constituting account elements, journalizing entries may represent an enormously complex mix of aggregation choices. A solution is to authorize only the lowest-level nodes to be used as constituting elements of accounts to which journalizing entries may be posted. By definition, all other accounts are summary accounts, much as Fowler defines them (see § 15.3). But this solution raises the question as to whether subject classification in journalizing entries should not be preferred to a multilayered chart of accounts. The answer is that constituting elements that are compositions in their own right (such as a homogeneous classification) cause more problems than they solve. Therefore, the pattern shown in Figure 17-8 should be interpreted as an attempt at testing conceptual limits, rather than as an operationally viable model. Through research into ever newer opportunities, persistent patterns result. Often, the earlier patterns are maintained, and sometimes a new pattern is substituted for an old.

17.4 Positional Exchange Rate Types

An important measurement of money is currency. The ratio needed to compute an amount stated in one currency into an amount in another currency is called the exchange rate.

Traditionally, transactions represented by journalizing groups and entries are consolidated into a general ledger using a single, fixed currency. Any calculations are applied before the consolidated registration. The ratio used is called something like consolidation (or registration) exchange rate.

Again, the increased processing power of information technology now warrants the conceptual conclusion that amounts in foreign currencies should not be transformed at registration. Instead, any calculations should only follow from the requirements of reports. Calculations at reporting times are also optimally oriented to relevant requirements.

When currency differences are always dealt with at reporting time (as often as a particular report is produced), transactions are registered with the original monetary amount and corresponding currency as properties. This improves the quality of the audit trail. In general, auditability is enhanced by eliminating as many constructs as possible that have gained conceptual status because of inherent limitations of manually administering large volumes of accounting information.

The application of modern information technology has also lifted a practical obstacle to frequent changes of exchange rates. The metapattern in particular makes such changes simple, since mechanisms for time management are inherently available.

Without any obstacle for frequent change, exchange rates can remain realistic. In many circumstances it is also realistic to distinguish among several types of exchange rates. As before, practical differentiation can be based on the concept of position. It could well be, for example, that one position applies different exchange rates for advances on business trips than does another position. The exchange rate type they have in common might be called advance/business travel. When those positions apply different exchange rate instances, it is only realistic that different positional exchange rate types be defined first (see Figure 17-9).

A variety of positional exchange rate types is useful for applications supporting organizational processes directly (as contrasted with the configuration of financial accounting systems that together make up the general ledger). Yet, when a transaction is consolidated into the general ledger, it must be possible to transfer amounts from rates in one exchange rate type to amounts specified in rates in another exchange rate type.

As suggested in § 14.5, it is efficient to define a particular currency as a base. A base currency is needed for each positional exchange rate type (with an explicit reference to another type possibly included when their base currencies are identical; of course, the positional exchange rate type must be regarded as an instance

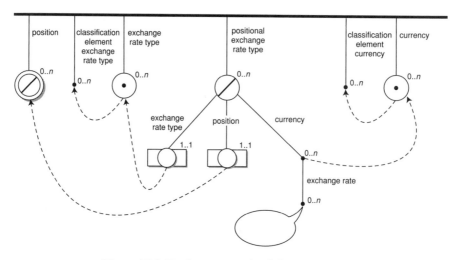

Figure 17-9 *Exchange rates for different positions*

of a parameter type, as explained in § 17.2). By definition, the exchange rate of the base currency equals 1. Then, the exchange rate of all other currencies need only be articulated with respect to the base currency (see Figure 17-10).

It may happen that the base currency changes. When this occurs at t_1, the exchange rate of all other currencies must be adjusted from that same point in time, relative to the new base.

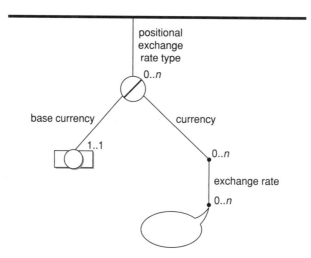

Figure 17-10 *Establishing a base currency for expressing exchange rates*

17.5 Defaults for Entries

We have shown that transactions may be ordered in many ways (§ 16.7 and § 15.3). One or more such orders may be used to simplify registration by first determining the structure and then (as far as possible) the contents of journalizing entries. The concept of process offers a general starting point, particularly when this concept is modeled by nodes in a homogeneous classification hierarchy.

As always in modeling, it makes sense to abstract from any specific process and investigate how groupings of processes may be useful, bringing the concept of process type into the model. A particular process type may then encompass one or more possible transaction types. Next, for a particular transaction type, a template may be defined to support that registration of journalizing entries about transaction instances (see Figure 17-11).

This pattern can be made more compact by assuming that an individual transaction is the smallest appearance of an individual process. It allows for process type and transaction type to be subsumed under a single concept, including its modeling implementation as a hierarchical classification hierarchy. Once achieved, the correspondence between the adjusted concept of process type and that already elaborated as the concept of transaction type in § 14.4 should be

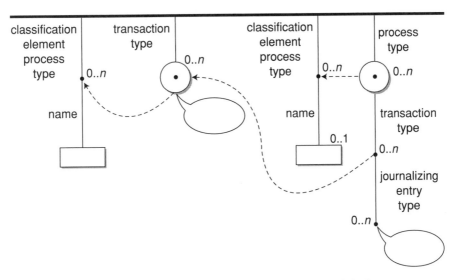

Figure 17-11 *Support of registration by supplying defaults*

clear. That original perspective is authorization, and an elegant enhancement for defaulting information is presented. Here, instead, defaulting is the original perspective. One area we did not deal with earlier is further differentiation to support journalizing groups and entries for financial accounting systems.

With the metapattern, it seems logical to specify defaults for entries *within* the context of a particular financial accounting system. But defaults are often more generally valid. The solution is to model, as one of the defaults, the reference to the financial accounting system to which the entry should be posted. This is the perspective for the pattern shown in Figure 17-12. The defaults *at the level of* a process type first determine "something" for the financial accounting system, then "something" for the whole journalizing group, and finally "something" for the individual journalizing entries. Default values for an entry are concerned with the account, the quantity, the dimensions, and the possible subjects (see Figure 16-7).

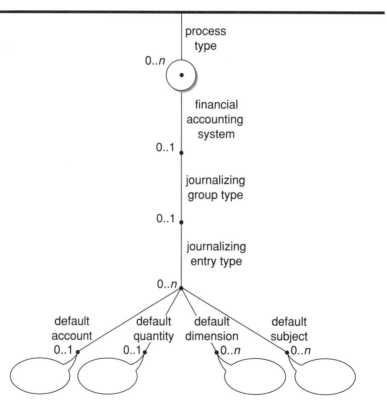

Figure 17-12 *Process as generalization for transaction*

At the level of process type, which now includes transaction type, what can be determined in advance as the contents of specific entries is mostly limited to categorical references. The account may almost always be fully specified for every future journalizing entry matching the criterion of process type (transaction type). But as far as quantity, default values will probably not exceed direction and currency. With respect to a subject, it is likely that a specific information object acting as subject instance is too detailed as a default. However, its subject type may be known and, according to the metapattern, that type already provides the context of the subject instances to be chosen for journalizing entries. Finally, for dimensions, the defaults contain values for what should be called, under scrutiny, dimension types—for example, references to investment dimension and cash dimension. The temporal information must be specified for each journalizing entry. Dimension types to be defined as defaults should correspond to the (internal) account relationship in which the default account participates. Validation of dimension type defaults should preferably occur at the time of their own registration, not each time a journalizing entry based on them is created.

As § 14.4 reasons from authorization to defaulting, the inverse direction here shows that a remark is in order about whether defaults are mandatory. Is a default merely a suggestion? Is there no room for any alternative? And why not refer to another information object, rather than copying? Because these are reasonable questions, such differentiation must be included in the conceptual information model. This can be achieved by explicit orientation of default nature, as shown in Figure 17-13.

The contents of future journalizing entries may acquire further details by changing the perspective from process type to process instance. Process at its most specific level equals a transaction instance, which means that all previously explained notions can be simply extended to apply to defaults for process instances. In Figure 17-14, the enhancements are sketched generally, and any overlapping and/or contradictory defaulting information is abstracted. Validation rules must be available to keep defaults for process type and process instance in line.

The subpattern for defaulting in the context of a process/transaction instance is identical to the one for process type (see Figure 17-14). The specification of default values is correspondingly more detailed for process instances than for process types. For example, it is expected that many subject references are known in detail for a process instance. This is also probable for the temporal aspect of dimensions. Suppose the context of journalizing is a particular investment project. This predefines, for all relevant journalizing entries, the period to be registered for the investment dimension. Again, this raises the question as to

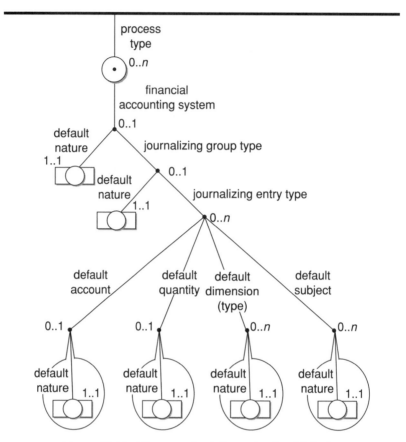

Figure 17-13 *Allowance for different kinds of defaults*

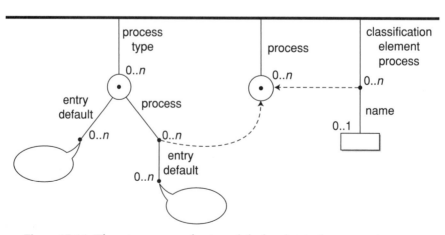

Figure 17-14 *The extreme case of unique defaults; that is, for process instances*

whether the (implicit) mechanism, offered by the homogeneous classification hierarchies for both process type and process, should also be exploited for the purpose of inheritance of journalizing defaults. They can, indeed, but it is advisable to limit such additional use to dimensions.

17.6 Conclusion on Case

The patterns presented in Part IV result from long, ongoing development. The first versions of what is called relational accounting, created in 1982, incorporated only successive phases in a single series. In light of the later extension by dimensions, the original was implicitly one dimensional. Starting in 1984, the Ministry of Foreign Affairs of the Netherlands successfully applied that version to its operational financial accounting. At the time, the author was employed by the ministry as an internal consultant and coordinator of information systems. In 1986, in his capacity as an external consultant, he revised the conceptual information model so as to accommodate the Fourth Amendment—then a draft proposal—to the Government Accounting Law of the Netherlands. The increased complexity was countered by the introduction of the concept of dimension, which greatly increased the variety of the pattern. In the Netherlands, implementation started in the late 1980s; the Ministry of Housing, Geographical Planning, and the Environment based its operational configuration of financial accounting systems on that extended pattern.

Although both are on a large scale, they remain thus far the only two operational applications. A familiar obstacle to acceptance of innovation that incorporates the advantages of digital information technology is that information processing is often still governed by strong traditions rooted in manual practices. This can only be changed when conceptual information models are even more conceptual. A sensitivity to truly conceptual models is often lacking. In fact, in the Netherlands, the Ministry of Finance recently coordinated development and publication of some reference models. But differences in meaning (contents) are still largely uncritically transferred to differences in form, so that the variety those "official" models support is far from optimal. An opportunity for renewed conceptualization has been missed.

The power of a phase-directed structure, on the contrary, results from acknowledging the different meanings (contents) that transactions derive from phases, as well as from establishing uniformity of registration—that is, of all transactions in all phases. With a phase ledger as a module, all modules are *formed identically*. Simultaneously, their contents have *different meaning* for each phase.

Without recognition of the possibilities of (very) different contents while preserving a single form, conceptual information models elsewhere continue to be based on differences in contents. The reasoning goes that a contract budget, for example, is something different from an actual contract and therefore separate modules are required. The first part of such reasoning is correct. Yes, there is a real, lasting difference. But the second part does not necessarily follow from the first. The abstraction into form makes even dimensions and phases into variables. This multiplies flexibility; more can be achieved with significantly less.

Another major advantage is in the area of dependency. After the single module has proven to function properly, all of its implementations are equally certain to perform. As mentioned before, all of this has been documented extensively in *Aspecten en Fasen*.

In the private sector, complex configurations of financial accounting systems can also be made more transparent and more manageable (thus keeping the focus), with variability based on dimensions and phases. To date, no operational applications have been reported. The conjecture seems safe enough, however, that systematic variables will greatly simplify such things as traditional charts of accounts in any sector.

The importance for financial information of robust mechanisms—for temporal references, reconstructing information, and for auditability—cannot be overstated. All are standard mechanisms with the metapattern. This provides strong support for the fourth hypothesis stated in the *Preface;* that is, that the metapattern is also eminently suitable for designing innovative patterns for financial accounting systems. In fact, previous pattern versions have been successfully applied. The improvements described in this chapter, made possible or, at least, inspired by the metapattern, have led to an even more powerful pattern (family) for financial accounting.

Part V

Metapattern
and Pluriformity

Chapter 18

Strategy

The fifth and final part of this book, consisting of this one chapter, is intended as a manifesto for conceptual modelers. It is not a summary of the book's contents. For that, the reader is referred to the introductory chapters.

The profession of conceptual information modeling is increasingly challenging. With some powerful basic ideas strongly related to the metapattern, professionals can greatly increase the quality of their contributions.

The subject of this chapter is not so much the metapattern itself or its application in designing specific conceptual information models and patterns, but rather the issue of how an organization or "position" can benefit strategically from applying the metapattern.

Here we raise several issues of a more strategic nature that occur along a spectrum. At one end, measures are aimed at incidentally serving particular information requirements; this is the extreme of a separate information system for each individual question. At the other end, all information resources are completely integrated. Thus, the question is answered from the same, all-encompassing source.

Of course, neither approach is satisfactory in the real world. The metapattern helps us find a balance between the extremes of, say, distribution and integration—that is, autonomy and coordination. The need for a conceptually realistic balance in creating, handling, and retrieving increasingly complex and often dynamic information is urgent, because the information society will most certainly continue to evolve at an accelerated pace.

18.1 First Priority: Differences

Conceptual information models are often required when a configuration of information systems or an individual system does not perform adequately, or when no previous resources exist to fulfill information requirements. More or less radical changes are almost always due. In this sense, an information model is a means to reach the end of improved information sets and the way they operate as integrated aspects of organizational processes.

For some time now, what has been introduced as a new tool (information system) does not exclusively substitute for an automated variety of previous manual operations. That information and its manner of processing must be viewed as integral and integrating aspects of overall processes. What was treated as a separate administrative function before, should now always be repositioned as an integrated administrative aspect. This explains why an information model increasingly reflects the informational aspect of overall, complete processes. It also clarifies why the use of the prospective tool must be included in the conceptual information models.

The integration of the administrative function into information management and process management greatly expands the horizon of information modeling. Until recently, the administrative function was given an almost completely separate position in organizations, working on the basis of exclusive laws, rules, and prescriptions. This period of (self) protection in a separate realm of activity, duplicating much work, should be declared to have permanently passed. Modern information systems are expected to contribute directly to overall processes. Only an integral strategy for information can reach this objective.

At the same time, as more reality must be taken into account, greater information is needed for planning and control of organizational processes. As the relevant part of reality grows, chances of conceptual diversity also increase. This hinders cohesion of information.

Attempts to establish an integral information model based on uniform concepts, when the world-out-there must be characterized by conceptual pluriformity, can only fail. Regretfully, examples of overoptimistic modeling exercises abound. Behind such failures is the mistaken reversal of means and ends. The real end should always be a configuration of information systems in the pluriformity of reality as experienced during the execution of organizational processes. Information models can only serve as real means to such ends, nothing more or less. A viable approach to conceptual information modeling, therefore,

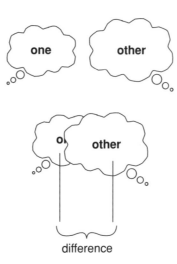

Figure 18-1 *Basic perspectives for understanding differences*

must start with the recognition of differences as they really exist. It deserves the highest priority. The focus on life comes first. Tools must be developed to develop life.

Figure 18-1 shows that two practical perspectives help discover specific differences. Suppose, in general, a certain difference is attached to one when compared to the other.

First, the one may differ simultaneously from the other. That is, they coexist with their difference. Or, to be more specific, their difference coexists. Figure 18-2 helps to clarify this.

Second, the one may differ consecutively from the other. In this case, they exist separated by time. And so does any difference they may entertain. Figure 18-3 sketches the principle of consecutive difference.

It should come as no surprise that both general cases represent the elementary categories of problems for traditional approaches to modeling. Part II, in particular, describes several problems and examples of multiple and dynamic classification. It shows how traditional object orientation does not succeed beyond incidental solutions, often going against the principles of the approach taken. Encapsulation in object orientation, for example, will suffer from differentiating subtypes to an object type.

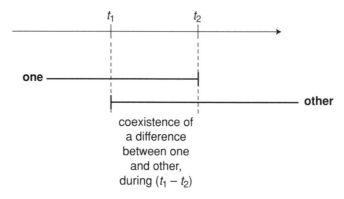

Figure 18-2 *Simultaneous difference*

The metapattern, however, starts from the premise of recognizing differences; this is its first principle. Yet another principle, the need for cohesion, is recognized by the metapattern. Both principles are joined by the ideas of a context and an object-in-context.

A *simultaneous difference in cohesion* is supported by different contexts. Traditionally, a specific context is kept from the information model; from within the model it can only be implied. When we apply the metapattern, we always specify contexts as integral, even integrating, parts of the conceptual information model. As a result, an overall object disappears as an entity in its own right,

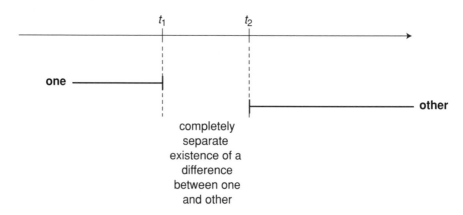

Figure 18-3 *Consecutive difference*

modeled as a collection of partial identities tied together to provide cohesion when and where necessary.

In this way, the metapattern removes the major obstacle to an integral strategy for the informational aspect of complex, dynamic organizational processes. As stated earlier, given the pluriformity of reality, developing an integral information model—or an integrated family of models based on uniform concepts (absolute object types)—will never succeed. An integral model, however, has become a realistic possibility (opportunity) when pluriform concepts are available. With contexts inside, not outside, the conceptual information models, pluriform concepts have acquired an operational, practical status.

For a *consecutive difference in cohesion,* the metapattern also provides fundamental mechanisms. The quantity of uniquely identifiable information contains, as part of its intext, one or more existence entries (and validity entries, too). This guarantees the dynamic operation of the information sets at the most finely grained level of modeled information. With a particular point in time in the past, present, or future as a criterion, a selection is made of the information that only then existed, exists, and/or will exist (and is/was registered as valid at that time).

The combined effect of context and time further guarantees that relevant differences can all be cohesively modeled. This feature extends beyond, say, first order information, for metainformation is also modeled using the metapattern. Therefore, even types are dynamic. A particular time of relevance does not lead directly to a selection of information corresponding to a fixed type. Instead, the relevant type is determined as it existed, exists, or will exist (and is/was registered as valid at that time).

The explicit recognition of simultaneous and/or consecutive differences, even at the metalevel(s) of information, makes the metapattern eminently suited for gradual development and introduction of related information sets. With existence and validity entries, fundamental mechanisms are available to correct information, even retrospectively. The audit trail is never compromised. In a most literal sense, the metapattern handles errors and their corrections constructively. It is possible to change information types, it is possible to change information relationships, and it is possible to change primitive information. Through its "forgiveness" to errors, the metapattern supports development by trial, thereby avoiding the many pitfalls of the blueprint approach to complex information systems. Cohesion may grow gradually, as insight into the pluriformity of concepts grows. Any unsuccessful trial can easily be controlled by correcting the errors encountered.

Underlying the metapattern's potential for integrated information systems is a paradox. Recognizing real differences and giving them first priority strongly promotes eventual cohesion. The most sensible way to begin applying the meta-pattern is not integrally, but marginally. As soon as a marginal information set is proven to fit the strategic scheme, which is a dynamic perspective itself, one or more specific, sensible integrating activities can be successfully undertaken. And so on, until no margin is left for trial and error.

Emphasis, however, should always also remain on the real pluriformity of the reality that the configuration of information sets addresses. In this respect, in most situations it is a sound idea to have a different look—that is, a metapattern-based look—at the organizational processes and existing information systems. Often, traditional modeling has imposed uniformity, not only on information systems, but by extension on organizational processes, too. This results in an obstacle to opportunities that require flexibility.

The metapattern can remove such limiting uniformity and provide space for relevant pluriformity. Seen in this light, the metapattern serves as a second generation tool for organizational process design.

When legacy systems are inadequate, another paradoxical intervention is not to start by replacing them. They can more easily be integrated by superimposing a meta-information application based on the metapattern. Only then should a gradual renewal or replacement of legacy systems be considered, if necessary.

18.2 Second Priority: Similarities

Differences are real in complex processes. For an operational information system to integrate properly into such a process, its conceptual information model must realistically contain corresponding differences. However, more differences than strictly required are ineffective. In mathematical terms, the optimum lies with what is *necessary and sufficient*. Of course, what is optimal may, and will, differ from situation to situation.

With the first priority in modeling being the recognition of real differences, the second priority is to avoid unnecessary differences. An unnecessary difference equals a similarity.

Tracing similarities can be accomplished through a method that often yields surprising results. In order to be successful, the professional modeler should consciously apply the difference between content and form, a method most people don't seem to apply in daily behavior. Of course, they experience real and immediate differences, from which it only seems logical to conclude *corresponding* differences to appear in the conceptual information model. The design-oriented difference between content and form, however, allows a more detailed analysis. By comparing two phenomena, the professional modeler raises the following question: To what extent, if any, does the difference in information contents demand that their corresponding information forms also differ? Part IV illustrates practical, simple patterns for financial accounting that show where a radical pursuit of such questions may lead. As far as their contents (that is, meaning) are concerned, a budget and contract are, for example, different. In the realm of meanings/contents, pluriformity rules, but the form in which those contents are registered can be considered uniform (and should be, whenever possible, for simplicity's sake).

When different contents are given identical form, however, an identifying criterion disappears, calling for an elaboration of the form. Usually a minimal extension, it should be kept uniform to accommodate the additional content that secures the real pluriformity. The additional variable will, in this case, contain a value to indicate whether the "other" information is about a budget or a contract. This small addition eliminates more elaborate, separate modules for budgets and contracts. By abstracting even more, *in the form* of a phase, a strong similarity has been designed for financial accounting and its configuration of information sets. Indeed, the (extra) surprise is that such an explicit concept, like phase in the financial accounting aspect of organizational processes, may consequently be used to redesign the logic of the overall system of (financial) planning and control. Again, the processing phase exerts a strong influence on the theory and practice of financial management. One similarity often leads to the discovery of another.

To maintain equilibrium, however, it is sometimes necessary to introduce new differences. In fact, what has been conceptualized as phase is a prime example. It also follows that, in general, equilibrium through modeling is dynamic. An investigation into similarities may thus lead to organizational process design. The designer can arrive at radical shifts in concepts—often too radical for other people involved. This points to limits to change, but a limit also exists with respect to the gradualness of change. Financial accounting is *yes or no*, based on explicit process phases. As the conceptual shift grows, the need increases for management to provide strategic overview and concurrent practical support to implement changes. A large shift provides extra risks and opportunities. The metapattern makes risks manageable through the possibility of more gradually developed change. This should help in deciding to benefit from opportunities.

The metapattern directly supports differences. Its influence in establishing similarities is more indirect, which is amply illustrated in Parts III and IV where various patterns (consolidated similarities) are presented. The fundamental concepts of context and time do not always appear explicitly. It is more that similarities in those patterns are sketched trusting that differentiation can always be reintroduced whenever necessary.

In addition, and partly based on the metapattern's characteristics, powerful types of compositions (patterns in their own right) are available. Such compositions, like the position concept, often encompass great complexity. Beginning with the similarities they assume, it is easier to recognize and model real differences in other information.

Another method aimed at designing similarities idealizes the ever-increasing capacities against ever-decreasing costs of digital information and communication technology. The idea is to use the surplus of technical processing capacity for conceptual surplus. What often begins as a luxury choice turns out to be a necessity. Address information may serve as an example. Under the general denominator of connectivity (see § 12.4), many addresses are properties (intext) of positions. It happens that a specific address is not absolutely valid as a property of a particular position. An address could only count as a property of one position *in relation to* another position. What is then more logical than to model address in the intext of positional relationships? Another modeling step makes the conceptual model more uniform again by accepting address *exclusively* as a property of positional relationships, eliminating address from the intext of single positions. With only one position determined and the other(s) empty, all previously single positions form a subset of positional relationships. Thus, all addresses that are valid for a single position fit better when more generally modeled as a property of positional relationships. The reader is invited to integrate the patterns from Figures 12-7 (connectivity) and 12-9 (explicit positional relationships) accordingly.

At first, extending the context of address from position to positional relationship might seem like a waste of processing and storage capacity. Why deal with the unnecessary information of an empty second position in a positional relationship when a single position suffices to identify an address? Instead of rejecting such conceptual surplus outright, consider it seriously. It could be sensible if relationship-based addressing occurs in the future; if not, the *model* will have achieved greater uniformity while supporting increased potential of pluriformity of *behavior* of the information set. The additional complexity for most users may be easily hidden by supplying them with application interfaces that feature what looks to them like single positions. In the background, a minimum of one empty position would be added to accommodate the more general context of positional relationships for addresses.

What can be seen as the precaution of conceptual surplus in modeling contradicts the gradual development of a system of information systems made possible (more easily) by the metapattern. Why extend the model now, when it is equally possible to do so later? The choice between now and later should always be a strategic one. Therefore, it should be made dependent on the specific strategic situation, including its dynamics. The metapattern doesn't cause such problems, opportunities, and so on: They always existed. With the metapattern, choices can be made more consciously, thereby improving results.

The tactics of conceptual surplus are enhanced by available patterns (when applicable). After operational performance has been sufficiently secured, a particular pattern deserves to be labeled "applicable" when any subset of its instances delivers the functionality required. Such patterns—reusable conceptual information models—*fundamentally* provide both wide and deep functionality, as presented in Parts II, III, and IV (often elaborating on the important work of other authors).

During the practical use of an information system, however, users should not be inconvenienced or hindered by provisions that are not required. Special attention to the user interface eliminates such problems. A user may register an address under the impression that it is a property of a single position, or even of a single person, while "behind the screen" (requiring some surplus of processing power) the context is generalized. Addresses of only positional relationships are actually registered, to offer one example.

Conceptual model pluriformity and user interface pluriformity are two different perspectives. The variety of use can never surpass the model variety. Particularly with context and time as fundamental categories, the metapattern supports the design of patterns from which highly specialized user applications can be developed while maintaining the advantage of compactness at the pattern level.

18.3 Boundary-Crossing Information Services

The coverage required from information systems is increasing rapidly along many dimensions. This growth will continue to accelerate for some time. With an approach like the metapattern contributing to the acceleration, more information of a diversified nature becomes integrally manageable, providing practical means for wider coverage, and so on. In light of growing complexity, it is illusory to think that high-level standards offer the proper means to control those systems of information systems. In a world fundamentally characterized by pluriformity, sooner or later strictly uniform rules are obstacles to further development. Again, it is more productive to start thinking from real differences (the strength of the metapattern is in its high uniformity to support pluriformity). Information draws its right to exist, in characteristic contents and equally characteristic form, from the actual processes that primarily create it; for their continuation, it is kept available as an integrating aspect. This characteristic content and form may, in principle, never be negatively imposed upon by the requirements of information services that cross the boundaries of the original processes (situations). In fact, boundary-less information services in particular benefit from recognizing specific boundaries. Without boundaries (contexts), no specific meaning exists. And without such meaning, information is essentially valueless.

Taking the originating process(es) seriously, we may take concrete measures that allow information to cross a specific boundary and still contribute to cohesive information beyond. It may even be reasonable to attribute more importance to information after crossing its boundary. When cohesion clearly becomes normative, the logical conclusion should be to abolish the original boundary, replacing it with boundaries that establish a wider process/situation. But, again, as long as processes retain their own character, this character should be awarded primary status; any crossing of boundaries comes second.

In the previous paragraph, some tactics were outlined showing how to benefit from differences in establishing similarities. Those modeling tactics are equally valid when dealing with information services across the boundaries of the processes that created the information. Boundaries, however, presuppose remaining differences, for if all differences disappear, boundaries serve no purpose.

With the metapattern, the behavioral rules for joint information services are given a separate place in the information model. The intext of a particular information object, acting as a type for other information objects, may contain information about specific boundaries. Any such property establishes another context. It provides the logical node to which corresponding behavioral rules for translation of contents and/or form needed to cross the boundary, can be attached as part of the next-level intext. Notwithstanding the overall governing limits, this mechanism is a uniform representation of joint information that individually originated at pluriform processes. Equilibrium is always required between the primary orientation at information-creating processes and the secondary orientation at subsequent information sharing. At first, this presents another paradox in conceptual information modeling. It disappears, however, when the modeler recognizes that necessary and sufficient differences amount to the maximum number of similarities. The metapattern provides the freedom required for modeling differences directly.

18.4 Technological Developments

Conceptual information modeling is an activity separate from construction modeling and the actual construction of an information system. This assumption was made to describe the metapattern as clearly as possible (Part I), as the metapattern is designed to support conceptual modeling. The underlying idea is that conceptual information modeling is a discipline in its own right. It is difficult to do well, which establishes the need for expert practitioners. This book attempts to support the further development of this exciting profession. The metapattern is presented as a characteristic tool for conceptual modelers. But what ultimately counts is whether practical results improve through applying the metapattern and its associated models.

So far, experiences are based on KnitbITs®, the first construction tool to directly support the metapattern, and on specific applications developed with it. Not surprisingly, it has confirmed that navigating a metapattern-based information set requires additional processing capacity, but such capacity is becoming cheaply available. It seems reasonable to extrapolate that metapattern-based information processing makes no more than realistic demands on current and future technology. Even better, metapattern-based information systems make improved use of increasingly powerful technology. The applications have also illuminated that an essentially higher level of flexibility and accountability is achieved. When all such reasons are taken together, it's clear that the flow of conceptual modeling should not be obstructed by technological limitations that are probably not even relevant. Conceptual modeling is about putting realistic information requirements first. Almost without exception, problems with the operational performance of information technology turn out to be nonexistent or, when they do occur with current technology, worth the price of improved functionality. As D. C. Hay remarks in *Data Model Patterns:* "[T]echnology and its limitations will change. An accommodation made today to relieve a particular bottleneck may be completely inappropriate three or five years from now." So, anyone aiming to build a competitive advantage in the private sector and/or improved government services should fully use the opportunities of conceptual information modeling with the metapattern.

18.5 Fifth Hypothesis

Each part of this book has been written toward making a particular hypothesis credible. All five hypotheses are stated in the Preface. The fifth, at first sight, is the subject of this final part. It suggests that the metapattern supports uniformity in an overall system of information systems while guaranteeing pluriformity in processing behavior where required (as is usually the case in complex organizations and organizations of organizations).

This final, short chapter does not attempt to establish extensive arguments to support this hypothesis, since the entire book is dedicated to proving this realistic claim.

Initially, the metapattern will be rather difficult to understand. As with any novel idea, however, such difficulties result from applying a different frame of reference, or paradigm. For example, the reader may unconsciously hold on to a world view in which context is not yet considered a first principle.

When a concept is no longer new, it becomes easier to handle. Such a learning process can be greatly assisted through practical exercises and application. The reader is therefore invited to start working with the metapattern, as she or he understands it, on familiar modeling problems. The specific patterns in this book will help in getting started. Soon it will be evident that resulting models are more elegant, compact, simple, and powerful. Practice will improve the quality of what the reader achieves. Such conceptual information models are an important, even vital, step toward flexible, accountable information sets.

The last few words of this book are personal. I want to thank you for studying the metapattern and looking at the specific patterns. I hope that you, as a professional modeler, benefit from your efforts. If you have any comments you would like to share, please contact me at pewisse@wanadoo.nl, or through the publisher.

Part VI

Appendices

Appendix A

Multicontextualism

Knowledge principles for differences in unity

I have tended the growth of some new philosophical roots.

How else can I state such an impossibly immodest hypothesis in a modest manner? A claim to such basic novelty definitely sounds pretentious. Wasn't the frontier of the philosophy of first principles closed long ago? Or will there always be space for fundamental discoveries? But, then, how did it come about that I was able to make some? Or is it only a rediscovery?

As branches of philosophy are concerned with, and comment upon, development of knowledge, philosophical roots must provide them with principles. Of course, such roots are essentially philosophical in nature. A clear distinction between roots and branches, therefore, is never possible. Earlier branches may lead to later roots; roots of philosophy grow from philosophy, too. Driven by an accumulation of actual problems, I arrived at what I propose here as today's new roots.

Regardless of realism or idealism, or of any intermediate world view, traditional theories of knowledge imply a singular relationship between information and what that information means to an interpreter. Its meaning is often denoted as knowledge about an object believed to exist autonomously or as an autonomous ideal (or ideal). Particular information is supposed to refer to a particular object only. Modern semiotics, with its familiar triadic foundation, does not escape the perspective of absolute objects, either real or idealized. Fair enough; it is recognized that the reference may be false. Even then, the fraudulent use of information relies on acceptance of singularity in correspondence between information and (non)object.

Much of philosophy has been dedicated to coming to terms with the problems thus generated. But such problems are best solved at the roots, with as wide a bearing as possible. As a principle of knowledge, the idea of mutually autonomous objects with corresponding supplies of information is just too simple. It does not support the increasing simultaneous and subsequent variety experienced during the encompassing life that a person, or, for that matter, many other objects, leads today.

Instead, I superimpose the concept of situation, or as its equivalent from the perspective of information, context. At any time, a multitude of contexts may be assumed. Next, a particular object may be thought to appear in some, or all, of those different contexts. Depending on the situation or context, the object will show a characteristic identity, with contextual properties (or, in general, contextual behavior). Information thus structured carries multicontextualism. As a matter of principle, there is no absolute, only contextual meaning. Different meanings may occur for the same object, presuming equally different contexts.

This epistemological approach, with its strong ontological flavor, I have named multicontextualism. Only by making context an explicit, primary, and operational concept for information is it possible to label traditional theories as monocontextualist. Thus, those earlier theories are not supplanted but, rather, enveloped.

Multicontextualism offers a powerful synthesis, a blend of analytical philosophy and structuralism. Or, as a friend remarked, it unites Wittgenstein I and II.

Multicontextualism holds that information is still related to an object, but the scope of the object's relevant autonomy, as meant by particular information-as-reference, is now strictly limited to a particular context (Wittgenstein II: language game). At the same time, contextual identities may be joined to form a supracontextual object. In its supracontextual capacity, however, an object does not entertain any characteristics. These are only made specific within contexts. Its minimal supracontextual relationships provide for an object's fundamental unity while its behaviors are equally and fundamentally different for correspondingly different contexts.

In any structured information set, some information must by necessity be primitive—that is, its explicit meaning is not contained within the set but must be interpreted from without (or has been implicitly given, as with genetic inheritance). Other information may be included with references to such primitive information, or to references specified earlier. As such, it is a straightforward matter to recognize that information objects, as the set evolves, constitute each other for the most part.

A succinct prescription for formalization of multicontextualism is presented in the first part of this book. The formalization's highly practical power is derived from the recursive application of fragmented information about contextual objects and relationships. Contexts, too, are formalized by such information, and resulting information models are both compact and flexible. The emphasis of design choices shifts to elaboration of contexts and supracontextual cohesion. It seems reasonable to expect that the full extra degree of freedom to represent knowledge supports a higher level of intersubjectivity; that is, of success in communication.

I originally developed multicontextualism as an approach to conceptual information modeling oriented at business and government processes. Traditional object orientation, I found, left too many problems unsolved, or without sufficiently elegant solutions. A much higher quality of such models, which includes ease of communication, is a prerequisite for constructing superior (digital) information systems for all sorts of administrative purposes.

At an early stage, I recognized multicontextualism's potential for fundamental and applied philosophical inquiry. Other disciplines besides information science may also benefit, the essential criterion being that conceptual information models lie at their hearts. Examples that come readily to mind are cognitive and social psychology, linguistics, and artificial or, rather, machine intelligence (expert systems). But, then, is not every science an attempt to model our world? Would it not help, also, to view light, behaving as either a wave or a particle, as a matter of context?

As in any mature discipline, the volume of philosophical work is overwhelming, making it impossible to ascertain multicontextualism's novelty. In fact, I learned from my readings that many thinkers over the course of centuries tried with various degrees of success to capture pluriformity. However, nowhere did I find a really comprehensive treatment and formalization that suited my own original purpose. Of course, when another author is shown to have made this contribution earlier I will gladly change my hypothesis, so boldly stated at the beginning of this short essay on multicontextualism. I will change it to the extent that the novelty is not mine, and give the other person(s) full acknowledgment for his or her achievement. In fact, from research on my new book *Semiosis & Sign Exchange,* I have already learned that philosopher J. Dewey (1859–1952) placed the concept of situation at the root of his logic as a general theory of inquiry. Then there is a so-called dialogical theory with M. M. Bakhtin and V. N. Voloshinov as goundbreaking theorists. Recent examples of attempts at mathematical formalization are publications by J. Barwise and K. Devlin.

Original or not, I will no doubt always strongly maintain that the approach to understanding along multiple contexts may be at the root of many fruit-bearing branches of philosophy—that is, of a great variety of applied disciplines—while providing opportunities for their advanced synthesis. As for myself, I will stay especially busy applying multicontextualism to conceptual information modeling for very practical results.

Appendix B

An Alliance of Metamodels

Metapattern meets RM-ODP

The metapattern is a powerful approach to conceptual information modeling. It is not, however, a comprehensive development approach for information systems. Therefore, it must be combined with other metamodels, methods, and so on.

The idea behind combining forces, or forming an alliance, should always be this: that a particular task must be fulfilled but it is too big for a single *unit* to complete successfully. When several units contribute their efforts, a task's critical mass may be, literally or figuratively, overpowered.

A Range of Alliance Types

Success by alliance comes at the price of coordination, though. This implies that an alliance is never totally homogeneous, as units contributing similar efforts would remain, by definition, uncoordinated. Many people can attempt to lift a rock. If their aggregate energy more than equals the rock's weight, then it is only when they apply energy simultaneously that the rock will move. Making people lift on the count of three, for example, would be a coordinating effort.

At the other extreme of alliances, as shown in Figure B-1, all efforts by units are completely heterogeneous. Coordination becomes prominent. Considering the characteristics of participating units, a task is decomposed into disjunct aspects. For the completion of the overall task, actual efforts are matched to such aspects.

In practical life, alliances lie somewhere in between. It depends on the requirement of coordination as the only different effort and, on the other hand, of all efforts being different. Looking at this range, it should be evident that *alliance*

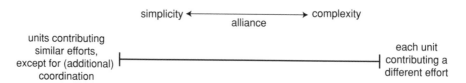

Figure B-1 *Spectrum of alliances*

and *organization* are synonyms. The term alliance helps stress the importance of contributions, whereas the term organization has become associated with the (static) structure of participating units.

Autonomy

We have purposely called participants of an alliance *units*. A unit suggests autonomy, making clear that every alliance exists *because of* a fundamental tension. The assumption is that, given the opportunity, a unit would rather execute the task by itself, exclusively reaping the rewards. An important aspect of coordination, therefore, is to counteract hegemony.

Ideally, units exhibit self-control. Aware that their particular efforts are insufficient for task completion, they recognize the contributions of other units. Each unit wants its autonomy respected, relinquishing in turn some of its original autonomy. It accepts coordination for the benefit of enjoying a fair share of success that would be impossible without contributing to the alliance.

Variety

The second reason to use the term unit is its generality. It covers a wide variety of phenomena. A unit may be an individual person or an organizational unit. Unit can also be given a less traditional meaning, such as that of method or paradigm.

The latest developments in the philosophy of science acknowledge that the complexity of reality cannot be explained or changed according to a single paradigm. This has led to acceptance of *multiparadigmatic* approaches. No paradigm (unit) may claim absolute priority. The proper alliance of such units supports the successful achievement of the specific, often complex (scientific) task.

Scientific Aspects

An application of the metaparadigm of multiparadigmatically coordinated efforts should be the development of complex information systems. Such development is never the mere deployment of scientific results achieved elsewhere. It follows from the need for innovation that a development process has scientific aspects, too. Without a scientific attitude—healthy curiosity—it would be impossible to gain sufficient understanding of the problem, opportunity, or situation. It would be equally impossible to design, construct, and implement an optimal information system as the solution.

Hegemony and Reduction

A scientific attitude alone, though, could be disastrous. For example, if the task is to improve the quality of service in a government agency, other aspects need to be recognized and treated accordingly.

Suppose that a particular unit would perfectly match some aspect x of the task, but would be unsuitable for aspect y. Suppose, too, that the unit one-sidedly declared its paradigm valid for both aspects x and y. (This often happens with the best of intentions: therein even lies the danger.)

Such a course of events is known in philosophical discourse as reductionism, or simply reduction. What happens is that understanding, and subsequent practice, of y is reduced to the theory and practice underlying x. The difference between an open alliance and reduction is sketched in Figure B-2.

Of course, reduction can work in any direction. It is equally harmful to view tool construction, including characteristic precision, as if the situation for its intended application must be charted. Such opposite reduction, when compared to Figure B-2, is shown in Figure B-3.

Reductionist practices in this sense are normal in human society, and not always bad. Someone visiting a doctor expects to be treated as a patient. But a doctor who does not also meet the patient as a person pursues professional reduction much too far—that is, she or he is *not* really a professional.

The saying that "To a hammer, everything looks like a nail" expresses the practice of reduction well.

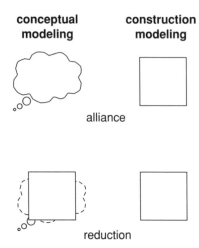

Figure B-2 *Reduction of conceptual modeling by construction orientation*

We can now restate a major issue of task coordination. An alliance can only remain successful when reduction by any participating unit is avoided or, when that is discovered as too ambitious, kept at an acceptable level. Ideally, every unit combats reductionist urges itself.

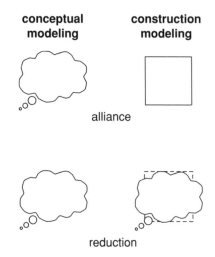

Figure B-3 *Reduction of construction by orientation at conceptual modeling*

Strength and Weakness

Coaches of top performing sports teams consistently select players based on their strengths. One such strength is the ability to avoid exhibiting eventual weaknesses. Thus, a team may be considered a combination of participating strengths.

Development of a complex information system is like a team effort. Units should be included on the basis of how well they match particular aspects. Any weakness concerning other aspects does not matter, as different units will properly match them.

Knowledge and Ignorance

A variation of this theme is that one unit does not have to be completely knowledgeable about the other participating units. Often, it is even counterproductive. What counts is optimal coordination of their task-oriented efforts. That makes it necessary and sufficient for a particular unit to know how to interact with other units. It can and, for the sake of effectiveness and efficiency, should be totally ignorant about how another unit internally acts to produce such contributing efforts.

Metapattern as Participating Unit

To develop a fitting information system, it is necessary to learn about the purpose(s) it has to serve. This entails acquiring an understanding of reality. Such understanding should be as rational as possible, in the sense that reality is viewed as essentially structured.

What *having a structure* (or its equivalent, *being a system*) assumes is that elements exist, with relationships between and among them. Special status is awarded to the element of the environment or, to be more precise, the rest of reality.

A strength of the metapattern lies in its support for *more realistically* understanding reality. It escapes the traditional limitation of direct synchronization between the concepts of an element (called a real object, or simply object) and its behavior. Usually, a one-to-one correspondence is defined. Because this correspondence is implicitly assumed, it is difficult to escape.

With the metapattern, an object may be attributed with a multitude of behaviors (intexts), with each behavior unambiguously defined for a particular context.

The metapattern includes a simple method for integrated visualization of multiple contexts, of partial objects each having its own behavior or intext, and of integration of partial objects to constitute an overall object.

The principle of contextual differentiation of object behavior opens the possibility of reflecting comprehensively on greater complexity of reality. Such conceptual models may be easily documented and communicated using the metapattern's simple notation.

The emphasis on conceptual modeling as a strength is a clear indication of the metapattern's weakness. It is *not* a paradigm, or metamodel, to support predominantly technological aspects of (digital) information system development. In full recognition of this weakness, we advise *not* applying the metapattern beyond the area of its evident strengths; that is, outside conceptual modeling. Otherwise, aspects requiring a characteristic paradigm for their optimal development would be reduced to what the metapattern allows. With the focus of the metapattern on reality, the equally necessary focus on tool technology would suffer.

Unit Candidate

With the metapattern optimally matched to conceptual aspects of development, one or more missing units are needed to successfully complete the overall development task. What are suitable candidates? Does a unit even exist that shows strengths for all aspects, including conceptual modeling? Such a unit would make it unnecessary to let the metapattern participate in development.

The number of methods, paradigms, or metamodels (call it what you will) offered as employable units for information system development has grown beyond reviewing capacity. Here, instead, only one unit is considered for alliance. This serious candidate must be introduced first.

Open Distributed Processing

A pervasive characteristic of Western society is its variety, occurring for reasons that range from free competition to state intervention. Competition creates some variety, offering consumers at least the illusion of choice. Historically, when a state intervenes, it is often without regard for resources elsewhere. A famous case involves different widths between rails, causing railroad carriages to be transferred at some international borders from one chassis to another.

At any rate, variety is a way of life; it's a reality. Information processing is no exception. As with a train strictly keeping to a proprietary track, information processing remains relatively simple when performed in isolation; that is, using stand-alone resources. Increasingly, however, resources are combined for information processing, because a counter-phenomenon to variety exists, exhibiting itself in cooperation and communication. Adding to the complexity is that many such resources have not been developed with an alliance of different units in mind. (The recurring theme of alliance is, we hope, not lost on the reader.)

Accepting the fundamental variety—even honoring it where it supports special requirements and/or promotes innovation—the question becomes how distributed, often heterogeneous resources can still be successfully combined for information processing.

Throughout the ages, the answer has been to establish an agreement on exchange format (Figure B-4). Such agreements are commonly known as standards. Digital information processing is no exception.

Standards originate from several sources. Official, or *de jure,* standards are issued by Standards Developing Organizations (SDOs) in which nations participate, usually represented by their respective national standardization bodies. Actively involved in *international* standards for information processing are the

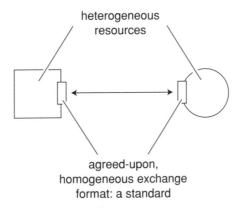

heterogeneous
resources

agreed-upon,
homogeneous exchange
format: a standard

Figure B-4 *The principle of standardization*

International Telecommunications Union (ITU), the International Electrotechnical Commission (IEC), and the International Standardization Organization (ISO). ITU and ISO have a long-established, healthy tradition of adopting each other's standards. More recently, ISO and IEC have joined forces as far as information processing standards are concerned; they work together through Joint Technical Committees (JTCs).

Over the years, many standards have been developed to combine resources over distance (telecommunications) and/or to bridge technical heterogeneity. A standardized framework for information processing—a metastandard—has been developed by ISO/IEC. It is called the Reference Model for Open Distributed Processing (RM-ODP). It goes without saying that RM-ODP is oriented toward *distributed* information processing. Otherwise, there would be no need for a standard. The standard's objective is for information processing to be *open*; that is, no obstacles for successful information processing will remain when all participating units conform with RM-ODP. It is, so to speak, the standard that secures the *opening* required for successful exchange between resources that may otherwise be different from each other. (An alternative name for RM-ODP might be reference model for allied information processing resources, which directly illuminates the critical issue addressed by the standard.)

Technical Orientation

The fact that official standards have a predominantly technical orientation is an early indicator that the metapattern and RM-ODP could complement each other. A related example would be a simple telephone connection; an agreement must be made about how to transfer elementary signals while preserving (more accurately, reconstructing) their original structure to represent higher-level signals. Not standardized is what such higher-level signals, or information, mean. The vocabulary of the conversants is also not subject to standardization. Again, it is the signals, at an intentionally meaningless level from the end user perspective, that are standardized.

It is this limitation—avoiding any attempt at standardizing interpretation by end users—that has spurred technological development. It is the perfect example of a successful alliance. The aspects of tool use and tool development meet when base signals are transferred.

A note of warning is in order. Aspects of communications such as phonetics, syntax, semantics, and pragmatics are relative. From a particular perspective, they all have a corresponding meaning. Thus, pragmatics are also relevant when applying a strictly technological focus. Pragmatics with a life focus, however, mean something different. At the minimum, levels are shifting. It seems reasonable to suggest that, for example, a tool's internal semantics are in many ways its user's external phonetics. Semantics, therefore, within a tool such as an information system, is a different concept from semantics as experienced and practiced outside by the tool user. Even though it is a simplification, thinking in terms of restraining descriptions of communication aspects by focus—and only then investigating how they might correspond—may eliminate much confusion between collaborating units. Figure B-5 shows a general example.

Figure B-5 raises awareness that some communication or behavioral aspects are *impossible* to translate between focuses. This cannot be changed; it's just the way it is. Such fundamental differences should be fully exploited, not denied—and that is why essentially different methods, metamodels, or whatever they are called, are required when a complex task may be characterized by a multitude of focuses. Success calls for an alliance of metamodels.

Again, meaning should not be reduced to a single focus. Such familiar use of similar terminology has unconsciously obstructed communication, rather than promoting it, as meanings can differ radically. Insufficient awareness of real differences often makes units believe they are competing whereas, in fact, they could act as allies to their mutual advantage.

focus 1	focus 2
phonetics	
syntax	
semantics	phonetics
pragmatics	syntax
	semantics
	pragmatics

Figure B-5 *Possible shift of communicative (semiotic) categories between different focuses*

Ambiguity

Earlier, we labeled the concerns of standardization bodies such as the ISO as primarily technical in nature. Does RM-ODP conform to this idea of a technical standard, even though it is a metastandard?

Two answers are possible. The first takes a point of view *outside* RM-ODP. For example, if viewed from the conceptual perspective of the metapattern, the technical nature of RM-ODP is obvious; the standard primarily addresses concerns of construction, implementation, and operational management of distributed tools for information processing—concerns not addressed by the metapattern. An alliance of both metamodels, therefore, can make complex development tasks feasible.

It may look different, however, from *inside* RM-ODP. It is not so much the claim that the information viewpoint is completely covered by the standard. Being a metastandard, an alliance could well consist of the metapattern supporting the development task of information views. In fact, this would be a real opportunity, except for RM-ODP insistence on the use of basic modeling concepts that show weaknesses for conceptual modeling when compared to the metapattern.

Comparison

A short overview of some of RM-ODP's basic modeling concepts may suffice to help you appreciate how its approach to conceptual modeling differs from the metapattern.

What is reality according to RM-ODP? First of all, in the formal recommendation document (see reference in the bibliography) reality is considered a universe of discourse. And "[t]he elements of the universe of discourse are entities and propositions."

An entity is defined by RM-ODP as "any concrete or abstract thing of interest." This would make an entity (or its synonyms, thing and element) the same concept as the metapattern's (real) object.

A proposition is "an observable fact or state of affairs involving one or more entities." This (last) sentence itself is a proposition. The ontology of RM-ODP, however, is difficult to extract. It seems that the "universe" is made up of entities, whereas the "discourse" about it occurs through propositions. The metapattern tries to separate views of reality, on the one hand, and views of reality's representation (information) on the other.

RM-ODP defines an object as "a model of an entity." With object equivalent to entity, in metapattern terms the question must read: What is the model of an object? The answer needs an introduction.

When a real object (entity in RM-ODP) is observed from a behavioral perspective, variety must be acknowledged. The metapattern states that an object is presumed to be an overall object, consisting of partial objects, each attributed with different behavior. Now, what is the model of an overall object? It is a configuration of information objects, specifying multiple contexts as required to accommodate diverse behaviors; the partial objects are represented by unique nodes in this configuration, connecting every context with a corresponding intext that specifies the partial object's static and dynamic behavior.

But doesn't RM-ODP accomplish the same result through naming contexts? It defines a name as "a term that, in a given naming context, refers to an entity." What multiple naming contexts do solve are problems of synonyms and, in particular, homonyms. They do not directly support, however, finely grained differentiation of behavior.

What about object interfaces in RM-ODP? Are they not equivalent to the metapattern's contexts? To some extent they are. It could be possible to express an interface in terms of other objects (metapattern: information objects) and their relationships. A disadvantage of this interpretation is that the concept of interface is no longer available to support different implementations of behavior within a single metapattern-based context. It would thus be wise to keep intact the technologically oriented meaning of RM-ODP's concept of interface.

Whichever way interface is interpreted, RM-ODP's weakness in conceptual modeling, when compared to the metapattern, should be apparent from a short comparison. A full review would be far beyond the competence of the author, anyway. In general, a professional conceptual modeler should retain a balance between knowledge and ignorance of technological issues.

Characteristic Meanings of Object

From this short discussion it may be observed that the use of the term object is typical for the shift that, by definition, occurs between focuses. In RM-ODP's terminology, object seems a pragmatic concept, corresponding, as it should, with RM-ODP's characteristic focus on tool technology. The metapattern does not even recognize that technically pragmatic concept as it concentrates on conceptual modeling. It puts forward the concept of information object to enable translation of conceptual models onto construction models. As such, metapattern's information object may well be labeled an intermediary concept, too. It paves the way for the specifications of tools that, when constructed and made available, are integrated into the whole of reality.

Within the metapattern, object is also a pragmatic concept. Indeed, terminology is highly isomorphic. But according to the metapattern, what is meant by this is an object behaving in the totality of reality. This is different from RM-ODP's object, which behaves within a particular information system.

Ideally, pragmatics of real objects are exhaustively mapped onto pragmatics of digital technology objects. But such a full representation is illusive. The Belgian painter Magritte (1898–1967) humorously exposed the core of the insoluble problem when he included the statement "this is not a pipe" in a painting in which he *figured* a pipe. Thus, in a metapattern-based conceptual model, the term by which another partial object is named should *not* share the nil identity with that partial object. Instead, the reference to the term must be considered a property of the partial object named. Otherwise, confusion sets in between the proper object and its representation. It is not the name proper that is an object's property in the sense of complete ownership; it is one object having or given *the use of* another object *for its name*. Remember that what is modeled concerning an object's name is, again, a representation. Out there in reality, the name is also an object.

It is difficult to illustrate the basic incongruence of real object and representation, but the reason for this problem is quite simple: any figure or model, would, by definition, imply the appearance of the real object through a representation. An opposite problem caused by the nature of a model is that infinite regression rules the representation of a representation. Therefore, a model of how a representational object stands to the real object it represents needs to be simplified. In Figure B-6, a choice is made for the real object 1 to be interpreted as a representational object. (The "real" cube represented must be understood to be missing by default.)

With real object 2 considered a name, it may be applied to represent real object 1. It is precisely this act of assigning representation that creates both relationship *and distance* between the two real objects involved. What their relationship amounts to has been extensively theorized about by disciplines such as semiotics. Now, with the metapattern, their preferred distance can also

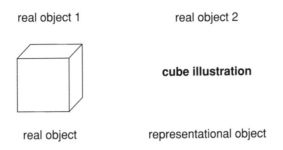

real object 1   real object 2

cube illustration

real object   representational object

Figure B-6 *Incongruence between object and representation*

be formally expressed. As indicated in the figure, it follows that a representation of a representation should be excluded from sharing the nil identity with the representation of the real object represented. To avoid behavioral confusion, they must not participate as partial objects in the same overall object. This is shown in Figure B-7.

Without such understanding, it is difficult to avoid substituting, rather than simulating, the behavior of the representational object for that of the real object. Starting the analysis from higher-order representations increases the reduction of reality even more. Is substitution, and its danger, not exemplary for technocratic approaches to reality?

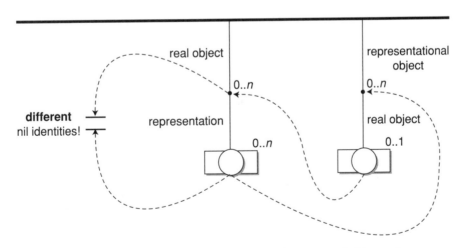

Figure B-7 *Constraint on the relationship between real object and representational object*

Conceptual modeling is least reductionist when based on, and performed using, an ontological, reality-oriented system of (meta)concepts. A technologically based metamodel can never be made to express what is different from its origin. RM-ODP, for example, can hardly be considered a metamodel of reality. All it presumes to exist are entities (things, elements). Structural elaborations are grounded in the tool technology. That focus must be complemented.

Only when the name-as-real-object is distinguished from the name's representation in the conceptual model is it possible to appreciate that, in reality, the object-object and the name-object are ontologically different objects (to use just two examples). They are representationally related, which is important. But, to repeat, it does not qualify them to be considered partial objects of one and the same overall object. Magritte made this perfectly clear long ago in his brilliantly immediate way. For C. S. Peirce (1839–1914) it was the principle of his semiotic philosophy.

Denying the fundamental dissociation of an object and its representation is also at the root of branches of, say, idealized artificial intelligence, which aims to equal and even surpass human intelligence. Of course, there is nothing artificial about intelligence. Instead, every real object should be considered to have its own, characteristic intelligence. Therefore, digital machine intelligence is a much better term. It acknowledges that a machine may be intelligent but essentially different from a human being.

Important choices about necessary limitations should be made through conceptual modeling. When conceptual information models are forced within a basically technical frame of reference (metamodel), it is almost a certainty that choices will never be optimal. This reduction is not yet fully evident with information systems for control of closed, technical systems. The unambiguity of technical system behavior is even, so to speak, preordained. Thus, there are no fundamental differences between the behavioral domains of the technical system and the controlling tool. The behavior to be modeled *is* the technology. (And that is why traditional object orientation is successful for information systems controlling technical systems.)

But a tool for use in an open, social, or sociotechnical system cannot escape the reality of different behavioral domains. Representational objects in the behavioral domain within the tool itself can *simulate* real objects in the behavioral domain of the wider social system, but they can never *substitute* for them. With substitution a pure impossibility, the range of possibilities for simulation indicates the risk associated with confusing real objects with tool-based objects.

One of the conclusions from this philosophical analysis should be that RM-ODP's basic modeling concepts may still operate satisfactorily for conceptual modeling of closed, technical systems. Then, the simple, one-to-one representational correspondence between real object (in RM-ODP, entity) and information object (in RM-ODP, object) will often not constrain what is to be minimally included in a conceptual model.

The expressive power of RM-ODP's basic modeling concepts are often insufficient, however, for conceptual modeling of social systems, characterized as these are by qualitatively greater variety and complexity of (real) object behavior. The metapattern's richer language invites the modeler to respect behavioral diversity of a real object, resulting in conceptual models with a closer simulation fit. In a good alliance, RM-ODP's basic modeling concepts should not be made to also conceptually model reality. They can be put to effective use starting with the creation of a tool-oriented construction model from the conceptual model created earlier with the metapattern.

Not Reduction, but Mapping for Alliance

The obstacle that RM-ODP has formally (with conformance requirements part of the standard) erected against a successful alliance can, in principle, be easily removed. At the same time, it is difficult to achieve, since it needs a change of perspective from inside to outside RM-ODP. The requirement for some basic modeling concepts to be universally applied in all of RM-ODP's viewpoints does not serve any real purpose. Actually, it risks *reducing* the quality of overall development by forcing the extension of technical interpretations on conceptual issues. This is a mistaken approach, encountered in attempts to extend the metamodel of software engineering to conceptual modeling. The isomorphism between what is seen with a focus on life and on tool technology, respectively, exists only with a single focus. A dual focus (or multiparadigmatic approach) reveals a superficial isomorphism at most, to say nothing about semantics or pragmatics. A small conceptual isomorphism is always insufficient to deal with issues that are qualitatively different *by nature*.

Again, reduction, in its philosophical sense, is difficult to defeat. It is seductive, and it seems easy to transfer success with one aspect to another. Why trust another unit to contribute? Why spend the extra effort on coordination? And why share benefits of success? It often takes an experience of failure to realize the benefits of alliance.

A standard is achieved rationally, and with the maximum guarantee of quality, when concepts can be successfully mapped between aspects (or focuses), one to another, or one to a configuration of others.

Source of Inspiration

When the strengths and weaknesses of RM-ODP are explicitly recognized, the metapattern may inspire some improvements in the next version of the ISO/IEC metastandard's.

The idea of multiple contexts lends itself to distributed information processing. What must be established is, if not an unambiguous procedure, at least a heuristic for mapping conceptual diversity—and the opportunities provided by it—to the relevant (distributed) configuration for information processing.

Other relevant issues are the metapattern's "standardized" conceptual mechanisms for time and validity control. With respect to time, for example, RM-ODP applies the epoch concept. It should be no problem to refine it to the level of control suggested by the metapattern.

What also must be developed in detail when an alliance is pursued are mappings between the metapattern and the schemata required by RM-ODP's information viewpoint. In many ways, what are called invariant, static, and dynamic schemata in RM-ODP are combined by the metapattern. What is still missing, if anything?

In preparing for and eventually evaluating an alliance, the overriding awareness should be that success comes through building on genuine strengths of participating units rather than through compensating weaknesses.

The metapattern must be open to continuous improvement. It is hoped that professional conceptual modelers will be inspired to make valuable contributions.

Bibliography

Bassett, Paul G. *Framing Software Reuse*. Upper Saddle River, New Jersey: Prentice Hall, 1997.

Fowler, Martin. *Analysis Patterns: Reusable Object Models*. Reading, Massachusetts: Addison-Wesley, 1996.

Hay, David C. *Data Model Patterns: Conventions of Thought*. New York, New York: Dorset House, 1996.

International Organization for Standardization and International Electrotechnical Commission. *Reference Model for Open Distributed Processing, Part 2: Foundations*. ISO/IEC 10746, ITU X.902 (recommendation), 1995. http://www.iso.ch:8000/RM-ODP/part2/toc.html

Kilov, Haim. *Business Specifications: The Key to Successful Software Engineering*. Upper Saddle River, New Jersey: Prentice Hall, 1999.

Martin, James and James J. Odell. *Object-Oriented Methods: A Foundation, Second Edition*. Upper Saddle River, New Jersey: Prentice Hall, 1998.

Maslow, Abraham H. *The Psychology of Science*. New York, New York: Harper & Row, 1966.

Odell, James J. *Advanced Object-Oriented Analysis & Design Using UML*. New York, New York: SIGs Books/Cambridge University Press, 1998.

Scheer, August-Wilhelm. *Business Process Engineering: Reference Models for Industrial Enterprises*. New York, New York: Springer-Verlag, 1994.

Vaihinger, Hans. *Die Philosophie des Als-Ob*. Berlin: Reuther & Reichard, 1911.

Wisse, Pieter E. *Aspecten en Fasen: aantekeningen over relationeel boekhouden, organisatorische informatievoorziening, verandering enzovoort en omgekeerd*. Voorburg: Information Dynamics, 1991.

Wisse, Pieter E. *Informatiekundige ontwerpleer: strategieën in objectgerichtheid*. The Hague: Ten Hagen & Stam, 1999.

Index